early years
training & management

Managing children's behaviour

Hannah Mortimer

Editor
Kate Element

Author
Dr Hannah Mortimer

Illustrations
Adrian Barclay

Assistant Editor
Jennifer Shiels

Series Designer
Mark Udall

Cover Photography
Mark Udall

Designers
Andrea Lewis, Micky Pledge

Acknowledgements:
Karen Bibbings for use of an activity 'The Lovers and the Glums' created by Karen Bibbings (Health Visitor, Stockton on Tees) © Karen Bibbings.
Her Majesty's Stationery Office for use of extracts from *National Standards for Under Eights Day Care and Childminding* © 2001, Crown Copyright (2001, DfES ref: 0488/2001).
Dr Hannah Mortimer for an extract from *Emotional Literacy and Mental Health in the Early Years* by Dr Hannah Mortimer © 2003, Dr Hannah Mortimer (2003, QEd).

Every effort has been made to trace copyright holders and the publishers apologise for any inadvertent omissions.

Designed using Adobe InDesign

Published by Scholastic Ltd, Villiers House,
Clarendon Avenue, Leamington Spa, Warwickshire CV32 5PR

Visit our website at www.scholastic.co.uk

Printed by Bell & Bain Ltd. Glasgow

1 2 3 4 5 6 7 8 9 0   4 5 6 7 8 9 0 1 2 3

British Library Cataloguing-in-Publication Data A catalogue record for this book is available from the British Library.

0-439-97130-6

Contents

Introduction

The aims of the series

The *Early Years Training and Management* series covers what managers and staff need to know about running provision, staff development, training and gaining qualifications. The aim of the series is to cover areas that would be of common concern to early years managers and professionals. Managing young children's behaviour is an area of concern to many and this book aims to provide early years managers with ideas and information for supporting their colleagues and developing their knowledge, skills and confidence in this area. You will find two other books in the series that complement this book: *Manager's handbook* and *Staff Training Activities* (Scholastic).

Who the book is aimed at

This book will be helpful for managers, Heads and special educational needs co-ordinators (SENCOs). Since 2001, many new early years SENCOs and area SENCOs have been appointed and each is to receive regular training under DfES guidelines. They suddenly find themselves not only having to plan approaches for children with behaviour problems, but also to persuade colleagues that it is *their* responsibility to actually meet the needs, and not that of the SENCO. While they can access books and resources about helping children with behaviour difficulties, both managers and SENCOs are challenged by the thought of disseminating this information to others in a practical way and supporting colleagues through the process. That is why there are activities throughout the book for staff discussion and a final chapter on training.

How to use the book

The book is divided into 12 chapters. Initially, you will need to read through the whole book in order because one chapter builds on another. When you are completely familiar with the contents, it should be possible to dip into the book for ideas of approaches or staff activities. There are 18 photocopiable pages at the end of the book containing planning sheets, observation charts, review forms, sample letters and workshop handouts. There are also four pages detailing useful books, resources and contacts.

Behaviour and feelings

Chapter 1 introduces the idea that children need to feel positively about themselves if they are to behave well. There is another theme in the book that staff members too need to feel positive about themselves if they are to be able to manage behaviour effectively. This chapter describes the link between self-esteem and confidence, and introduces the concepts of emotional literacy and emotional intelligence. The thrust of the book is that each and every child is entitled to a full and balanced early years curriculum and that it is up to early years workers to plan approaches and

interventions that are going to make this possible. The book promotes an inclusive approach in which children are not excluded on account of their behaviour.

Ages and stages

If staff are to be able to manage behaviour effectively, they need a clear idea about what behaviour is typical for each age and stage. This helps them to understand that they should plan how to change problem behaviours rather than problem children. Chapter 2 covers issues surrounding expectations and how to share these. There are ideas for helping staff members to develop clear, unambiguous language when talking about behaviour, how to observe and describe problem behaviour objectively, and details of a consultative model that can be a useful approach to adopt.

Getting ready

Chapter 3 helps you to set the scene in your setting for behaviour management. It covers the standards that you need to meet and provides background information to help you plan your behaviour policy. Behaviour management includes thinking about the whole context in which a behaviour takes place and there are ideas for planning the environment, room management and for planning activities and routines.

Promoting mental health

Mental health is defined by the document *Promoting Mental Health within Early Years and School Settings* (DfES ref: 0112/2001) as the ability to:

- develop psychologically, emotionally, intellectually and spiritually
- initiate, develop and sustain mutually satisfying personal relationships
- use and enjoy solitude
- become aware of others and empathise with them
- play and learn
- develop a sense of right and wrong
- resolve (face) problems and setbacks and learn from them.

There is now a great deal of research on the links between early experience and mental health. Chapter 4 covers the risk factors in childhood that lead to mental health problems later on and provides suggestions for reducing this risk. Children who have experienced separation and loss, who have been bereaved or who have been through a period of trauma are at particular risk and there are helpful approaches to share with staff members. There are also ideas for approaches that have proved effective for emotionally vulnerable children, including nurture groups.

Defining problems

In Chapter 5, there is information to help you advise staff on when a child's behaviour becomes a significant problem. Various methods of observation and assessment are described and the training activities in Chapter 12 follow this up with practical

opportunities. You will have coped with a wide range of behaviours in your setting because children come to you with different experiences and levels of maturity. You will be able to manage most of these simply by patiently teaching appropriate behaviour through personal, social and emotional development in the early years curriculum. However, sometimes a child's behaviour is so extreme, so immature, so disruptive or potentially dangerous that you need to plan additional or different approaches. These children fall into the description of having special educational needs (SEN).

Planning changes

There are ideas for planning general interventions in Chapter 6. These are the types of interventions that staff should be regularly trying in the setting as part of their day-to-day behaviour management and teaching. The most common behaviours that need management in early years settings are those shown by children with low confidence or anxiety, children who cannot follow rules, children who throw regular tantrums, children who play aggressively, children with toileting problems and children whose behaviour causes problems at meal and snack times. All of the interventions suggested in this chapter have been tried out in a large number of early years and Sure Start settings and have been considered helpful.

Changing behaviour

In Chapter 7 there are suggestions for teaching behavioural approaches to staff members. These are based on the idea that all behaviour takes place in a context. There is something that will have led up to and triggered the behaviour, be it in the environment or from within the child. There will also be a certain consequence of the behaviour that will affect whether that behaviour is likely to happen again. Armed with this knowledge, staff can be helped to plan changes in antecedents or consequences in order to change a difficult behaviour. There is information to help staff to use rewards and praise effectively.

Special educational needs

Chapter 8 provides information that will help you to decide when a behaviour has become a significant enough problem to require additional and different approaches. There is a brief introduction to the SEN *Code of Practice* and the need for individual education plans, which this book refers to as individual behaviour plans. Most staff will need support and guidance when planning Early Years Action and when setting targets, and so there are ideas for a step-by-step approach to planning. It can sometimes be difficult to involve parents and children in reviews and there are suggestions for keeping children central and parents or carers on board. You will find fuller information in another book of this series, *Manager's Handbook*.

Disabling conditions

Most of this book concerns the management of the usual range of behaviour difficulties seen in three- to five-year-olds. There is also a smaller group of children whose behaviour is sufficiently unusual or 'different', that they might go on to be diagnosed with a particular condition such as autism, Asperger syndrome or attention deficit/hyperactivity disorder (AD/HD). Chapter 9 describes these children, what staff might observe and what they can do to help and support them. You can read about these more fully in the *Special Needs in the Early Years* series, also from Scholastic (see page 141).

Supporting families

One of the most demanding aspects of working with challenging behaviour can be communicating with parents and carers in a constructive way that will bring everyone on board. Chapter 10 covers this area and provides ideas for useful ways of talking with parents and giving them a positive role. The idea of home-setting behaviour plans is introduced and information about when to seek further support from outside agencies or professionals.

Supporting staff

No book on behavioural and emotional difficulties would be complete without an acknowledgement that successful behaviour management depends on the emotional literacy of the adult as well as the child. Chapter 11 describes the effects of challenging behaviour on staff and provides information on stress at work, assessing risk and providing clear information. There are approaches for stress management and for anger management. It is also important to consider your own safety, and that of your staff, when dealing with anger and there are suggestions for measures you can take.

Training others

Each manager or SENCO has a responsibility to pass on information about behaviour management to staff members through training and ongoing support. Chapter 12 will help you to plan some introductory sessions and to support staff members as they make their own observations and interpretations about difficult behaviours and plan interventions. There are five training activities altogether and you will be able to supplement or adapt these by using the many case examples and discussion points throughout the book. You will find the book *Staff Training Activities*, also in this series, very useful for more general training on topics such as SEN, equal opportunities and inclusion.

Chapter 1 Feeling good, behaving well

- **Feeling successful**
- **Self-esteem**
- **Entitlements for all children**
- **Creating the right ethos**
- **Useful approaches**
- **Circle time**
- **Meeting individual needs**
- **Emotional literacy**
- **Appropriate behaviour**

This chapter highlights the links between children feeling successful, children gaining in confidence and the growth of positive self-esteem. There are ideas for helping staff to think about the entitlements that all children have, and therefore how to provide more inclusive support for any child who has behaviour difficulties. It provides examples of how to create the right ethos in your setting and to encourage the right expectations from the staff. There are also practical suggestions for building children's self-esteem and developing emotional literacy.

Feeling successful

Children need to be confident if they are to cope with all the various challenges they will meet in their world. Confidence and learning seem to be bound together: if a child tries something and succeeds, self-esteem and confidence are raised and they are likely to try again next time and to learn. On the other hand, if a child tries something but cannot succeed, self-esteem and confidence are lowered and they are less likely to try again next time and to learn from it. That is why it is so important that the approaches we design for helping children's behaviour and social development to change should remain positive and should leave the children feeling good about themselves.

In just the same way, staff members need to be confident if they are to cope with the various challenging behaviour they will meet in their setting. Because confidence and learning are bound together: if a staff member tries an approach for managing a difficult behaviour problem and succeeds, self-esteem and confidence are raised and they are likely to try again next time and to learn. That is why it is so important that the approaches we design for helping staff to manage children's behaviour should again be workable and effective, and should leave staff and children alike feeling positive.

We are also going to provide better behaved young people if we can design approaches that give children a feeling of some control over the way they behave. Otherwise, children tend to 'behave' in whatever way they are behaving until someone else stops them. In this book, you will read many ideas for helping staff to manage challenging behaviour that will avoid mental health problems developing as the children grow. The success of these ideas depends on positive approaches, they ensure that children's self-esteem remains positive and gives them the skills for behaving differently.

Useful tip
Try to help staff understand that they are dealing with difficult behaviour and not difficult children. Behaviour management involves reducing difficult behaviours but also teaching children new and more appropriate ways to behave instead. Therefore you cannot separate behaviour management from the teaching of personal, social and emotional development.

Not all children who have behaviour or emotional difficulties have boisterous and challenging behaviour – you should be just as concerned about the child who is very quiet, withdrawn or whose behaviour suddenly changes. Children can show emotional difficulties for many different reasons. Some of these will stem from their past, their life changes or their relationships with others. In Chapter 4, you will read about some of the risk factors that make children vulnerable to emotional and behavioural difficulties and to mental health problems. All staff should also have a basic awareness of the risk factors associated with abuse, be it physical, emotional or sexual. The need to act on any concerns about child protection override all the suggestions in this book and always need to take priority, however difficult it may be at the time.

Useful tip
Make sure that the professionals in your group are up to date with child protection procedures and basic child abuse awareness training by contacting your local Social Services Department, Early Years Development and Childcare Partnership (EYDCP) or NHS Trust.

Self-esteem

What is meant by the term 'self-esteem'? It is usually used to mean that people have a favourable opinion of their own worth or 'are happy in their own skins'. Very young children may not have even reached the developmental stage of being self-aware and being able to see themselves as separate little people. So in an early years setting, it is helpful if we use it in a similar way to self-confidence and to look at the behaviour a child is showing as a way of interpreting whether self-esteem is high or low (see page 11).

Why is self-esteem important?

Why is developing positive self-esteem such an important aim for your setting? The Rowntree Foundation commissioned a report that drew together all the available research evidence on self-esteem. It found that low self-esteem is strongly linked to mental health problems later on in life and also to being bullied by others. Low self-esteem can be influenced by the ways in which families bring up their children, and it is reasonable to assume that there are also lessons that could be learned within settings. For example, permissive parenting styles in which children are allowed to behave how they wish actually lead to lower self-esteem. Children benefit more from clear boundaries and a firm but loving structure. Children also do best where parents value the child as a contributor to family life and decisions. Finally, children do best where explanation is used to control behaviour rather than enforcement. It seems that the best balance is where parents or carers have the ultimate say in what a child does, but that the child is offered choices within that boundary.

Guiding principles

Below are some guiding principles that could be used at a staff meeting as a discussion point. It helps if staff can share some basic principles and visions concerning their work with young children who have behaviour and emotional difficulties. Here are some examples:

- We encourage the children to behave appropriately using positive approaches that encourage their self-esteem.
- We manage the children's behaviour with a proper respect for the children themselves and their parents or carers. We respect their culture, their ethnicity, their language, their religion, their age and their gender. The approaches we

Children with low self-esteem:
- ➤ usually have a strong need for reassurance and praise from others
- ➤ feel insecure and lack trust in their own ability to do things or to succeed
- ➤ have problems in trying out new experiences or in learning
- ➤ seem to expect things to go wrong for them and appear powerless to change this
- ➤ are reluctant to express ideas or make choices for themselves
- ➤ over-react to failure
- ➤ find it hard to accept correction without hostility or over-reaction
- ➤ find it hard to accept praise
- ➤ seem not to trust others.

Children who have high self-esteem:
- ➤ usually behave more appropriately
- ➤ are more willing to take risks when learning new things
- ➤ appear to be more confident
- ➤ are better motivated to try
- ➤ make friends more easily
- ➤ view other people positively
- ➤ can accept correction or suggestion without giving up
- ➤ develop a good sense of what they are good at and when they need help.

use for managing behaviour must be respectful of all children regardless of their gifts, abilities or specific learning needs.

➤ Behaviour management and the personal, social and emotional education of young children are not two separate, discrete activities. As a consequence, when we work with young children's behaviour, we will attend to their whole development and lives and not to certain aspects of it.

➤ We believe in the principle of the 'loving use of power'. Early years educators inevitably have power; this needs to be acknowledged and used lovingly, wisely and well.

➤ The interests of the children are paramount. Changing their behaviour in any way must enhance their lives, their learning and their development. It must 'work' for the child.

➤ We also recognise that children will thrive best only if their families thrive and we aim to work in close partnership with families and the community.

Things to consider:

➤ Think about each of the statements above.

➤ Now design your own set of guiding principles for your work with difficult behaviour in your setting.

➤ Choose wording that you could include in your setting's positive behaviour policy (see the photocopiable sheet 'Our behaviour policy' on page 126).

Entitlements for all children

It can be a useful exercise for staff to think about the rights and entitlements of all children before they start becoming too involved in what makes a particular child's behaviour difficult or different. What could a 'good' entitlement and provision look like from the perspective of the child?

- They are entitled to be cared for by a small number of familiar and consistent people who understand and are sympathetic to their needs.
- They are entitled to opportunities to form mutually respectful relationships with a range of other children and adults.
- They are entitled to be safe from emotional and physical harm.
- They are entitled to a sense of well-being, to feelings of self-worth and identity, and confidence in themselves as learners.
- They are entitled to contribute their individual and unique thoughts, feelings and ideas, and to be respected for the choices and decisions they make.
- They are entitled to opportunities to take on a range of responsibilities in the setting, progressively becoming more aware of what is involved in being a member of a group.
- They are entitled to opportunities to learn through their senses and physical activity, through active involvement in first-hand experiences and play.
- They are entitled to express their feelings and emotional needs to others.
- They are entitled to opportunities to think, to understand, to ask questions, to learn skills and processes, and to pursue their own interests and concerns.
- They are entitled to opportunities to learn about themselves and others, to become critically aware, and to grow to recognise and challenge bias, stereotypes and discriminatory behaviour.

Creating the right ethos

If you accept this kind of approach, based on entitlements for all children rather than a singling out of 'difficult children', then ways of creating the right ethos develop naturally. Straight away, colleagues can be helped to see how isolating a child or preventing them playing with others are not as desirable as teaching the child how to behave appropriately. It is clear from the entitlements that all children need to be supported in their learning by staff who:

- work with parents and carers with trust, respecting each other's concerns, circumstances, practices and traditions
- are respectful of differences between individual children
- provide an environment, indoors and outdoors, that is healthy, interesting, involving, safe and fun and that allows children to be physical
- have high expectations of all children's developing capabilities, giving them opportunities to take risks, to experience success and failure, and to reflect on their own learning and achievements
- value them for their religious, ethnic/racial, cultural, linguistic and sex/gender identities, and for their special needs, aptitudes and interests
- welcome their contributions to the group and to the activities
- sensitively extend the range of each child's responsibilities
- listen, watch, take time to understand, welcome children's curiosity, follow where children lead, and provide time, space and opportunities for extending children's thinking, imagining and understanding
- treat everyone with respect and equal concern.

Case study

This case study could be used at a staff meeting as a discussion point. It is based on a true story.

Mrs Johnson was given a new class to teach in the USA. She was told that it was the most difficult class in the school but if anyone could help these children make progress it was her. She started the school year with some trepidation and found that she was getting nowhere. The children's behaviour was terrible, they refused to do any work and they were always disrupting the lessons.

One day, she crept into the headteacher's study and looked at the pupils' confidential files where it was the system to record their IQs. She had wondered whether many of the children had learning difficulties and that was why they were misbehaving. To her surprise, she saw that they all had figures in the 120s and above, even though the average IQ is 100. Suddenly she understood – she had been under-stimulating the children and they were bored and disenchanted because they were all so bright.

Mrs Johnson went back and pushed the children to achieve more. She made her lessons stretching, interesting, and she followed a more structured approach on managing their behaviour. She showed all the children how much she valued them and how far she felt each of them could go. Later, the Head asked how she had been so successful with the class. She confessed to looking in the children's files at their IQs. The Head smiled, 'Those were the pupil's locker numbers,' he replied.

Things to consider:

- Why did the children make progress?
- How important are our own expectations of how the children can learn and behave?
- What can we learn from this?

Useful approaches

What approaches can staff use in order to promote high self-esteem and confidence in all children?

- Use circle time to promote self-esteem and confidence. Within the circle, children learn to look and to listen, to learn from each other and to develop an identity with the rest of the group.
- Try using flexible start or finish times so that certain vulnerable children and parents or carers can avoid the usual rough and tumble, and have a chance to settle in earlier or later than the other children.
- Appoint a key worker to act as a 'secure base' for any vulnerable child, supporting their play and keeping a watchful eye on their emotional needs.
- Work and play in small groups to help a child feel less socially 'overloaded' and more secure.
- Plan activities that allow you to talk about feelings and about behaviour.
- Plan little responsibilities for children so they can develop pleasure in helping.
- Encourage staff to offer children choices in their play.
- Use positive behavioural approaches, praise and encouragement to promote more appropriate behaviour.

➤ Try to help staff see that praise has got to be specific and truly meant – if they are using blanket praise, children soon realise that their efforts have not been fully noticed or truly valued.
➤ Try teaching social skills including how to play with a friend and how to resolve conflicts.
➤ Have a 'quiet place' to withdraw a child to when things seem too much. Try to use them before the behaviour becomes difficult to manage. Sometimes these areas have comfortable cushions, gentle light displays or even opportunities to listen to relaxing music.
➤ Plan sheltered nurture groups (see page 48) to provide extra nurturing and to allow these children to express their feelings through sensory play.

Circle time

Why have circle time approaches proved to be so helpful in developing children's self-esteem and confidence? There appear to be positive benefits for all children, and particularly those experiencing emotional and behavioural difficulties. The process of circle time involves key skills required of any individual belonging to a social group: awareness (knowing who I am); mastery (knowing what I can do); and social interaction (knowing how I function in the world of others).

Authors such as Jenny Mosley have designed whole-school circle time models that involve regular circles with all the children, circles for encouraging staff self-esteem and morale, and smaller therapeutic circle times for children who do not benefit from the usual approaches. You can also use circles to deliver the early years curriculum across all Areas of Learning. You will find suggestions of books and approaches on page 141.

Useful tip
The most manageable way of identifying children who have behavioural and emotional difficulties is to use or adapt the assessment you would use for all the children in the area of personal, social and emotional development.

Meeting individual needs

We have already seen how you cannot separate personal, social and emotional development from managing children's behaviour in early years settings. The one should lead to the other and vice versa. By developing approaches for assessing the personal, social and emotional development of all the children, you will already be gathering information about each child's confidence and behaviour. This in turn can be helpful if you need to plan individual approaches for any child whose behaviour is challenging, inappropriate or who seems to be emotionally vulnerable. The case study on page 15 is an example of how an assessment can be developed that would be appropriate to use on all the children but that would also lead to more detailed assessment and planning for a child with highly individual needs.

Emotional literacy

The term 'intelligence' has been controversial, mainly because it seems to imply that gifts such as cleverness are pre-programmed and unchangeable. It is probable that there are some members of staff who still view it in this way and may genuinely believe that there is nothing they can do to teach a child to become cleverer. It now seems that, although the range of our potential intelligence might be 'fixed' by genetic make-up, it alters with life's experiences and by what is learned and practised. Over time, environmental influences have been seen as having a significant impact on a child's intellectual development: it is not just what you are born with, it is the way you are taught and the

Case study

This simple assessment could be used in a staff meeting to assess the personal, social and emotional development of a child causing particular concern. Use it to plan what you would do and discuss why you would do it.

Confidence
- Does the child enter your setting with confidence?
- Does the child join in with activities?
- Does the child join in conversations?

Self-respect
- Does the child look pleased when you offer praise?
- Is the child proud of his or her achievements?
- Does the child accept suggestions positively?

Relationships
- Does the child relate well to other children?
- Does the child relate well to familiar adults?
- Does the child co-operate within a small group?

Concentration
- Does the child play independently for 15 minutes on an activity of their own choosing?
- Can the child persist in a difficult task?
- Can the child work independently for five minutes on a set task?

New situations
- Can the child cope with a change of routine?
- Can the child adapt flexibly to new activities?
- Is the child eager to explore new learning?

Personal independence
- Can the child manage his or her own coat?
- Can the child pour juice and drink from a cup?
- Can the child use the toilet independently?

Independence in play
- Can the child choose an activity?
- Can the child ask for help when needed?
- Can the child think up ideas on their own?
- Can the child select the resources needed for a simple activity?

Thinking of others
- Can the child recognise feelings in others?
- Does the child show concern for others?
- Is the child helpful to others?

Sharing
- Can the child take turns with one other?
- Can the child wait for a turn?
- Can the child share in a group?

Behaviour
- Does the child respond to 'No'?
- Does the child follow a direction when asked?
- Does the child follow simple rules of behaviour when reminded?

Right and wrong
- Does the child understand how to behave appropriately?
- Can the child tell you what is right and wrong?
- Can the child attempt to explain why?

Living things
- Does the child treat animals gently?
- Can the child help to look after younger children?

Surroundings
- Does the child look after his or her own property?
- Does the child show respect for nursery property?

Things to consider:

- Does this child need approaches and support that are 'different and additional' to what you already offer in the setting?
- How will you plan next steps for this child?
- Can this kind of assessment be used for all the children?

Appropriate behaviour

What behaviour are you hoping to encourage in your early years setting? If you are going to speak of 'difficult' behaviours, it would be helpful to be clear about the appropriate behaviours you are hoping to encourage in the first place. It is probable that you would like children to be able:

- to feel motivated and confident enough to develop to their best potential
- to respect themselves and other people
- to make friends and gain affection
- to express their feelings in appropriate ways
- to 'do as they are nicely asked'
- to make a useful contribution to the group
- to develop a positive self-esteem.

The Early Learning Goals for Personal, social and emotional development describe the goals to aim for by the end of the Foundation Stage and are useful to keep in mind when developing your approaches for assessing and supporting the children's behaviour in the group.

Experience tells us that appropriate behaviour is most likely if children know what is expected of them. Some children may be coming to your setting with the idea that 'play' is synonymous with 'rough and tumble' or chasing each other around. They may need to be shown how to play appropriately, and helped to understand the right and wrong times for more physical behaviour. They respond best to a familiar structure with a calm and purposeful atmosphere, but it may take them a while to become familiar with your routines and to understand that play can be purposeful and intrinsically rewarding.

Children also respond best where there is mutual courtesy, kindness and respect, making it easier for people to work and play together. Again, this might need to be learned in the context of your setting with the adults constantly modelling courteous and kind behaviour to each other and to the children. 'Please' and 'thank you' come much more easily when they are part of the daily exchange rather than when children are confronted with constant demands to 'say the magic word'. When the children are behaving appropriately towards each other, each individual enjoys maximum freedom without threatening the freedom or enjoyment of others. This will be most likely to happen when there are observant and interested adults ensuring that each child's needs are met, and where children are encouraged and supported while they learn self-discipline. Appropriate behaviour is also more likely if positive approaches are used to raise and maintain children's self-esteem. Children who are 'nagged' constantly with 'don't...' and 'no', tend to stop listening or trying after a while, and come to see themselves as 'naughty'. Children whose appropriate behaviour is noticed and praised, are more likely to repeat the behaviours that are attracting your admiration and to see themselves as helpful and kind, 'Good to see you sharing the bricks, Tariq!'.

Chapter 2 Sharing expectations

- **Ages and stages**
- **What to expect**
- **Individual differences**
- **Seeing behaviour objectively**
- **A consultative approach**
- **Sharing expectations with others**

This chapter outlines the typical ages and stages that young children go through when they are learning to behave appropriately. There are ideas for sharing this with staff in order to help them develop the right expectations and to be clearer about what constitutes 'problem' behaviour. Your staff need to use clear and unambiguous language when talking about behaviour so that they can plan how to change it and recognise when there are results. There are exercises and discussion points to help them develop this skill. One method of helping staff to communicate clearly about behaviour is to use a consultation framework, and a simple version of this to use in your setting is described. Finally, you will be given ideas for sharing all of your expectations with parents and carers in the most effective way.

Ages and stages

If you have had experience of working or living with very young children, then you will know that there are wide differences in the ages at which they reach new milestones. Walking and talking are classic examples of this – without there being anything wrong with children, they might begin to walk at eight months or at almost two years. Some learn to crawl very early on and others are content to lie and watch the world go by for several months, perhaps bypassing the crawling stage altogether and perfecting an efficient 'bottom shuffle'. Some are using several single words by the time they are one year old. Others use very few and speak 'gobbledegook' until they are two, when they suddenly produce whole phrases!

In the same way, children learn appropriate behaviour at different stages and this will be related both to the dispositions they are born with and the experiences they meet in their world. It is constructive if you help staff gain a clear idea of the stages that children go through when they are learning how to behave. It is useful to look at the evidence from research studies in order to show staff how they can link research and theory to their day-to-day activities. This research not only tells you about how children develop, but also what interventions and approaches have proved useful in encouraging that development.

What to expect

Learning to separate

The two-year-old is typically very dependent on a parent or carer, and finds it difficult to separate unless the situation is very familiar. The three-year-old child might need to explore your group with a parent or carer there, even if they are in the next room. The older pre-school child can separate more easily, although might at first attach themselves to a particular helper or an older child; this is absolutely normal. Sometimes a 'cuddly' or favourite toy is used to bridge the confidence gap until it is no longer felt to be needed. Sometimes you will notice children 'regress' to a younger stage of separation if there has been an important event in their lives – perhaps the birth of a sibling or an illness. Be aware of sudden changes in behaviour so that you find out the reasons for this or take steps to monitor the child's well-being and protection.

Learning in a group

Direct observations of children in their early years show that they engage mostly in solitary play, in which they pay no attention to other children, and later in parallel play, in which they play next to each other but do not interact. After the age of three, children typically play together but not sharing a goal or mutual roles. The four-year-old child becomes able to negotiate play with another child, so that each of them has a say in how the game develops. Also, as they become a little older, children become more willing to take part in joint efforts and often work together successfully to solve simple problems. Imaginative and role play provides some excellent opportunities for developing these early stages of playing co-operatively.

Problem solving occurs when children figure out how to use available material or resources to achieve a goal. This becomes easier with both age and experience of the play materials and tools. The role of staff within the group becomes one of ensuring that there is a wide range of resources for the children to use flexibly and imaginatively, with their own ideas adding to their menu rather than prescribing the approach. Research tells us that children who have had this experience solve practical problems more quickly than those who have not. Also, children who have positive self-esteem have the confidence to explore both their physical and social worlds more easily.

Developing concentration

Concentration and attention appear to develop gradually over the first five years. First, young children must learn to control their attention so that they are not constantly distracted by what is going on around them in the busy group. Then they must learn to switch their attention so that they can focus on what they are doing, but also switch to what you might be saying to the whole group. They need to plan their attention so they can switch it themselves depending on the information they need to gather for their work or play. Finally, they learn to extend their attention and concentration for longer periods. All of this is very challenging for the developing child and by understanding these stages, you will be able to help in the right way. You cannot suddenly expect socially immature children to concentrate on your own agendas if they have not learned how to master the stages in between.

Becoming independent

The one-year-old child typically will begin to help co-operatively when being dressed and undressed, moving on to managing simple articles of clothing without difficult fastenings within the second to third year. Shoes and socks can usually be managed by the three-year-old in pre-school, if laces are not involved. Many three- to four-year-olds master shoe-buckles and can put on a coat, although the pre-school child will often require help to place the zip into its foot.

Toilet-training is usually completed by two-and-a-half, although there is enormous variation in this; bowel control usually being managed just before bladder control, girls just before boys, and daytime before night-time. It becomes meaningless to talk of typical ages as so much will depend on whether, and how, the skills have been taught or encouraged, whether the child is striving to be independent and any emotional experiences bound up in the process. Children can learn to perform at very different levels of independence at home and in the group, and it makes sense to keep communicating well with parents and carers.

Getting on with others

Friends are security givers, standards against whom one can measure oneself, partners for activities that cannot be engaged in alone, guides to unfamiliar places and apprentices who confirm one's developing sense of competence and expertise. As such, the processes of peer friendship and relationships are bound to affect the development of the child's self-respect.

There are developmental stages in children's concepts of friendship. In the early years, friends tend to be 'momentary playmates', that is, whoever the child is playing with at the time. By the age of five- to seven-years-old, playmates are the children seen most frequently who share things, act in a pleasant manner or are fun to be with. Staff are well-placed to nurture these early friendships by encouraging children to spend time playing together – this will help to build up the children's social confidence and independence. Most young children seek out and enjoy other children. If they find themselves on their own, they will tend to join an ongoing group or activity, particularly if there is an interesting adult there too. During the early years, there are sharp increases in the strength of children's attachment to peers generally, and social relationships, particularly within gender, become closer, more frequent and last for longer.

Sharing

Children of two years old are able to offer and accept toys from each other, and at three they can play co-operatively and take turns. Spontaneous sharing, however, is rare unless another child requests it and this same child has shared in the past. Therefore sharing and turn-taking actually have to be taught and in a very concrete way – the children need to be shown as well as told. So often, very young children are disciplined for 'not sharing', with no idea at all what this word actually means or how it can be fun and enjoyable. The adult's role is to give the children strategies to share, modelling how to do this and setting up games and activities that are even more fun if they are shared. For example, if a child tends to snatch another child's toy, tell and show them how to ask for that toy instead. If a child has difficulties taking turns, teach them to play a simple game of football that involves kicking the ball from one child to another. Sharing and co-operating can enhance relationships between different ethnic groupings, develop positive social relationships and make groups a more positive experience. Moreover, when children experience structured co-operative learning (such as working together to create a model or on a project), they are less likely to develop prejudices against others.

Right and wrong

In the group, you would expect children to base most of their moral judgements of 'right' and 'wrong' on the code of rules already given to them. New rules will need to be learned in your group: new behaviours learned from scratch and inappropriate behaviours stopped and replaced. Some children might need to learn fresh that 'doing as you are told' can be as fun and attention-getting as behaving inappropriately. Managers and staff cannot assume that their new intake will have the same concept of being 'good' or 'naughty' as they do and will need to be positive and clear in their instructions. Moral reasoning with very young children about what is right and what is wrong is usually ineffective; helping children to understand what the consequences are is likely to be much more successful in changing behaviour.

Useful tip
Encourage staff to put children's behaviour into context by helping them to remember typical ages and stages. You want them to stop seeing difficult behaviour as a 'problem' and need them to focus on teaching and encouraging appropriate behaviour instead.

Learning self-control

What interventions have proved effective in encouraging self-control in young children? Self-control makes its initial appearance in the form of compliance. By the age of three, children can usually wait a little while to have their needs met and are open to reason. They can learn to control their behaviour with your help, but self-control will still be difficult, particularly if there are distractions or temptations in the way. Young children are generally anxious to win approval and respond well to your praise. As they grow older, the task for your staff becomes one of encouraging them to develop an intrinsic enjoyment of their play, learning and behaviour, rather than to perform for adult approval alone.

Feelings

Between the ages of two- to five-years-old, children learn to recognise and label different emotions from facial expressions and situations, usually discriminating between happy, sad and angry feelings. Increasingly, they understand that the source of an emotion can be from within as well as from without, and that emotions can endure over time or be related to memories and imaginations. Children appear to learn emotional responses through a number of routes: some seem to be present from birth and appear across differing cultures, others may be learned from parents and through experiences. Watching others can be a potent way of learning how to react, ways of expression and what to call these feelings, and it can also be used to help children cope with stressful situations and events.

Early years children are able to express concern over each other's welfare and show great interest when a child is upset or hurt. Emotions are bound together with all day-to-day interactions and relationships. Learning to be aware of one's own emotions, to recognise other's feelings and to express emotions genuinely and appropriately are important aspects of early social adjustment. This will be covered further in Chapter 4.

Behaviour: what is normal?

This chart of typical behaviour problems shows which are normal at which age. Use this at a staff meeting as a discussion point.

These figures were taken from parents' descriptions of their children's behaviour and show the percentage of the age group described as still having that kind of problem.

Behaviour	**Age 2** %	**Age 3** %	**Age 4** %
Fights or quarrels	72	75	92
Hits others or takes things	68	52	46
Stubborn	95	92	85
'Talks back' cheekily	42	73	72
Disobedient	82	76	78
Tells 'fibs'	2	26	37
Constantly seeks attention	94	48	42
Cries easily	79	53	58
Temper outbursts	83	72	70
Active, hardly ever still	100	48	40
Wets self during the day	75	14	7

You will find more of this kind of information in *New Toddler Taming* by Dr Christopher Green (Vermilion).

Things to consider:

- ➤ Are you surprised by any of these figures?
- ➤ How can we share this kind of information with parents and carers in order to help with their expectations?
- ➤ What activities could we plan to help the children overcome each of these difficulties?

Individual differences

During the past 30 years fashion has changed on how we view temperament and personality. At one time, personality tests were widely used and fostered a belief that you could not influence a child's behaviour much as it was all 'in the genes'. Then professionals and researchers began to see behaviour as mainly the product of the environment and pointed out that siblings brought up in very different situations developed very different patterns of behaviour. The research on early emotional attachments provided support for this idea.

Today, we regard both genetics and environment as playing an important role, the one interacting with the other. While children are influenced greatly by the way they live and the way in which they are brought up, we can also distinguish very different temperaments and individual differences between

Useful tip
'Personality clashes' between adults and children are a real phenomenon. Be aware of the different teaching styles of your staff and the different learning styles of the children so that you can match these appropriately.

Planning a behaviour consultation

➤ Agree a time limit to discuss each child – perhaps 15 or 30 minutes.
➤ Find a quiet area where you will not be disturbed and can switch off your mobile telephones.
➤ Make sure that you have arranged a time when those members of staff who know the child best will be present.
➤ Use the photocopiable sheets 'Behaviour consultation' on pages 123 and 124 to direct the discussion.

The first behaviour consultation

➤ Help staff put into words what it is they are concerned about and why. It helps if you can encourage them to find clear unambiguous words to do this. You can also help them to find phrases that are not judgemental in any way – this skill takes time, practice and professional support and encouragement from managers and SENCOs.
➤ Encourage the staff to talk about what approaches they have tried so far. The very fact that you are meeting regularly in this way encourages staff to see difficult behaviour not just as a problem to be spotted and identified, but as a problem to be worked on.
➤ Ask them what effects they have noticed following their interventions. It will be helpful here to have the voices of different members of staff who might have seen the problem differently or have tried other approaches with differing success. Again, the fact that behaviour consultation is a regular part of the management process will make the experience one of staff sharing approaches rather than staff feeling threatened.
➤ Ask staff how they would like things to change and begin to talk about how this might be done, building on the staff's own ideas and your own knowledge of good practice.
➤ Explore whether there are other factors you think might be important.
➤ Talk about how parents or carers are involved in the problem and their feelings about it.

➤ Make a note of any other agency involved and what their input has been or might be in the future.
➤ Make sure that you end up with clear conclusions, strategies and actions, and that everyone understands what these are.
➤ Keep a record of the discussion – this may become part of your 'evidence' for monitoring any SEN in the future.
➤ Meet up again in three weeks to review any progress and decide on 'next steps'. You can use the photocopiable sheet 'Consultation follow-up' on page 125 for this.

The follow-up meeting
➤ Start by reviewing the original cause for concern.
➤ Make a note of the child's progress since you last met.
➤ Discuss how your approaches worked.
➤ Decide what your current concerns are.
➤ Decide what you will do next – one of the options would be to change your approaches. Another might be to involve parents and carers more fully, or to plan approaches that are 'additional' or 'different' under the SEN *Code of Practice* (see Chapter 8).
➤ If you feel you need to meet again, then plan another time.

Useful tip
By holding a regular behaviour consultation session, you will disperse some of the staff defensiveness that sometimes goes with having to discuss difficult behaviour and what you did about it. The meetings can be a valuable source of support to colleagues and help boost their self-confidence.

Sharing expectations with others

It is one thing to support your staff in developing reasonable and shared expectations of the children's behaviour. It is another thing to work in partnership with parents and carers to establish a common language and expectation about their children's behaviour. The following suggestions provide ways to begin to share your own expectations between home and setting, and will support the staff in doing the same:

➤ Look for opportunities to share with parents and carers information about the activities you are doing in the session and why. This helps to give them clearer expectations about what stage their child has reached, for example, 'Young children have to be taught how to share so we play simple turn-taking games to make this fun'; 'Most children use silly words if they notice people paying them attention. That is why you will find us ignoring some words that they say'.
➤ Share the chart 'Behaviour: what is normal?' on page 23 – this can be a real eye-opener to parents who might feel that their child is the only one with the 'problem'.
➤ Use positive questioning to find out the parents' or carers' views. For example, 'How do you feel he is doing in the group?'; 'What's going well?';

➤ Physical punishments, or the threat of them, are not used.
➤ Adults do not use any form of physical intervention, for example, holding, unless it is necessary to prevent personal injury to the child, other children, an adult or serious damage to property. Any incident is recorded and the parents informed of the incident on the day.
➤ There is a named staff member in the setting who has the responsibility for behaviour management issues and has the skills to support staff and be able to access expert advice if ordinary methods are not effective with a particular child.

(DfEE *Full Day Care – National Standards for Under Eights Day Care and Childminding.*)

There are also other Day Care standards that should influence you when deciding how you will manage behaviour in your setting.

Providing equal opportunities

Standard 9 of the Day Care standards covers equal opportunities and states that 'the registered person and staff actively promote equality of opportunity and anti-discriminatory practice for all children'. In other words, you should plan steps for any child who has not yet learned to behave appropriately, to have the same opportunities as the others when accessing the Foundation Stage curriculum. While you can believe this in principle, it is more difficult to achieve in practice because you are also balancing the needs of the other children in the setting. This is why you are reading an entire book on the subject! How would you know that you were meeting this standard? The Day Care standards give the following supporting criteria:

➤ The registered person has, and periodically reviews, an equal opportunity policy that is consistent with current legislation and guidance. All staff and volunteers understand and implement this policy and it is available to parents.
➤ All children and adults are treated with equal concern and the registered person has regard to relevant anti-discriminatory good practice. The registered person promotes equal opportunities with regard to employment, training, admission to day care and access to the resources, activities and facilities available.
➤ The registered person liaises with parents to ensure that all children's records contain information that enables appropriate care to be given.

(DfEE *Full Day Care – National Standards for Under Eights Day Care and Childminding.*)

Meeting special educational needs

When a child's behaviour needs approaches that are additional and different in order to manage it and make it more appropriate, you may decide that the child has special educational needs (SEN) and make plans under the SEN *Code of Practice* (2001). You are bound to find overlaps between your behaviour policy and your SEN policy. In fact, you will by now have a SEN policy in place that can be adapted easily to embrace a range of behavioural issues – you will see an example of this on the photocopiable sheet 'Our behaviour policy' on page 126. Standard 10 of the Day Care standards states that 'the registered person is aware that some children may have special needs and is proactive in ensuring that appropriate action can be taken when such a child is identified or admitted

to the provision. Steps are taken to promote the welfare and development of the child within the setting in partnership with the parents and other relevant parties'. How would you know that you were doing this effectively? Here are the supporting criteria:

➤ The registered person has regard to the *Code of Practice...* for the identification and assessment of special educational needs.
➤ The registered person has a written statement about special educational needs that is consistent with current legislation and guidance and includes both special educational needs and disabilities. It is available to parents.
➤ Staffing arrangements are designed to meet the needs of individual children who attend and have special needs.
➤ The physical environment is, as far as is reasonable, suitable for children with disabilities.
➤ Children with special needs attending day care have access, alongside their peers, to the facilities, activities and play opportunities provided whenever reasonable, in order to promote their welfare and development.
➤ The registered person consults with parents about the need for any special services and equipment for the children in their care.
➤ The registered person ensures the privacy of children with special needs when intimate care is being provided.

(DfEE *Full Day Care – National Standards for Under Eights Day Care and Childminding.*)

Partnership with parents

Working in partnership with parents and carers is covered in Standard 12 of the Day Care standards and this is also relevant to your behaviour policy. It states that 'the registered person and staff work in partnership with parents to meet the needs of the children, both individually and as a group. Information is shared'. For example, if a child is identified as a 'child in need' (section 17 of the Children Act 1989) the registered person, usually with parents' permission, gives appropriate information to referring agencies.

A positive behaviour policy

Once you have decided how these standards can be met in your own setting, you will be in a position to draw up your behaviour policy. Each registered setting should have a behaviour policy that shows how your group promotes good behaviour using positive approaches. This should be a workable and accessible document that draws together all the things that you do in your setting to encourage good behaviour in the children. It makes common sense for it to flow out of your other policies, and in particular the policies you have on SEN and equal opportunities. Usually the same factors that promote inclusion, confidence and a sense of belonging also promote good behaviour. Here are some of those factors, although you will probably have more arising from your other policies.

Key factors for a behavioural policy

- Encouraging all the children to feel enthusiastic in their learning.
- Making sure that all children and adults feel included in the setting.
- Finding ways of showing that you value each and every child.
- Supporting children as they arrive, depart and go between activities.
- Developing each child's sense of worth and confidence.
- Making sure that adults feel confident and develop skills for handling difficult behaviour.
- Making the transfer between settings or into school go smoothly.
- Finding ways in which each child can learn successfully.
- Teaching children to work and play within groups.
- Showing children how to listen to and communicate with each other.
- Building up children's concentration and teaching looking and listening skills.
- Providing positive role-models, especially through the adults' own behaviour.
- Making sharing enjoyable and successful.
- Findings ways of motivating each child.
- Providing nurturing and comfort where needed.
- Working in partnership with parents.
- Using approaches shown to support self-esteem, such as circle time.

What should your behaviour policy contain?

The policy would begin with a clear set of aims followed by details of how you would achieve those aims.

The aims of the policy

Your policy needs to begin with a list of your aims. You might wish to say that you recognise and support the principles of the various current codes and standards. These would probably include the Care Standards Act 2000, the Children Act 1989, the Education Act (Amendment) 2000, the Special Educational Needs and Disability Act (SENDA) 2001 and the SEN *Code of Practice* 2001. You have already considered many of these principles by thinking through how you will meet the Day Care standards. You will read more about the SEN *Code of Practice* in Chapters 8 and 9. You might wish to comment on your learning environment. You could talk about how you provide a stimulating, calm and inclusive setting and how the staff have positive attitudes, always trying to remove any barriers to learning. You could mention how you use your resources, both within the setting and beyond, to help the children become active and valued members of their community. You could also mention how you ensure that staff are kept up to date with new approaches to help them promote appropriate behaviour and manage any difficult behaviour effectively.

Useful tip
You will find the section on special educational needs policy on page 165 of the *Manager's Handbook* (also in this series) very useful when putting together your policy or statement on behaviour management.

Case study

Below is an example of a behaviour policy that could be used at a staff meeting as a discussion point. Use it as a basis to design your own positive behaviour policy. You might find the form on page 126 helpful.

Daisychain Nursery School: Our behaviour policy

Our aim

- We aim to provide a setting where each and every child feels accepted and valued.
- We want each child to feel happy and to grow in confidence, whatever their needs.
- We want all the children to develop friendly and helpful behaviour.

How we do this

- We try to make each play and learning experience enjoyable and make sure that each child can succeed.
- We use positive praise and show the children that we value what they are doing using praise, photographs and displays.
- We warn children before an activity is going to change.
- We show them how to behave in a friendly way as well as tell them.
- We sometimes work in small groups so that we can teach the children to join in and to share.
- We use a daily circle time to teach the children personal and social skills.
- The children help us to agree just a few clear rules, which we encourage the children to follow with helpful reminders.
- If we need to tell a child to behave more appropriately, we do this away from an audience whenever possible.

How we respond to children who have emotional or behaviour difficulties

- If a child does not respond to our usual approaches, we talk with the group's special educational needs co-ordinator, whose name is Ella S.
- She discusses the child's behaviour with parents or carers, helps us to assess what the difficulties are and helps us plan our approaches.
- We design an individual behaviour plan to suit the child, based on positive approaches.
- We can call on the advice of the Behaviour Support Teacher if needed, and always notify parents or carers first.

How we involve parents and carers

- We believe that the best approaches will come if we can use the expertise of both home and setting.
- We always value what parents and carers have to tell us about their child's behaviour and can use this information to plan our approaches.
- If a child's behaviour needs an individual approach, we will discuss and share the plan with parents and carers and review it regularly with them.
- These staff have training in behaviour management and emotional difficulties: Ella S., Zach N., Sue B.
- We review this behaviour policy each September at the annual management meeting.

Things to consider:

- How can you design your own policy to reflect your own aims and codes of behaviour?
- How could you involve the children in planning your behaviour policy?
- How will you share your behaviour policy with parents/governors/inspectors/supply staff?

Useful tip
You will find ideas for a staff training session on designing a positive behaviour policy on page 98 of another book from this series, *Staff Training Activities*.

You would mention how you work towards keeping the behaviour policy up to date and how you are always aiming to improve the service you provide for encouraging positive behaviour in your setting.

How to implement the policy

Your policy should then describe how you are going to carry out the behaviour policy in your setting. You might wish to include these points:

- How you ensure that all staff understand and implement the behaviour policy.
- How staff respond to children who have emotional or behaviour difficulties.
- Any particular roles and responsibilities of staff members.
- You would name the person who has special responsibility and knowledge of behaviour management issues. Usually this is the SENCO or the manager.
- You would list any special training in behaviour management that the staff had received and how you plan and monitor their training needs.
- You would also state how you worked with parents and carers to design, implement and review the policy.

Planning the environment

Young children behave best when they feel secure and valued and when they are aware of the routines and boundaries in your setting. The starting point for encouraging appropriate behaviour is to think about how you structure the environment so that:

- there is a familiar structure that leads to an atmosphere of calm and a sense of purpose
- each child will be happily engaged and at ease
- children know what is expected of them
- children know how to behave appropriately
- each individual enjoys maximum freedom of choice without threatening the freedom or enjoyment of others in the group
- there are adults who are observant and supportive, making sure that each child's needs are being met
- there is an atmosphere of mutual courtesy, kindness and respect
- the children are encouraged to develop self-discipline as well as to 'do as they are nicely asked'
- there are a few simple and meaningful rules that have been developed with children and families, rather than many rules with frequent confrontations
- appropriate behaviour is noticed, valued and commended by positive staff members.

If you are going to encourage 'good' behaviour in your setting, you need to be clear with the staff and children about the behaviour you are hoping to encourage. It is all too easy for adults to leave well alone when children are behaving and concentrating beautifully, only to intervene when there is trouble and strife.

The ultimate message to the children is that they need to misbehave in order to get attention, and adult attention is usually the strongest reinforcement they can be given when learning how to behave. You will probably wish to encourage these behaviours in your setting:

- Children and adults are kind to one another and do not hurt each other.
- Children help to look after the group's property and do not damage it.
- Children and adults respect each other and themselves.
- Children 'do as they are nicely asked'.
- Children understand and try to follow the rules, especially those on safety.
- Children learn to share and take turns with each other.
- All children join in and have access to the curriculum.

Useful tip
Think about how you use physical spaces. Make sure you have large spaces for physical play as well as small areas for quiet play. Make the most of soft surfaces and cushions to absorb sound and keep the general noise (and stress) levels down.

Encouraging good behaviour

Here is an exercise that could be used at a staff meeting as a discussion point.

If you are going to encourage 'good' behaviour in the setting, you need to be clear about the behaviour you are hoping to encourage from the children. Make a list together of the behaviours you think are important in your group.

Things to consider:

- How will you encourage each of these behaviours?
- What will you do when you see the children behaving in this way?
- How will you make sure that you give the children positive reinforcement when they are behaving in this way, rather than reacting more when they misbehave?

Room management

If you are going to have observant staff ensuring that each child's needs are being met, then they need to be sure of their roles. It can be helpful to manage their time effectively by giving them different roles. These roles can be rotated to provide everyone with the same experiences or volunteers/parent helpers might be used to provide extra pairs of hands for some of the roles. The idea of 'room management' is important when there are several children whose behaviour is causing you concern. For example, supposing there are four adults in a room of lively two- to three-year-olds, then you could define four distinct roles for the helpers:

- The activity facilitator, who plans and organises a structured activity, engages and supports the children as they take part and stays mainly in one place for the duration of that activity.
- The play facilitator, who moves around the room supporting and engaging all the children in their choice of free play.
- The nurturer, who remains in the soft cushion area and is available for comforting and for sharing story-books or songs.
- The care facilitator who moves around ensuring safety, helping the children mop up spills, managing any 'accidents' and so on.

Depending on your situation, these roles may need to be combined. If a child has additional support because of their special educational needs, you might also have a 'support worker' who will be keeping an eye on the needs of the child

Useful tips

➤ Remind staff that being bright does not mean that the child is socially more mature. Providing extension activities means far more than moving children further 'up' the curriculum.

➤ Point out to parents and carers that bright children are always likely to learn quickly – but there is a real danger that they will miss the concrete and practical experiences on which to build their later learning if they are pushed on too quickly.

with SEN, ensuring that this child can access the curriculum and is fully included. Where the SEN involves behavioural and emotional difficulties, this role might include putting into effect any positive behaviour programme that you might have agreed for the child (see Chapter 8). Room management works best when it is used as the ideal structure, and when staff are also encouraged to be flexible and use their shared expertise and common sense to support each other.

Planning activities

You really can avoid many behaviour problems by making sure that the activity is at a suitable level for the children, it suits their style of learning and that the expectations that adults have are appropriate to them. Young children are at different stages of maturity and developing their learning styles, and you need to plan activities that suit all of the children inclusively. For example, some older children find it easiest to attend and concentrate when they are listening. Others need to look, while others still need to handle and manipulate. At the Foundation Stage, you need to plan the activities in a multi-sensory way so that young children can listen and think, can observe and inspect and can also feel and manipulate – in other words, to plan a learning experience that is visual, auditory and kinesthetic.

This also applies to how the staff present the learning activities. The ideal teaching style will be to:

➤ show the children what to do (modelling the activity or providing picture, real objects or concrete examples)
➤ tell the children what to do (giving clear and simple instructions, emphasising key words or providing a simple running commentary as the child plays)

Case study

This case study can be used at a staff meeting as a discussion point. Talk about what you would do and why you would do it.

Matthew was nearly three years old and known to be a very bright little boy. Because of this, he was moved from the nursery room for two-year-olds to a rising five-year-olds group where he could take part in the early reading and number activities that he already found so easy. However, his behaviour became very difficult to manage. It was the custom to blow a train whistle every ten minutes and for the four-year-olds to form themselves into a long train and 'chuff' to the next play area. The staff felt this would prepare the children for a more structured school timetable. Matthew would not finish playing when the whistle went and threw a temper tantrum when staff tried to move him on. He would also break away from the 'carriages' to touch and fiddle at every opportunity, even when the staff explained that their display was 'for looking' and not 'for touching'. He was referred to a psychologist for advice.

Things to consider:

➤ Why do you think Matthew was misbehaving?
➤ What would you suggest?
➤ How could you design play activities that would be suitable for Matthew?

➤ give the children something to do (making the activity practical and encouraging the process of the learning as well as the product).

The activities themselves need to be child-centred (tuned into their values and interests), need to allow the children an element of choice and help them feel successful in their learning and playing.

Routines

Children need to feel secure within a setting and this will come from a regular and familiar routine. While you will always wish to retain the flexibility to respond to a learning opportunity as it arises ('Quick everyone! Come and look at the rainbow!'), you need to aim for a familiar pattern or routine that will provide the children with the security to cope with any new changes and demands within it. This will involve a regular start and finish to your session, as well as regular staff members with whom the children can feel familiar.

In some areas where there are many changes and caregivers in the children's lives, managers find it useful to adopt a 'key worker' system. A named adult has particular care and concern for a small group of children. This might allow you to have smaller group times within the larger group session and provide a 'secure base' from which the children can operate and play. Within the smaller group, staff can provide nurturing, can help the children plan and review their day, can use a regular welcome and farewell circle time, and can keep a watchful eye to make sure that each child is fully included. Children can be encouraged to make choices in their play and conflicts can be handled with guidance and support.

Useful tip
Encourage staff to follow a 'do as you would be done by' approach to their behaviour management. Their power over the children needs to be used lovingly and wisely and their own attitudes and behaviour in the setting should lead by example.

Staying safe

Your particular knowledge of a child's behaviour is bound to influence how you plan for everyone's safety. Under the SEN Disability Act, you will be expected to make 'reasonable adjustments' for any child who has a significant difficulty on account of behavioural or emotional needs. On a day-to-day basis, there are many considerations that will help to keep you 'a step ahead' of incidents that might affect safety:

➤ Make sure your premises are secure to keep unwanted visitors out and energetic children in.
➤ Make sure that physical play is supervised and safety matting is used where appropriate with large equipment.
➤ If a child throws objects continuously, remove dangerous items and supervise the safety of younger children.

➤ If major tantrums are a problem, set up a quiet area for a member of staff and the child to withdraw to for 'cooling off'.
➤ If there is a lot of kicking, consider encouraging all the children to wear slippers indoors.
➤ Make sure staff are trained in lifting and handling techniques.
➤ Use safety gates on kitchen spaces, or stairways and safety catches on closed cupboards.
➤ Make sure that staff and unsupervised helpers have the appropriate police checks.
➤ Make sure that all staff are kept regularly up to date with child protection procedures.
➤ Use room management approaches to provide additional supervision and support for children whose behaviour is a risk to themselves or to others.

Feeling secure

In Chapter 4 you will find ways of helping vulnerable children feel more secure and confident in the group. This usually goes hand in hand with more appropriate behaviour – or at least behaviour that will respond to your usual methods and approaches. If a vulnerable child behaves in a way that is inappropriate, you will still need to manage that behaviour. You cannot allow staff to think, 'Well, he can't help it because he's emotionally vulnerable so we'll just let him be'. You still need to help that child to develop more appropriate ways of behaving. However, knowledge about the child and the emotional vulnerability will help you to plan more effective strategies for both changing the behaviour and helping them to feel more secure. Staff will understand this concept if they can learn to see behaviour management as teaching and not sanctions.

Useful tip
You will find information on creating a safe environment in the *Manager's Handbook*, which is also in this series.

Case study

This case study could be used at a staff meeting as a discussion point. Talk about what you would do and why you would do it.

Ama is four and arrived in the nursery very distressed. She had fled with her family from Zaire. When staff approached her, she froze. If other children were near she crawled beneath the table and, if they came too close, she would squeal and scratch them. She did not communicate and seemed to be in a frightened world of her own. The only play she would engage in was a pretend game of washing the clothes, just like she had done in refugee camp. She was already receiving help from the local Child and Family Service who supported resettled or traumatised refugee families.

Things to consider:

➤ What could you do to help Ama feel more secure? (You already know that she is receiving specialist help.)
➤ Why might she be behaving in this way?
➤ What would you do to manage her behaviour?

Chapter 4 Vulnerable children

- **Promoting mental health**
- **Risk factors**
- **Avoiding risk**
- **Getting it right**
- **Separation and divorce**
- **Bereavement**
- **Supporting children after trauma**
- **Tried and tested**

In this chapter, you will think about the needs of the more vulnerable children in your setting and consider how you can support staff as they promote the positive mental health of all children. There is information about which children might be at risk of mental health difficulty and how you can reduce these risks. In particular, there are suggestions for how staff can support children who are bereaved, whose family has separated or who have experienced trauma. Finally, there are some tried-and-tested approaches that have been helpful for vulnerable children and their families.

Promoting mental health

The document *Promoting Children's Mental Health within Early Years and School Settings* (DfES ref. 0112/2001) provides guidance for LEAs, schools, early years settings and Child and Adolescent Mental Health Services. It starts by defining 'mental health' as the ability to:

- develop psychologically, emotionally, intellectually and spiritually
- initiate, develop and sustain mutually satisfying personal relationships
- use and enjoy solitude
- become aware of others and empathise with them
- play and learn
- develop a sense of right and wrong
- resolve (face) problems and setbacks and learn from them.

It goes on to describe the types of mental health problems experienced by children such as attachment disorders or conduct disorders and links this back to the term 'emotional and behavioural difficulties', suggesting that the one has a greater risk of leading to the other. It stresses the link between children's emotional well-being and learning well.

Useful tip
Make it clear on your policy documents that your setting is working to make all children feel valued and successful. Draw staff's attention to the fact that working preventatively in this way can actually reduce behaviour difficulties in the setting – many staff do not make this connection automatically.

In other words, if you can take steps to make sure that children's mental health is as strong as possible during the early years, then you actually have a chance of reducing the behavioural and emotional difficulties in your setting. Clearly there is only so much you can do in your group and setting, but the move now is towards cross-agency 'joined up' working so that everybody can tackle this issue in community, home and setting. Many of the recent Sure Start initiatives and Centres of Excellence attempt to do just this.

Risk factors

The more that you find out about mental health, the more possible it becomes to identify certain children who are at risk of developing these problems later on in life because of their particular childhood experiences and pre-dispositions. We now know that the more risk factors faced, and the more severe the risk, the more likely the child is of developing a mental health problem. There is also research that suggests that, unless steps are taken to counteract this, depression and mental illness will soon cause more days off work than any other illness. It is so important that staff begin to see behaviour difficulties not as difficult and demanding children but as behaviours that certain children display because of their particular life experiences. Not only will this put them in a better position to understand that behaviour, but they will also be more aware of the steps they can take to prevent later difficulties.

There are a number of risk factors for young children that increase their chances of experiencing mental health problems later on. These are:

- loss or separation, perhaps because someone in their family has died, their parents or caregivers have split up, there has been a long period in hospital or there have been many changes of home and caregivers
- major life changes, such as the birth of a new brother or sister in the family, moving house or changing families ('looked after' children are particularly vulnerable)
- traumatic events, such as violence, accidents, war, natural disaster or abuse
- having a 'difficult temperament' or very low self-esteem, perhaps not being flexible enough to adapt to different social situations
- having learning or communication difficulties
- socio-economic disadvantage and homelessness.

Useful tip
Where there are several risk factors for a child, it would be reasonable for you to plan approaches with colleagues that act preventatively, avoiding behaviour and social difficulties before they have a chance to develop. Make sure you have a system for gathering information so that you know whether the children are vulnerable.

While many children with risk factors will grow and develop with no mental health problems whatsoever, risk factors do seem to 'stack' up.

Avoiding risk

It is also possible to identify certain resilience factors in children, families and communities that are going to make these children less likely to develop mental health problems later on. Again, it makes sense for staff to be aware of these so that you can build on what is known about avoiding risk. These are the resilience factors:

- Children who have enjoyed secure early relationships with their parents or carers.
- Children who were seen as 'easy' babies by their caregivers and who were therefore responded to with warmth.
- Children who have developed good ways of communicating with others.
- Children who have been brought up with humour, affection, thoughtfulness and optimism.
- Children whose parents and carers support their education.
- Children from families where there is harmony and mutual support.
- Children from good housing, a good standard of living and a positive ethos in the community.

While some of these resilience factors will be hard to influence, staff can be helped to see just how important it is that each and every child should develop a positive relationship with at least one caregiver, and, where necessary, this must be within the setting.

Seeing this wider viewpoint also helps staff to see the reason for the various community projects that are now developing – it makes sense to 'break the cycle' of mental health problems and difficult behaviour by offering support at the level of the child, the family and the wider community.

Case study

Here is a case study that could be used at a staff meeting as a discussion point.

John is three years old and lives with his gran. His mum lives in the home too but there is a Social Services Supervision Order and she is not allowed to be on her own with him because of an incident in which he was scalded – the full details were never known. He is a lively little boy who seems happy to be cuddled and played with. His attention span is very short. His gran finds him very hard to manage. He is easily distracted and does not use much language. He can sometimes kick and hit out if he wants a toy that another child has. If thwarted, he can become very angry with himself and everyone else.

Things to consider:

- Is John emotionally vulnerable?
- Why do you think this?
- What could you do in your setting to make him less at risk of mental health difficulties?

Useful tip
Find out about local community schemes in your area for parenting and support. Could you perhaps link together to support your own families and is there current funding that you might tap into?

Getting it right

How can settings develop approaches for promoting children's mental health? Early years staff can do this through:

- stable childcare arrangements so that children interact with just a few primary caregivers in any one day
- low staff turnover so that children are cared for by the same individuals over several years
- good staff training in child development
- adequate staff to child ratios (as set in the National Standards for Day Care)
- positive approaches for behaviour management.

Early years staff can also plan interventions that can be used to support individual children and families who are experiencing difficulties. These include:

- home visiting
- parent 'drop-ins'
- courses run for parents in such areas as literacy and computing skills
- parenting classes that enable parents to build on their strengths and learn new ways of engaging with their children
- work with small groups of vulnerable children, or vulnerable children individually, on strategies to promote positive behaviour, social development and self-esteem
- the teaching of interpersonal problem-solving skills to young children
- compensatory nurturing experiences for vulnerable children (such as nurture groups).

Separation and divorce

One of the most familiar 'risk' factors for the children you work with is family breakdown. At least one in four families in the UK has one parent absent, and in 90 per cent of these families, it is the father. About one child in eight is likely to experience family divorce before the age of ten, and about a third of these children are under five. For some children, a family breakdown may have become accepted. For others, feelings will still be raw and sensitive, and you will need to plan how your staff are going to support that child most effectively through the next few months.

Encourage staff members to understand what family breakdown means from the child's point of view. A family breakdown can take them utterly by surprise and cause misery and bewilderment. At a time when the parents will be absorbed in their own conflicts and emotions, the child can be left feeling isolated and even in some way responsible for the split. Make

sure that your setting is an important 'constant' at a time when home life might be confusing and unsettled. Keep to your familiar routines and make allowances if the child wants to play with very familiar or less demanding activities for a while. Explain to staff that some children may be feeling very miserable or cross; this does not mean that they are setting out to be 'naughty'. Others may behave as if nothing is wrong, but show a delayed reaction later or may show you through their atypical behaviour that they are unsettled.
Ask staff to make allowances for difficult behaviour and to stay calm and reassuring, but at the same time to handle it firmly, consistently and lovingly.

Sometimes you may be approached by parents for advice and it is helpful to be aware of research findings in this area. Children adjust best to the change if they continue to feel loved and valued by both parents, even though they live apart.

Children whose parents discuss with them what is going on appear to cope better. They need clear information in a way that they can understand. Typical questions asked by children may be:

- Where is everyone going to live?
- When will I see Mummy or Daddy next?
- Is he still my daddy?
- Was it because I was naughty?
- What about Grandma and Grandad?

It is important that parents do not expect the child to support one against another, no matter how rejected, angry or guilty the remaining parent feels. Children must feel 'allowed' to talk about the missing parent, even if this is distressing for the partner remaining. A photograph album of their previous and present life can be a useful talking-point for the child to reach for whenever they feel a need to talk about things.

It will be helpful for you to gather the facts from the parent and establish what the child knows. If you feel you have to, share what you know about ways to help children through recent family breakdown. Agree the factual information you may need to give the child, and agree one carer in your setting who is going to be giving particular support to the child.

Ask colleagues to concentrate on making the child feel secure and comforted during the session; they will probably be feeling rather at a loss themselves and so it is helpful for you to give them a role. Ask staff to help the child find words to express what he or she is feeling, even if these feelings are coming out as challenging behaviour or particular quietness. They should not force the child to talk, but just be there, close by, as an extra comforter and listener as needed. If you are also able to offer a listening and impartial ear and practical help to the parents themselves, you may be helping them find the emotional resources to help their children through this difficult time in their lives.

Useful tip
Remind staff that families come in many different shapes and sizes when carrying out any activities on a 'families' theme. Ask them to make sure every child and family feels accepted and valued.

Bereavement

From time to time, you may have to support families, other children and staff following a bereavement of a child. Though child mortality rates have fallen dramatically during the past 30 years, some of us are still likely to face the death of a child, or a sibling of a child in our care, at some point in our careers. The greatest cause of death in a pre-school child in this country is bacterial meningitis and respiratory disease. Road accidents are the most common form of fatal accident. Approximately 40,000 families worldwide experience the death of a child every single day.

When a child in one of the families attending your setting dies, everyone will have their own grief and distress to cope with. Try not to let your fear of not knowing what to say get in the way of speaking to the family. It can be devastating for them if, as well as the traumatic loss of their child, all the usual sources of friendship and support withdraw. Let your care and concern show, and express your sorrow about what has happened. You are unlikely to be able to say that you understand what they are going through unless you have actually experienced such a loss yourself. Even then, everyone reacts to grief in their own individual way and at their own pace. Be aware that if you or your staff have any recent experience of bereavement, your personal feelings will become sharper as memories are revived.

Avoid giving direct advice and platitudes such as 'time will heal' or 'you're taking it well', but be sensitive to what practical help you can give. Perhaps you can provide support to any siblings or friends in your setting who are grieving in their own and individual ways. Never be frightened to mention the child's name; you will not add to the grief that is already so poignant, but it will provide opportunities for recognising the child as a continuing part of your memories.

Be there to listen. Allow the family's grief to show and be ready to talk about the child they have lost. Find happy memories to share and continue to talk about the child even after those first days of raw pain. If you have lost a child in your nursery or class, find ways of at least offering the chance for regular contact with the family well into the future. You might think of a particularly appropriate and practical memorial within the group: a rocking horse, a special chair or a toy tractor. This is all the kind of advice that is helpful to share with staff who might be feeling at a loss for what to say and do.

Ask staff to give extra attention to brothers and sisters who will be feeling confused and sad at a time when parents may not have the time or emotional resources to comfort them. Encourage them not to be afraid to talk with the children about what has happened in clear, concrete terms, and to play alongside the bereaved child providing opportunities for them to act out some of their feelings. One nursery helped a brother and sister to draw pictures for their baby brother to say 'goodbye' and these were taken to the hospital to be placed beside him.

Other children in your setting will want to talk about things. Remind staff not to be put off if any children seem almost callous in their response. The news is usually taken at a very practical level with concerns such as 'Who will his mum collect from playgroup now?' or 'Who will get his bicycle?'. Encourage staff to avoid using expressions that will confuse children. If you talk of death being like 'going to sleep forever', you can leave children very frightened about what will happen if they allow themselves to fall asleep at night. Remember that the siblings may be feeling quite frightened that they too will die, and you may need to seek advice from the health visitor or specialist nurse on how to present the medical facts to the bereaved sibling.

Do encourage the family to take things steadily and not try to do too much at once. They may need continual reassurance that what they did was right and the best for their child. Siblings may need reassurance too so that they do not feel they caused, or could have prevented, the death in some way. Never suggest to parents that their other children will bring comfort; this cannot replace the child that is lost. Above all, continue to listen and support the family; it will be a huge comfort that all the relationships formed when the child was with you can still go on. No-one can erase the child that was and the memories that continue.

Case study

Here is a case study that could be used at a staff meeting as a discussion point. Talk about what you would do and why you would do it.

You have heard on the local radio that there was a major accident at the weekend and one of the families who come to the setting was involved. The mother and little brother were both killed, and the four-year-old has some broken bones and will be in hospital. The father was not injured. Many of the children who come to the setting are neighbours of the family and so will be very upset tomorrow. It is now Sunday night.

Things to consider:

- What should the manager or nursery leader do to prepare for the next day?
- How should staff respond on Monday?
- What kind of support should they offer in the longer term?
- How will they prepare the children for the return of the four-year-old to the group?

Supporting children after trauma

Occasionally, you may have children in your setting who have been traumatised by a sudden or major event in their lives. Perhaps a close family member of one of the children has died suddenly. Perhaps they have a close friend or important figure in their lives who has been killed or seriously injured. The child itself might have been involved in a major incident such as a bombing, a train crash or other traumatic event. Perhaps you have children from refugee families who have experienced war or natural disaster.

It is helpful if staff can be made aware of the emotional symptoms of post-trauma and they feel prepared to support the children through major incidents before such incidents happen. Every child goes through their own process of readjusting to a traumatic event. It is like travelling a journey; it does not get better day by day, but each day is another step towards its end. Some children may display intense emotions and others may behave as if nothing was different. All are normal responses. Some will behave as if they were younger, wanting constant cuddles, thumb-sucking and throwing tantrums. That is normal too.

Useful tip

Have a box with resources that you might need if your setting was ever the subject of a major incident. Hopefully you will never need to use it, but you will need accessible and practical information about what to do and who to call on if you find yourself having to cope. As a manager, keep a summary at home with you of what you should do that you can reach for quickly if called in to help.

Provide a 'secure base' for the child through their period of readjustment. Spend more time with the children and let them be more dependent on you. The need for constant reassurance and physical comfort might be there for several months. Encourage staff to use play experiences to help the child to relieve tension. Younger children find it easiest to share their feelings and ideas through play rather than words. Provide imaginative play, small-world play and picture books that help to make sense of their situation. Be there to support the play and do not be surprised if play sequences are repeated over and over, perhaps with strong emotion. Keep a diary of their play for a while.

Be there to listen, to comfort and to support family members, perhaps long afterwards. Staff themselves might need to 'debrief' with you if they have been working with a bereaved or traumatised child and, in turn, you yourself will need someone to talk to for peer support. Even when the world is back to normal and people expect a family to be 'over it', there will be feelings and emotions triggered in the least expected ways. Do not be surprised to find the family still on a 'rollercoaster' of emotions.

Above all, encourage staff to stick to familiar routines and sameness. The importance of this explains why children will come into your setting soon after a traumatic family event. Being with familiar people in a familiar and secure setting is all part of helping them realise that their basic security and their sense of who they are is still intact. Tell staff not to be afraid to share memories. The charity Barnado's produces the 'Memory Store' and 'Memory Book' for children facing separation, loss and bereavement. These help a child to hold on to their family history and to become clearer about what has happened to them. You will find the address on page 142.

Tried and tested

In this section, you will find out about some interesting projects and approaches that appear to work either within early years settings or as part of the local provision.

High/Scope

A series of well-evaluated American studies showed that early intervention could indeed be effective in improving the outcomes for disadvantaged children. The best-known was the High/Scope Perry Pre-school Project that followed a cohort of students through to the age of 27. These adults had significantly higher monthly earnings if they had received the High/Scope education. They had a higher percentage of home ownership, a higher level of schooling completed, a lower percentage needing social services, and fewer arrests for drug-related crimes. In the High/Scope curriculum children learn to be

self-critical and to set high goals while seeking objective feedback. There is a deliberate encouragement to think about what they are doing and how well it is going. The children are gently encouraged to develop persistence in the face of failure and a calm acceptance of errors and mistakes. The High/Scope curriculum is also characterised by the active and ongoing involvement of parents in their children's education, enhancing their interest and confidence and breaking down institutional barriers.

Starting early: PIPPIN groups

The PIPPIN project (Parents in Partnership – Parent Infant Network) brings together mothers and fathers during the last three months of pregnancy, seeking to provide the 'secure base' that was not sufficiently available to them during their own childhoods and is not present for them in their current relationships. They meet in a non-judgemental setting in which they can explore their feelings, deal with issues and learn more about their own relationships and patterns of behaviour. Though this can be a painful process, it can help them to understand how to respond appropriately to their children in a particular situation. Parents who have attended the PIPPIN classes say that they are less anxious, less vulnerable to depression, enjoy their babies more, develop better relationships with their partner and generally feel more confident, child-centred and skilled in coping with the ups and downs of family life.

Joined-up approaches: Centres of Excellence

These are expected to exemplify how early education and childcare can be combined with a number of other services designed to support families (such as the teaching of parenting skills, family learning and adult basic skills) and to stimulate good practice by other providers in the surrounding area. Most Centres of Excellence see the emotional welfare and self-esteem of the children, particularly those who are vulnerable, as paramount. For example, many life events can affect the families of children attending nursery. By using semi-structured interviews with the parents, the staff can try to keep up with these. Children respond in many different ways to major life changes such as separation, violence or homelessness. Some of them may appear withdrawn or full of grief, some may be angry and aggressive, some may be distracted or find

Useful tip
Even if you do not have these projects locally, there are things you might be able to learn or adapt from them. For example, invite staff to design and set up a 'nurture corner' complete with soft surfaces, gentle music, picture books, sensory play, soft lighting and an available adult ready to offer positive and unconditional time.

it hard to relate to others, many find it hard to concentrate, and many become needful of constant attention. Staff need to encourage each child to form a close attachment to a key worker and to work creatively to support children through these changes.

Providing a secure base: nurture groups

These were developed 30 years ago in the Hackney area of London by psychologist Marjorie Boxhall. As an approach, it has been shown to reduce the number of children excluded from schools on account of their behaviour. The groups attempt to replicate a form of 'family life' based on intense personal interest and positive support from the teacher or classroom assistant. Each child in the setting is helped to feel special and valued. There are shared meals and an emphasis on early sensory play and familiarity. Outings are arranged with parents and there are 'coffee days' for parents to come in and share notes about their children.

Reducing risk: Sure Start

'Sure Start' is a cross-departmental government initiative aimed at children under three years old and their families in a small targeted area of disadvantage. It concentrates additional resources and additional services in this tightly defined area in order to achieve seamless provision of preventative services. It involves all aspects of their lives including their health, education, social and leisure time. It brings together many different agencies and organisations in the statutory, private and voluntary sectors aiming to break down barriers and ensure co-ordinated and 'joined up' provision.

The Sure Start initiative is based on what is known from current research, including what is known about early attachments and early emotional development. A review of research on prevention and early intervention concluded that there were four groups of protective factors that helped children in adverse conditions achieve good outcomes. These were an adequate standard of living, temperaments or dispositions that attract and encourage caregiving, dependable caregivers, and networks of community support. Sure Start is therefore grounded in evidence from child development and attachment theory, as well as what works in supporting parents and young children within local communities.

Useful tip
Try to become involved in any Sure Start scheme from the early planning stages so that you can combine your service and bid for any funding that is available to help you extend the work you already do with the families and younger children. The local Early Years Development and Childcare Partnership (EYDCP) should have details of what is happening in your area.

Chapter 5 Problem behaviour

> ➤ **What is a 'problem'?**
> ➤ **Criteria for problem behaviour**
> ➤ **Observation and assessment**
> ➤ **Working it out**

What is a 'problem'?

In this chapter, you will be given ideas for helping staff members to decide when a behaviour becomes a problem. There is practical advice on how they can gather information about that problem in order to plan an intervention for changing it. If staff talk to you about 'a problem child', you need to spend time with them to help them redefine the problem as a 'problem behaviour', rather than something that is within the child. You can then help them sort out to whom the behaviour is a problem and whether your usual approaches should be effective. For example, if you have a child in your setting whose behaviour is causing concern, ask yourselves the following questions before you decide on whether there really is a 'problem':

➤ Has the child had time to settle into your group? Some children take longer than others to settle into new routines, so the behaviour might settle once the child is used to your approaches.
➤ Has anyone talked with parents or carers yet? They know their child inside-out and can contribute useful information and ideas. What they say might allay your fears or at least help you to understand what is going on. Perhaps there are changes at home that will inevitably leave the child unsettled for a while. What they say might also lead you to feel that you need to use more special approaches or advice. You always need to be vigilant for any child protection issues and follow your usual procedures.
➤ Have you considered that poor self-esteem and confidence might be at the root of any problem? If so, use a key worker to befriend and support the child, using positive encouragement and support to enable them to feel more confident and 'tuned in' to the rest of the group.
➤ Has the child not yet learned to play calmly and socially? This might not be a behaviour problem, but more a case of teaching the child another way to play and behave. Look for strategies to make play extra fun and rules clear. Play alongside the child with one or two other children showing that playing socially can be safe and enjoyable.
➤ Is the child not yet at a developmental stage where he or she has learned sharing, turn-taking, asking for things and so on? It might be that the behaviour problem is related to the fact that the child is still at a young stage of development.

Useful tip
It is very possible that the same behaviour in one setting can be a serious problem whereas in another setting it would not. In other words, how serious a behaviour problem appears is related to the staff ratio, the particular mix of children, the environment, the expectations and the experience of staff. Help staff to look at all these variables first before they are tempted to label a child in any way.

You can find out more about the 'problem' by trouble-shooting and finding out which approaches bring an improvement. Identifying a behaviour problem and planning an intervention should be inextricably bound together so that knowledge of the one informs the other. You will find ideas for planning a range of interventions in Chapter 6. Start by choosing a few clear rules that the children have contributed to. Talk about them in circle time. Look for opportunities to praise children in a specific way ('Thank you for giving that crayon to Freddy') for following the rules. Help children who do not follow the rules by showing them what to do instead and then praising it.

If a child has had time to settle with you and still is not responding to your usual encouragement and boundary setting, despite all the approaches above, then you might consider talking to parents about using approaches that are additional or different to the usual. Consider entering the child's name on your special needs register and putting together a within-setting individual behaviour plan (see Chapter 8).

Criteria for problem behaviour

There are four main criteria for helping you decide that a behaviour is abnormal or problematical:

- Fixation: a behaviour has continued beyond the age where it might be considered appropriate. For example, many one-year-olds throw toys but it becomes a problem if a four-year-old regularly throws them.
- Regression: a behaviour might have been achieved successfully at an appropriate age and the child then reverts back to behaviour characteristics of a younger age. For example, a child might have settled beautifully into the setting and then begins to cry inconsolably for no known reason.
- Failure to display: a behaviour that should have developed by a particular age has not done so. For example, a four-year-old might find it impossible to share or to take turns, or a three-year-old might not be able to play with a toy without throwing it.
- Exaggeration: a normal behaviour such as a burst of temper might become exaggerated into a full-blown temper tantrum in which other children get hurt. Also, a behaviour might have become greatly exaggerated in order to gain attention, such as hitting the younger children.

Observation and assessment

The first step with a behaviour difficulty is to gather information by talking with the family, any other professional involved and by observing the behaviour itself. Not only does this provide you with useful information but it gives you 'thinking time' to work out what you can do about it. Once a problem has been identified, everyone will be expecting you to 'do something'. When you gather information, you are clearly doing something even though you do not have a plan of action formulated. Sometimes the very act of standing back a little and observing what is going on gives you the emotional distance to think about the problem more objectively. There are various ways in which you can help staff observe and record problem behaviour. When this is done prior to a behavioural intervention it is called collecting 'baseline' information.

Case study

Below is an extract from an article that could be used as a discussion point in a staff meeting. Talk about what you would do and why you would do it.

'Your child's a biter!' stormed a furious mother at our village fête as she scooped up her family and left my two-year-old firmly in charge of the entire climbing frame. I can see his face now, still growling like the tiger he had become, yet with a gleeful glint in his eye that told me that he was entirely pleased with how things had turned out.

Biting works for the child because it can feel satisfying when you are feeling angry or distressed. It works because it can help a child win a dispute over a toy or leave them to enjoy the apparatus alone. It works because it can make life very exciting and attention-getting for a while. Our task becomes one of making sure that biting does not 'work' for the child and of ensuring, as far as we possibly can, that our children do not hurt each other in the process. This will be done most easily if we do not react in shock and horror, and if we handle this behaviour as calmly and consistently as we would any other.

Why do we tend to react so extremely when one child bites another in the setting? It is almost as if we see biting as something inherently primitive and bad within children. Instead of talking about biting behaviour, we slip easily into a labelling process that suggests that this child is a biter, will remain so, and therefore the behaviour cannot be handled or changed. This is simply not true. The very fact that biting is a primitive and animal-like behaviour should make us view it with far more understanding; it should not surprise us.

Why do children bite? My son (the one who now eats burgers instead of other children) told me it was because other children were in his way and he 'needed' to have a particular toy. Children at two- to three-years-old simply cannot see the world from any other point of view than their own. This does not make them 'naughty', it is simply the stage they have reached. Therefore, we need to teach them about the effect that their behaviour has on other children, and make it clear that they should not hurt others.

Sometimes very young children bite out of pure affection. Another child of mine at the age of one headed only for a certain blond and curly-haired child. There was no other provocation than the fact she was there. If you asked who he liked best at toddler group, it was this child. In a similar way, six-month-old babies can sometimes give a particularly loving and painful nip when breast-feeding.

The most common cause of biting at age two and three is frustration. The intensity of feeling at this age can be enormous, yet they lack the words to express what they are feeling or to negotiate the situation. Biting or striking out becomes the immediate and natural reaction when the words do not come. This is why we so often see behaviour improving dramatically when children learn the words to use instead. We can help this process along by putting in our own words ('I can see how angry you feel. How can I help you?') and showing children how to share or take turns. In the same way, if a child is hearing us shout, or seeing hitting and aggression used regularly in any situation, that will be what is learned.

Hannah Mortimer

Things to consider:

- When does biting become a problem behaviour?
- Why do you think people label children who bite as 'biters'?
- How would you gather information to help you decide why a child was biting?
- What general things can you do to prevent biting behaviour within the setting?

ABC diary

Ask staff to keep a diary recording of what the child was actually doing, what seemed to lead up to it and what the consequences were. Encourage them to write clearly and objectively, describing observable actions and using non-judgemental language (see page 25). This is called an ABC diary because it records:

- A – the antecedent. What led up to the behaviour or what was happening just before it? It might be that the child was playing with the tractor and another child took it. It might be that you had said 'no' to a request the child made. It might be that the child's mum had just arrived with the baby brother.
- B – the behaviour itself in clear, unambiguous words. Encourage staff to use words such as 'hit', 'threw' and 'screamed', rather than 'was aggressive', 'was disruptive' or 'was naughty'.
- C – the consequences of the behaviour. This would include what happened to the child as a result, for example, another child hit back, and what the member of staff did next, for example, led Poppy away and comforted Rea.

Useful tip
The observation method you select should serve the child and serve you. Do not bog staff down with complicated information-gathering unless it is going to be useful and usable.

Make sure that staff members do not just list a chronicle of behaviours without the antecedents and consequences. A list of trouble times can be used to tell someone else how bad the situation feels to the recorder, but it goes nowhere towards helping you plan for change or adopt the right mind-set for changing behaviours.

You can encourage the right frame of mind in staff by asking them to keep a similar diary for times when the child behaved really well – or at least better. What seemed to lead to the improvement and what did you all do as a result? This will help you look for the behavioural patterns that will help you plan your early years action.

Counting or measuring the behaviour

Sometimes a behaviour is so evident that you can actually count the number of times it happens during a session. This is only possible if you have all agreed what constitutes the problem behaviour and when you will count it as happening. One staff member's 'temper tantrum' could be another's 'grumble' – in other words two people can observe the same child doing the same behaviour and describe or interpret it in very different ways. Behaviours that might lend themselves to a frequency count include throwing toys, upsetting toy boxes, kicking, climbing onto the tables and so on.

Other behaviours can be measured in terms of their duration – perhaps a child screamed for ten minutes today, or played happily for twenty minutes continuously. The whole point of measuring the behaviour in some way is:

- to enable you to see change
- to enable you to monitor the intervention you have planned.

Unless you have recorded that you started with six major temper tantrums each session and that you are now (three weeks later) down to three, you would never appreciate the success you are having. Instead, you would have become so focused on these temper tantrums that you would be wondering why, after all your hard work, they were still very much in evidence. Only by seeing that you have in fact reduced them by half can you commend staff for their efforts and assure them that they are on the right lines.

Spot observations

With older children, we sometimes use spot observations to see whether a child is 'off task' or 'on task' – this becomes meaningless in early years settings because all play is 'on task' and learning and play should be synonymous. However, there are occasions when this can be a helpful approach, depending on the behaviour being observed. For example, you could ask a staff member to collect these observations. Suppose that staff were worried about a child whose behaviour was very solitary. Each five minutes one of them could observe the child briefly and record whether they were playing on their own or with others. This would again give you a baseline against which you could measure positive change. Perhaps your baseline observations show that the child was playing on his own for 10/12 observations. After you have worked on encouraging more group and social play, you might be able to record a 'post baseline' of only 3/12. You will find a possible framework for taking five minute observations on the photocopiable sheet on page 127. The whole observation need only take one hour of quick five minute spot checks. Repeat it in different situations and during different sessions so that you are sure you have a meaningful sample.

Useful tip
Use a timer such as an egg timer to prompt staff to record their five minute observation.

Useful tip
By asking staff to gather information about appropriate behaviour as well as problem behaviour, you are helping them develop a positive expectation that things can change.

Behaviour charts

An ABC chart can help to identify any factors that may be affecting the child's behaviour. Like the ABC diary, it allows you to gather information about all kinds of behaviour and not to identify the problem behaviour in advance. Ask the staff to record significant incidents of difficult behaviour on a chart such as this:

ABC behaviour chart

For every problem behaviour, collect information about an appropriate behaviour as well.

Time	What led up to it?	Behaviour	What happened next?

By recording the antecedent (what happened before the behaviour took place), the behaviour (exactly what the child did) and the consequence (what happened as a result of the behaviour), a clearer view of the context of the behaviour can be gained. For every entry of a difficult behaviour, staff should be asked to record one occasion when the child was behaving appropriately or especially well. This provides you with information about the situations that work well for the child as well as those that are not so successful.

Case study

Below is a case study that could be used as a discussion point in a staff meeting. Talk about what you would do and why you would do it.

Here is an ABC chart for a child who was having difficulties in behaving appropriately with other children.

Time	What led up to it?	Behaviour	What happened next?
	Jack was playing with the cars and Tammy asked for one.	Jack kicked Tammy.	Tammy cried and Jack tipped all the cars on to the floor. Mrs Smith comforted Tammy and asked Jack to say 'sorry' and pick up the cars, but he ran off.
	Jack was climbing on the frame. He called to Sam to watch.	Sam joined in.	Jack and Sam played together for a few minutes.
	Jack was playing in the outside play area.	Jack ran up to Mrs Smith and pushed at her back, swearing.	Jack was sent in.

Things to consider:

- What would you suggest doing to help Jack?
- What other information would you gather?
- How would you know if your suggestion was working?

'Fly on the wall' observation

Ask a member of staff to observe a child during a continuous period of time (say 30 minutes) and to write down what they are doing and how they are interacting in clear, unambiguous terms. Ask them to record the time in the left-hand margin so that you will have an idea of how long the child was playing in a certain area, with certain other children or demonstrating a certain behaviour. Arrange for extra help so that the observer can be released for this length of time. Ask other staff to carry on as if the observer were not present and not to rely on that person to manage any incidents. Suggest that the observer sits to the side of the room and moves discretely from area to area in order to keep the child in view. It soon becomes possible to develop the knack of observing from the corner of one's eye and recording as you watch. If other children approach, the observer should keep their eyes down and explain briefly but politely, 'I'm doing my writing today. You will need to ask... instead'. Later, you can look through the observation together and identify any patterns to the behaviour.

The use of check-lists

There are some check-lists available to help with assessments of behaviour and often these are compiled by a setting. If a check-list is standardised it tells you what particular skills or behaviours are typical of a certain age or stage, such as in the Portage Developmental check-list (nfer-Nelson) (see page 144 for contact details). Some managers and SENCOs feel that this helps them to know what is 'normal' and when to be concerned.

However, there is such a huge variation in the ages and stages at which children develop different behaviours, and so much depends on the child's personal experiences and the context, that other managers prefer not to use these. Instead, they prefer to look at their curriculum (such as the Personal, social and emotional Early Learning Goals and Stepping Stones), set out to teach to any weaknesses, and to become concerned when progress is not forthcoming despite planned support and teaching.

Useful tip
If staff are using standardised check-lists, make sure that they do not lose sight of individual differences and ranges of development – each child is unique with a unique set of experiences.

Working it out

There are certain behaviour problems that are noticed on a regular basis. These are the behaviours that you see with:

- children who have very low confidence
- children who cannot take 'no' for an answer and cannot follow rules and routines
- children who regularly throw major temper tantrums
- children who display aggressive behaviour.

It is worth looking at each of these behaviour problems in turn. Use this information to help staff to put the behaviour into context and to help them to think about the problem in more depth. By answering the questions together you will be gathering the information you need to begin to work out the antecedents and consequences for the particular child and situation with which you are working.

Children with low confidence

What you need to know:

- Approximately 43 per cent of seven- to twelve-year-olds talk about having fears and worries so it is quite normal for little ones to be worriers too.
- At the age of four, all children tend to be frightened of strangers, of things that might happen to them in the future and even of imagined events that might happen.
- Children younger than four tend to worry most about separation from their parents or carers.
- Children with a positive self-image are more likely to be more independent, better socially adjusted and more likely to achieve academically.

➤ Children with positive self-esteem are more likely to try new things, meet with success, and develop the confidence to try again.
➤ Developing confidence is therefore largely a matter of developing the positive way children think about themselves.

What are your concerns?

➤ Some children seem highly anxious in new situations. Is this the case for the child you have in mind?
➤ Some children have difficulties separating from their main carer. Is this the worry?
➤ Some children are very quiet in the group even if they are noisy at home (and sometimes vice-versa). Does this difference in confidence concern you?
➤ Some children's confidence is very easily knocked. Is this the case for the child you are working with?
➤ Some children have all sorts of fears, or have anxious mannerisms such as constantly chewing at sleeves or biting knuckles. Does this worry you?
➤ Some children seem to spoil their toys and their work, and act as if it does not matter when you praise them. Does this concern you?

Children who cannot follow rules and routines

What you need to know:

➤ About 80 per cent of four-year-olds still have some help when getting dressed in the morning.
➤ Three-quarters of four-year-olds are still largely dependent on their parents for help with dressing, undressing, feeding, going to the toilet and so on.
➤ Children become most confident and independent in new routines if they have warm, affectionate relationships with their parents. It is worth working on the parent's relationship with the child if you aim to improve things.

➤ Children become independent faster if they feel good about themselves, that is, if their self-esteem is positive.
➤ Children develop independence most quickly if you adopt a democratic style of caring, offering them choices but retaining the final say yourselves.

What are your concerns?

➤ Some children never stop or listen when you ask them to and do not listen to what you ask of them. Is this the problem for you?
➤ Some children tend to play out of sight if they can. You worry that they may not be safe, or may be causing damage or getting into trouble. Is this the case?
➤ Some children insist on more independence than you feel they are ready for. Is this a problem for you?
➤ Some children are reluctant to do anything independently and rely on you for everything. Is this your concern?
➤ Some children find it very difficult to play independently. Is this a worry?
➤ Some children find it very hard to know that 'a rule is a rule' and will always try to stretch it and test their boundaries. Is this a problem in your situation?
➤ Some children never seem to do what you ask them. Is this a worry for you?

Tantrums and doing as you are asked

What you need to know:

➤ Approximately 80 per cent of six- to twelve-year-olds still lose their tempers at least monthly, 48 per cent at least twice a week, and 11 per cent every day, so it is not unusual for younger children to do so.
➤ Temper tantrums are the biggest behaviour problem reported by parents of children under five.
➤ Young children feel emotions such as anger and fright very intensely indeed. They have not yet learned the words to talk about these feelings, so it can 'come out' in the form of a tantrum.

What are your concerns?

➤ Some children's tantrums are so severe that they can bang their heads, hold their breath and even pass out for a moment or two. What does the child you are working with do during a tantrum? How often are they happening?
➤ Some days may go much better. What is happening on the 'good days' when the child is not throwing tantrums?
➤ Some children become very frustrated because they are thinking faster than they can talk or because they might have difficulties in hearing or communicating. Frustrated children have more tantrums. Is this a worry in your child's case? What do you think is causing the frustration?
➤ Although almost all children go through a phase of temper tantrums, some develop this into a fine art in order to get what they want, because they have learned that tantrums sometimes 'work'. Is the child trying to use temper tantrums to get what he or she wants?
➤ Some children appear to be terrified during a tantrum. Is this child very frightened too? How do you know this?

Children who play aggressively

What you need to know:

➤ Most four-year-olds play together with other children their age, although they may not develop a 'best' friend until they are seven or eight.
➤ Boys are a little more aggressive than girls, though girls tend to use words more than physical actions in their quarrels.
➤ About 72 per cent of four-year-olds 'talk back' and appear 'cheeky'.
➤ Approximately 37 per cent of four-year-olds tell 'fibs'.
➤ Young children need to learn the skills of turn-taking and sharing through playing with other children.
➤ Children often go through a phase of biting but sometimes the biting becomes part of their regular behaviour pattern. There are many different reasons why little children bite – because it feels good, because they feel frustrated, because they are feeling excited, because they like to put things in their mouth and even because they feel hungry!
➤ You need to investigate the reasons behind the aggressive behaviour in order to plan the best approach for managing it.

What are your concerns?

➤ Look at the child's social skills. Have they learned yet how to be friendly? For some children, 'playing' means fighting, and that is exactly what they do whenever they meet another child. Is this a problem for this child?
➤ Some children do not know how to make friends or are very shy. Is this the case for your situation?
➤ Sometimes you feel as if certain children never stop quarrelling and fighting. Is this a worry?
➤ Some children tend to hit or throw things at other children. Is this a worry?
➤ Some children swear a lot and are cheeky.
➤ Some children steal things or tell lies a lot. Are you concerned about any children who do this?

In the next two chapters, you will read about how you can support your colleagues in planning changes for difficult behaviour. In Chapter 6 these four areas of behaviour will be revisited with possible solutions to discuss with the staff. We will also consider toileting problems and difficult meal times.

Chapter 6 Trying interventions

- **Children with low confidence or anxiety**
- **Children who cannot follow rules**
- **Tantrums and doing as you are asked**
- **Children who play aggressively**
- **Toileting problems**
- **Difficult meal times**

Supporting staff as they try out interventions for difficult behaviours takes sensitivity and a degree of subtlety. When a child's behaviour is particularly problematical, the adults who are trying to deal with this are already feeling stressed, emotionally vulnerable and perhaps defensive. You may feel that, as a manager or SENCO, you are being asked for 'the answer' and you too may be left feeling frustrated and inadequate. All of these feelings can lead towards exclusion rather than inclusion of the child and the child's individual needs. It can be helpful to bear these points in mind:

➤ There are no 'right answers' – only individual solutions. Therefore it helps to explore each situation and come up with the best ways forward (the consultation approach described on page 24 helps you to do this).

➤ You will be helping colleagues to be more effective managers of behaviour in the future if you help them reflect on the behaviour problem and work out some of these ways themselves. That is why you will read in this chapter of six areas of frequent behaviour problems with suggestions for thinking through the problem with the staff members concerned, and a range of possible interventions to try based on all that you have read so far.

Children with low confidence or anxiety

Things to think about:

➤ Think about the child's self-esteem (see page 10). We all vary in our self-esteem from day to day, but would you say that low self-esteem is a problem for this child?

➤ If so, think about ways in which you can encourage and support them. Perhaps they are feeling under pressure in some way. Can you think of anything that would help this? Can you perhaps expect a little less of them for a while, and boost their confidence as much as possible?

➤ If you are the key worker is it possible that the child is picking up any anxiety or tension from the way you are handling the situation?

➤ Sometimes children learn that one adult has one rule and another adult has another. Might this be a problem? Are the children 'playing one off against the other'? If so, think about talking together as a staff group and agreeing what you want from the children's behaviour. Back each other up so you all know what is going on.

➤ If a child has started to steal, think about what might have triggered this. Are they feeling very angry about something? Do you need to talk about this together? Are they feeling unsettled and confused about something: a new partner in the family, someone being away from home and so on? Try to tackle the underlying reason as well as the behaviour itself, because the stealing might be just a symptom of something else that is going on for the child. Help them put back what is taken, say 'sorry' and restore the damage.

➤ Some children are confused about what they are allowed to take home from the group (for example, a picture, some craft material) and what they are not (a toy car, a set of crayons). Can you think of ways of explaining these rules?

➤ If a child appears to be lying a lot, is it because they think it does not matter? Some children still confuse fact from fiction, and enjoy making up their own versions of reality just to make life interesting. If they are obviously not telling the truth ('The giant took it, not me'), then you might lighten things by smiling and saying, 'Yes, just pretend', showing that you know this is made up. Try to separate this kind of 'non-truth' from the other definite 'lie' that is usually given by an older child to get out of trouble.

Possible interventions

➤ Once you have decided on your rules, stick to them. Repeat them calmly if you need to and try not to become cross or be drawn into an argument. If children are squabbling, do not be drawn in or you will be involved for ever more. Instead, let them sort it out but step in if the rules (for example, 'no hurting') are broken.

➤ Take time to tell the children when they are sticking to the rules, and find a way of making them feel you are really pleased with them.

➤ There will be times when you all feel run-down or tired and it is difficult to help the children stick to the rules. Do not give up, you can only do your best. Start each session with fresh intentions to stay positive and to stay calm.

➤ Decide in advance what will happen if a rule is not kept, for example, if a child hits another child, they will need to sit quietly for four minutes and then you will help the child to say sorry, and help them begin to play at something more appropriate.

➤ If you are using quiet times in this way, the rule of thumb is one minute per year of age, for example, three minutes (which feel like forever) for a three-year-old child.

➤ Find ways of making it easier for the children to stick to rules. For example, find ways to help them know when to come in or how far away to play. Also, they are more likely to play happily if each is occupied, if one is helping you with an activity, or if you are playing and talking to them as you work, making it more interesting.

➤ Children will test you to see if a rule is a rule. You will need to be extra consistent at first. If you give in, they have learned to push you harder to get what they want the next time. Stay calm and patient too; the children are still very young and do not learn things first time.

Useful tip

Encourage staff to make routine tasks into a race or a game, 'I bet you can't put these cars away before me'.

➤ If a rule is broken, repeat the rule calmly, give the child a slow '1, 2, 3...' to do it on their own, and then gently but firmly help the child to do it. Praise the child for co-operating. This '1, 2, 3...' warning gives the child time to decide to do it independently and it reduces confrontations.
➤ Try to build up regular routines for doing things like sharing the toys or putting on aprons. If there is a regular routine, children argue less.
➤ However, if the child is so dependent on routines that they are frightened if these are broken in the slightest way, find ways of reassuring them and gradually introducing change, step by small step.

Tantrums and doing as you are asked

Things to think about:

➤ If you are seeing a lot of tantrums in the setting, it is worth thinking about why the children might be feeling so cross with themselves and the world. Are they frustrated? Do any of the children have any difficulty that needs looking at by a professional such as a hearing difficulty or a slowness in learning to talk clearly? Talk to the parents, carers or health visitor if you are concerned.
➤ Is the child seeing anger in other people and copying? Is there a chance that the child is seeing loud arguments between other people and learning that anger is an appropriate way to show feelings? Some children cannot make sense of the anger around them and become angry themselves as a result, without really understanding why.
➤ Some children are very frightened by the intensity of their own tantrums. Perhaps you need to tell the child that it is alright to feel angry and cross at times, you do too, but we all have to learn ways of being angry that do not hurt other people. Spend time recognising and talking to the child about feelings. Look for ways of allowing the child to get rid of pent up anger or energy by running around in a playground, beating a cushion, banging on a metal bowl with a spoon, shouting up a tree and so on.
➤ Is there a chance that a child has learned that tantrums can achieve a desired effect? For example, if the child threw a tantrum because there were no bikes left to ride, are you tempted to 'give in' for the sake of peace and because so many people are watching?
➤ Is there a chance that the child is gaining lots of attention for throwing tantrums and this is what is keeping them going? Does the child do it when lots of people are watching? Are they enjoying being the centre of attention?
➤ Look at what is happening leading up to the child's tantrums. Try to work out what is causing them. Keep a diary of the big tantrums, making a note of:

- what led up to them
- what the child did
- where it happened
- what you did
- what happened as a result of this.

Then try to work out a pattern. Perhaps they are happening when you say 'no', or when another child has a toy the child wants. Try to work out how the child is feeling during the tantrum. Is the child very angry, or very frightened, or a mixture of both? In general, children elicit in you the feelings that they have inside – if you are left feeling confused and muddled by a child's behaviour, it is likely that the child is feeling confused and muddled too. If you are left feeling angry at the child, then it is likely that the child is feeling angry too.

➤ Do you think that the child knows that when you say something, you really mean it? Sometimes, children switch into a tantrum as soon as they are told they cannot do something, believing that you are bound to 'give in'. If this a problem in your setting, think about how you can introduce rules and boundaries that are going to leave everyone feeling more secure and less fraught.

Possible interventions

➤ If you have worked out what leads up to a child's tantrums, you can sometimes plan things differently. For example, instead of saying 'no' and 'don't', you can give the children ideas about what they can do instead.

➤ It is better to help them to complete a request rather than doggedly insisting that they must do it themselves. This way, tempers are less frayed and the child has learned how to do it with your help.

➤ If the child is in a full tantrum, then shouting or even reasoning will only keep the tantrum high. When children are very angry or emotional, they have a surge of hormones in their blood that makes it very difficult to listen or calm down. If the bystanders get angry too, the child's hormones will stay at a very high level. Instead, the child needs a chance to calm down first (and so do you). Deal with the tantrum calmly, with minimum eye contact and words, calmly removing the child from the room and staying close until everything 'cools down'. This is easiest when you have a separate, safe and rather boring place to retire to together.

➤ When the child is calm again (and it can take a while), turn to the child and offer comfort. Start by praising the child for calming down. Talk calmly about what happened and what can be done about it. This is the time for reasoning and explanation. Then distract the child with something else.

➤ This 'cooling off' period is also known as 'time out'. It should not be a punishment but a means of giving everyone the chance to calm down. Do not be concerned if 'he didn't see it as a punishment'. This is fine; the point is the child has calmed down and now you have a chance of addressing the problem together.

➤ You will need to decide with your colleagues exactly what constitutes a tantrum so you know when to intervene with your 'time out'. Your setting, private nursery chain or Education Authority probably have clear guidelines for using 'time out' approaches and you will need to make sure that all staff members are aware of these.

➤ Make sure that the children are getting more attention from the adults around when they are behaving appropriately, rather than when they are throwing tantrums. If not, they will throw tantrums as the best way of getting your attention.

➤ Distraction can sometimes work. Offer them a little jar and invite them to fill it with tears for their mum. Or give them a cushion to bang all their crossness into, then ceremoniously take the cushion to another room and say 'goodbye' to the crossness. Ideas like this might be worth a try.

Useful tip
Try to distract and 'jolly' the children along, reducing confrontations if you can. A sense of humour can do wonders if yours is not already in tatters!

Children who play aggressively

Things to think about:

➤ Consider where the child might be learning about fighting and aggression. Has the child seen much of this going on? You may be tempted to blame home or the neighbourhood, but the children will be seeing it on the television daily. Is there anything you can do to make sure that they are not experiencing or watching too much violence? A lot of fighting at this age is linked to 'acting out' favourite television or cartoon characters. Contact the health visitor or any family support worker if you are concerned about aggression and violence in the home, and always abide by the Child Protection procedures.

➤ Decide ahead what you are going to do about squabbling in the setting and try to stick to it. You might decide to use each incident as an opportunity to help the children negotiate and resolve disputes, or you might decide not to intervene unless the children are being hurt or upset. Whatever the case, listen to both sides of the story first and help the children find a way through the problem.

➤ Think about the times of the session when the fighting is most likely to happen. It might be when you are busy with the tidying up and everyone is a bit tired. Can you set things up differently? Perhaps some of the children could help you more or perhaps one of the adults could keep the children occupied in some way with a final story or music session.

➤ If a child is biting or hitting out at other children, keep a note of what is happening by keeping an ABC diary (see page 52).

➤ We know from looking at lots of children's behaviour that swearing is often done because of the effect it has. It is easier to ignore swearing at home than in a busy group, although you could consider making it clear that it does not impress you by turning away and not reacting.

➤ Occasionally, children swear because they genuinely do not know that the word they are using is a swear word. Discuss this with parents and carers, then take time to explain to the child which words should not be said, and which are alright to use.

Possible interventions

➤ When you have decided on your rules (such as 'no hurting each other'), stick to them. Repeat them calmly if you need to and try not to become cross or be drawn into an argument. Help the children sort out their disputes and step in if the rules (such as 'no hurting') are broken.

➤ You may need to play with them for a while, helping them to share and to take turns. It may help to do something organised together like visiting the swings or playing a game of football. Try to find times when the child can succeed in playing with another child, even if it is with your help and supervision.

➤ Does the child need more opportunities to mix and play with other children in order to learn the social skills necessary for making friends? It is tempting to avoid social situations if a child is being anti-social or extremely shy, but perhaps they need more. Exclusion is always counter-productive for a child who has not yet learned how to be sociable.

➤ Take time to explain to the child how the other children are feeling and offer solutions to their problems: 'Perhaps another child is sad because you took their bike'; 'Perhaps the other children would like to take turns on the train-set'; 'Perhaps one of you could push and the other ride'.

➤ Give clear rules about 'no biting' and so on, and make it clear what will happen if they do (for example, they will have to come inside) and what will happen if they do not (for example, you will tell their mum that they have played well all morning).

➤ If a child is behaving very anti-socially (like stopping all the other children coming anywhere near the sand tray or lashing out), consider removing the child immediately from that social situation. When things have calmed down, talk together about what went wrong and make sure that the child understands what should be done instead. Watch that child carefully next time and give praise for doing better.

➤ Look for opportunities to praise each child for sharing, taking turns, handing round the snacks or waiting patiently. In other words, try to notice when the children are behaving appropriately as well as when they are behaving anti-socially. Tell them why you are so pleased with them.

Useful tip

Never deal with aggressive behaviour by being aggressive back, even if it is just with your tone of voice. Everyone's adrenaline becomes stirred and nobody can think clearly. Be clear, assertive and firm but do not show anger.

Toileting problems

Things to think about:

➤ If a child 'wets' during the day, find out from parents or carers whether that child has ever been 'dry' in the past? If so, then you might be seeing wetting because of some change in the child's life. Have they been poorly recently? Is there a new baby in the family? Have they just started in the setting? Think about what might be unsettling the child. Use a special five minutes talking time each session to encourage the child to share any worries, or to make it clear how special they are to you.

➤ If you feel the child was never really toilet-trained in the first place, then you might need to think about teaching them. Discuss this with parents and carers and agree a way forward. Keep a diary for a week or two of:

- when the child wets himself or herself
- what was happening at the time
- where it happened.

Look for a pattern to this.

➤ Do not keep asking the children if they want the toilet – they will usually say 'no', especially if they are too busy to stop what they are doing. Instead, ask any child who is having 'accidents' regularly to go and 'just try' for you at regular intervals. Be aware of the signs – the wriggle or the hold – that signals that the toilet is needed.

➤ If there is a soiling problem, try to work out what is causing this. Perhaps the child has never really managed to use the toilet successfully yet and has always 'held onto it' in the setting and used a nappy at home instead. Perhaps they constantly dirty their pants with overflow because they are so badly constipated. Talk to the parents and carers about wanting to help them sort this out, and speak with the health visitor if you feel that extra advice is needed.

➤ Consider the child's diet. Might constipation be a problem or is constant diarrhoea a problem? Consider asking parents or carers to add more fibre (potato-skin wedges, baked beans, breakfast cereals and bananas are popular choices) and more fruit and vegetables (orange fruit juice, raw carrots, apple juice, finger fruits) to the diet.

Possible interventions

➤ At first, praise the child for trying; later you can use stickers and so on to praise successes.

➤ With daytime wet pants, do not get tense over the accidents, but ask parents to provide them with a spare pair of pants to take to the group and a bag for bringing them home. Encourage the children to see to themselves as far as possible so that they do not get embarrassed.

➤ If you are toilet-training a child for the first time, use your diary record to decide when you need to remind the child to 'go'. Make a chart for yourself to remind you to keep it up. Before each snack time or before going home may be the best times. Look out for the tell-tale signs that the child needs to go.

Useful tip
Make the cloakroom area a pleasant and child-centred place to go to with colourful spaces and the right size and level of fittings.

➤ If you are encouraging little boys to urinate standing up and to aim in the right place, consider placing a ping-pong ball in the water to aim at. This rights and cleans itself when you flush!
➤ If older children won't put on a coat or wash hands without you, accompany them for a while but do not actually do everything for them when you know they can do it. Stay close by to reassure and praise that they are doing it 'all by themselves'. Try to stay calm, positive and reassuring.

Difficult meal times

Things to think about:

➤ Fussy eating is a very common problem in young children. It is not a serious problem so long as the child is putting on weight steadily. If you are worried about this, talk with parents and carers or the health visitor. Most children manage to balance their diet on a very narrow range of food. Think of ways of offering them choices, providing smaller quantities or about how you present the food in order to tempt them.
➤ Think about your own reaction to the problem. We know that getting tense about meal times and toileting can make problems much worse, so you may need to look for ways that keep these occasions as relaxed as possible.

Possible interventions

➤ Introduce variety gradually, with little tastes that the children can try. Praise them for trying, even if they have not finished. Look for compromises, for example, split the remaining food into two piles, 'You can leave this and eat this'.
➤ If a child shows difficult behaviour at meal times, make sure that you have a definite routine for meal times. Are your rules clear? Children need to know what is expected of them.
➤ Keep meal and snack times relaxed – a happy and social time for enjoying being together and talking together.

Chapter 7 Changing behaviour

- **Behavioural approaches**
- **Staying positive**
- **Using rewards effectively**
- **Planning changes**
- **Changing the antecedents**
- **Changing the behaviour**
- **Changing the consequences**

Behavioural approaches

Behaviour management is just one of the many tools that you can use in order to change difficult behaviour. You have already considered many ways of looking at and responding to children's behaviour in this book. Behaviour management is based on the theory of behavioural psychology and makes use of positive encouragement and reward. Although you would feel uncomfortable basing your entire Foundation Stage teaching around the premise that children only behave in a certain way in order to gain rewards, there is a definite place for it when a particular child is displaying very difficult and demanding behaviour that has not responded to your usual approaches. In other words, you have already decided that something 'additional and different' is required. Behaviour management gives staff a definite job to do at a time when they might be feeling disempowered or unconfident because of the child's behaviour.

In essence, a 'behavioural' theory states that:

- if you do something, and something pleasant happens to you, you are more likely to do that thing again
- if you do something, and something unpleasant happens to you, you are less likely to do that thing again.

So far, this should make sense to everyone. Suppose, for example, that you move to a new job and pluck up courage on the first day to say 'hello' to a new colleague in the corridor. If that person smiles and responds with a 'hello', then you are likely to continue with a regular greeting and perhaps get to know each other. However, if the person looks away and does not reply, then you are likely to feel less confident and not so likely to say 'hello' the next time you meet. In other words, what happens to you affects what you are likely to do in the future.

What of the child whose behaviour becomes worse after a 'good telling off'? Should it not follow that when something unpleasant happens (like the telling off) the child should be likely to behave better? In reality you know that this does not always follow! For some children, behaviour is directed at attracting any kind of reaction or attention, even if it comes in the form of being told off. In other words, you cannot decide that the telling off is a punishment for the child unless it actually reduces the behaviour. Each child and situation will be different. Therefore it is helpful to explain to staff that rewards are not rewards because of what they are (eye contact and a cuddle, a clap in front of all the other children, a special food treat) but because of what they do (they make the behaviour more likely to happen in the future). Similarly, punishments are not punishments because of what they are (a reprimand, being sent to another room) but because of what they do (make the behaviour less likely to happen in the future):

- The pleasant event is called a reward, simply because it makes the behaviour increase.
- The unpleasant event is called a punishment simply because it makes the behaviour decrease. Nowadays we use the expressions 'negative consequences' or 'sanctions' instead of 'punishments' because there are less overtones of physical violence.
- Negative consequences need not be something unpleasant that happens; they can simply be that the child was expecting a certain reward to happen and it never did (for example, the temper tantrum did not bring the expected tractor ride or the bite did not lead to being able to play with the train).

Case study

This case study could be used as a discussion point in a staff meeting. Talk about what you would do and why you would do it.

Ben used to attend a small nursery regularly. His speech and language skills were a little delayed and the speech and language therapist worked with the setting to support him and provide ideas to help him. The nursery assistants were keen to make each and every child feel welcomed and secure when they arrived at the setting. One of them would stand at the door and bend down to the children's level, greeting them warmly and effusively. Unfortunately Ben was sick on the doormat each morning as he arrived.

Things to consider:

- Think of all the reasons why Ben might have been sick on a regular basis.
- Was the greeting helping Ben?
- Does that mean that greeting children is wrong in every situation?
- Later, the nursery assistants found out that part of Ben's language difficulty meant that he found it hard to handle direct eye contact and transitions between one situation to the next. How could staff plan his arrival differently?
- Could staff have planned these changes anyway, or was it necessary to know about Ben's particular difficulties first?

Staying positive

It sometimes comes as a surprise to newly qualified or inexperienced staff that we should be using positive approaches for dealing with what might appear to be very negative behaviours. Your first task as manager or SENCO will be to explain what is meant by a positive behavioural approach and provide some evidence to back up why you are suggesting such an approach.

Positive behavioural approaches do these things:

- They make sure that the child's self-esteem remains positive. This is because the child is given the message that it is the behaviour that is unacceptable rather than the child.
- They are based on the use or removal of rewards and pleasant happenings. Negative consequences may work in the short-term to control or stop a difficult behaviour, but they will not help the child to change behaviour in the longer term. Instead, they lead to children behaving inappropriately until an adult intervenes, rather than learning self-control.
- They aim not only to remove or alter an inappropriate behaviour but to replace it with a more positive and appropriate behaviour. As you are all in the business of delivering the Foundation Stage curriculum for personal, social and emotional development this makes obvious sense. You know that children do not arrive in your setting with good behaviour ready packaged – behaviour and social skills need to be learned and developed just like everything else.

Case study

These statements about behaviour management could be used as a discussion point in a staff meeting.

- Why do we have to use positive approaches for Megan who is being really naughty?
- If we stay positive aren't we just teaching Kyle that it is alright to be naughty?
- What Caitlin needs is a really good telling off – she needs to know who's boss.
- It's no good praising Feras – he just becomes silly and over-excited.
- Using rewards is insulting – it's just like teaching a dog tricks and children are worth more than that.
- It's only when I get really cross that Jon stops being naughty.

Things to consider:

- Talk about each statement and decide on some arguments you could use to suggest alternative views.
- Do rewards work for us in everyday life?
- What are the problems with using a word like 'naughty'?

Using rewards effectively

Rewards are happening all the time in your setting. Adults smile at children, give them eye contact, make approving comments and give encouragement. All these are done quite naturally and provide motivation for the child to behave in that way again. Day by day, children receive the message that kindness, creativity, friendly conversation and happy and constructive play are all behaviours that are regularly rewarded and valued by the people around them.

There are several different categories of rewards that the children will already be used to in their daily lives:

- Social praise: smiles, eye contact, a cuddle, verbal praise, laughter, clapping hands, cheering.
- Food and drink: favourite snacks, drinks, fruit, meals.
- Toys and playthings: being able to play with the digger, the group's teddy, enjoying a new set of toys.
- Activities: going to play outside, having the slide out, enjoying a story, playing on the computer.
- Sights and sounds: a musical CD, a kaleidoscope, coloured lights.
- Physical: a cuddle, a swing, a brush of the hair, a gentle blowing of a fan.

If staff can recognise that rewards are a fact of daily life then they will feel more comfortable about using rewards in order to change particularly challenging behaviour.

If a reward is going to be effective it has to satisfy these conditions:

- It must happen immediately. It is no good saying, 'You can have a treat tomorrow' – young children need your praise and recognition straight away.
- It must be something that catches the child's attention. It is no good saying, 'That's wonderful Ruben' in a dead-pan voice that Ruben will not even notice. Sometimes (with some children for whom praise has not been given regularly) you have to be extreme in your expression – 'That's FANTASTIC Ruben!'.
- It has to work for the child. Some children (perhaps because they have social or autistic spectrum difficulties) genuinely find eye contact and strong praise difficult to handle. It might even cause them to behave in a way to avoid it. In other words, one child's reward might be another child's sanction.
- It has to be given consistently at first. When you are introducing behavioural approaches, staff need to realise that they should reward or praise every single time a child behaves in the targeted way. Later, as the new behaviour becomes established, rewards can be given every now and again and gradually phased out.
- If a concrete reward (such as food or a special toy) is given, perhaps because that is the only thing a child will work for at first, then social praise should always be given as well. After a while, the concrete reward can be faded out as the social praise remains. In time, the child will come to find the social praise alone to be rewarding. The aim is that as the children get older they will be behaving in the appropriate way through self-control and self-discipline.

You can use your own knowledge and experience of the child in order to work out which rewards will be effective. Parents and carers will also be a useful source of information. Perhaps their child collects certain stickers at home or loves a certain play activity. Perhaps they are on their very best behaviour when they are looking after their pet. Perhaps they love yoghurt snacks. Perhaps they love to be the family clown and to be cheered and applauded. Remember that each child is unique.

Planning changes

The best way for staff to change children's behaviour is to change what they are doing. Here are some simple steps for helping staff design a simple behaviour management programme in order to change a particularly difficult behaviour. The photocopiable sheet 'Behaviour planning' on pages 128 and 129 is a useful tool for staff to collect the information that they need for planning changes:

➤ Step 1: ask staff to describe the behaviour(s) they are concerned about. Help them to use clear language and to reach concurrence so that they are all clear about the behaviour that they wish to work on.
➤ Step 2: ask staff to observe the behaviour. If you are going to change a difficult behaviour into a more appropriate one, you need to know from where you started and when you have 'got there'. Your starting point is called the 'baseline'. It gives you a clear picture of how difficult or frequent the behaviour was before you started your plan to change things. You can measure behaviour in the different ways suggested in Chapter 5. You should end up with a clearer picture of the antecedents, the behaviour itself and the consequences (the 'ABC' of behaviour).
➤ Step 3: gather information – it is helpful to find out more about the child's behaviour in different situations. Speaking with parents or carers is the obvious starting point. Behaviour can sometimes be a sensitive area to discuss with families without arousing defensive feelings. There are more ideas about this in Chapter 10. There might also be useful information to be gleaned from any other professionals involved such as a health visitor, family support worker, community worker, social worker or child psychologist. Perhaps the child used to attend another group; what was the behaviour like then and what approaches helped this child?
➤ Step 4: select just one behaviour to work on first. When staff begin to gather information about a child's behaviour, they might end up with a whole list of difficult behaviours and situations. They can feel daunted unless you reassure them that they need to start somewhere and the best place to start is on just one behaviour – perhaps one that is easy to change (such as running into the kitchen area) or one that is causing most disruption (such as biting). You can reassure them that this approach can help other behaviours too by starting a 'positive spiral' of better behaviour, more positive self-esteem and a much happier child.
➤ Step 5: work with staff to decide on a hypothesis. What do you all think is keeping that behaviour going? Is the child behaving like this to seek attention? Is it because the child cannot yet play co-operatively? Is it because the child has not yet learned to share? Is it when their mum brings the child to the group and not their gran?

➤ Step 6: draw up a plan to change the antecedents, the behaviour or the consequences. There are more ideas below and also a range of more general interventions in Chapter 6.
➤ Step 7: monitor progress during three weeks and then review your hypothesis and your interventions if you need to. Behavioural approaches take a little while to work. If, for example, you have drawn up a plan to reduce attention-seeking behaviour by reducing the amount of eye contact and reaction you are giving the child, the behaviour is likely to become worse before it becomes better as the child will be 'testing the boundaries' for a while.

Useful tip
Help staff start by concentrating on just one or two behaviours causing the most concern.

Changing the antecedents

What are the most common approaches you can advise staff to follow for changing the antecedents to a difficult behaviour?

Avoid likely situations

When staff begin to collect information about a difficult behaviour using a diary or ABC behaviour chart, they may well begin to see a pattern emerging. Perhaps the child behaves worst in particular situations or places, or with particular other children or staff members. Perhaps the child becomes disruptive during story time, or very silly in front of certain helpers. You can 'break the cycle' of the difficult behaviour by avoiding the situation altogether for a while. There is an element of any difficult behaviour that has become a habit, and it is helpful to set up the situation differently so that the habit is broken for a while. It also helps everyone, child and staff alike, to feel more relaxed and confident. You are not being defeated by taking this avoidance action; this is clever management because you should then have a plan to move the child towards the stage when they can cope without misbehaving. For example, if a child cannot tolerate close proximity from certain other children without fighting them, you can distract the child away from those children for a while but later set up structured and supported play activities where you are helping them learn other ways of playing together.

Distract rather than confront

Distraction is one of the most powerful tools we have for managing young children's behaviour. Just at the moment when a squabble is brewing, we direct their attention to a new exciting event or opportunity, defusing the situation altogether. Again, do not feel you are side-stepping the issue; it is clever management to use distraction in early years settings. Again, staff can note 'problem times' and plan other opportunities for helping the children learn more appropriate ways of behaving.

Make sure the activity suits the child's level

So often, children who are referred to support services with behaviour difficulties turn out to be experiencing difficulties in learning as well. It is also true that many children are seen to have behaviour problems simply because the expectations of the staff were too high. A classic example is the tall, rather active and boisterous two-year-old who is perceived by adults to be older than he is. If staff respond to his behaviour as they would a four-year-old, that child is going to find it hard to 'get things right'. Another example would be a child who has not yet learned how to concentrate for longer than a minute or two who is expected to sit at a table and complete a worksheet. You will find more on expectations, ages and stages in Chapter 2.

Attract full attention before giving directions

If necessary, encourage staff to bend down to the child's level, say their name or gently touch their chin to ensure eye contact before giving instructions. Young children find it hard to realise that instructions given to a whole group also mean them, so staff need to cue in individual children to what they are about to say. Very active children tend to act without thinking and staff will need to teach looking skills and listening skills before they can expect the children to pay attention to what they are saying.

Give positive attention before trouble happens

Many children who appear to seek a lot of attention genuinely need a great deal of positive attention. Ask staff to look for ways of providing that attention when these children are behaving appropriately (they do not have to be especially good) and target their praise specifically – 'Thank you for sharing the paint, Ahmed!'. You may find that certain children behave more appropriately for some staff than others, and it could be that some staff members tend to give more attention to misdemeanours than to appropriate behaviour. This is quite understandable and you can commend the staff member for wanting to see better behaviour in the children, and then teach them the behaviour management skills that will help them balance their attention more effectively.

Give warning of changes of activity

Young children become so engrossed in what they are doing and have not learned to attend to more than one thing at a time. It can be very helpful if staff can give regular warnings about what is about to happen so that the children have a chance to prepare themselves for a change of activity – 'Nearly time to tidy up now, then you can play outside'.

Anticipate problem times and be a step ahead

Difficult behaviours often occur when children are in a 'vacuum' between activities or waiting for something to happen, such as at 'going home time'. Make sure that the children know not only what they can be doing now, but what they can do next. Helping children to plan and review their activities is a useful strategy here. You can also use visual timetables (a sequence of photographs illustrating the key activities and routines of the session) as a way of focusing certain children on what comes next. If a child with poor listening skills finds group story time difficult, then plan ahead by asking a helper to take him into the book corner for an individual story time. Gradually increase the number of children there until that child can listen within a group.

Give clear directions

Staff members know that children need full reasons and explanations if they are to learn about their worlds, yet there may be times when that is not appropriate. Help staff to choose what they want to say, for example 'no kicking' and repeat that, making the rule simple and clear. This is sometimes known as the 'broken record approach'! Sometimes, the more that staff elaborate, the more attention they are giving the child for behaving inappropriately. Instead, suggest that staff look for other times of day when they can talk together about reasons for behaving in a certain way and learn about behaving kindly.

Show what to do as well as saying it

Young children are usually too absorbed in what they are doing to respond to adult directions from across the room. Encourage staff working with young children whose attention is short to approach these children and model to them what to do. These children might find adult language difficult to understand, and staff can add meaning to their words by showing children what to do. For example, if a child throws the toys into the box at tidy-up time, show that child how to make a game of 'parking' the cars gently or putting the musical instruments back so that not a sound is made.

Choose a few simple rules and stick to them

These rules are especially useful when the children have contributed to them too, perhaps as a circle time activity. Suggest that staff stick to three or four rules at the most, perhaps relating to not hurting others, to being kind and to listening. Ask them to spend time with the children talking together about what it means to be 'kind' and to 'help'.

Changing the behaviour

You can help staff plan interventions that directly affect the child's behaviour.

Stop it if you can

Some behaviours can be anticipated and stopped from happening. If you know that a lively child is going to join your setting who tends to behave impulsively and has little sense of danger, then you would make sure that your boundaries, doors and gates were totally secure. You might need to fit safety locks to certain cupboards and you would carry out a risk assessment of how safe your setting was, making sure that safety features such as electric plug covers were all in place. You can also take a look at the way your spaces are organised. Wide open spaces with wheeled toys call out to lively children to move at great speed. Consider how you can draw their attention towards the near distance rather than the far distance by dividing up the space, adding 'road' lines and making suggestions to channel their play.

Teach the child a new behaviour opposite to the first

When a child is playing constructively with another child on the car mat, he cannot at the same time be fighting. In other words, some behaviours are incompatible with others. You can use this fact to great advantage. Help staff to decide ahead what behaviours they wish to see in place of the problem behaviour, and then set this as a target for teaching. Suddenly staff have a positive plan of action and are not focusing entirely on the negative behaviour. For example, staff might decide to work hard to build up a child's level of concentration, to help them play in a supervised group or to help them play alongside another child. In other words, they are managing the difficult behaviour by delivering social skills training.

Praise another behaviour incompatible with the first

Sometimes, a child is already demonstrating appropriate and friendly behaviour as well as the difficult behaviour. This gives staff a clear starting point for their behaviour management. Help them to use all the approaches already discussed to plan antecedents that make the problem behaviour less likely to happen, and then selectively praise and give attention at times when the child is behaving appropriately. There will still be good times and bad times, but usually the proportion of good times steadily increases.

Changing the consequences

The third option is to plan interventions that change the consequences of a child's behaviour, making it less likely to occur in the future.

Be absolutely consistent

This is the most difficult part of behaviour management. If it is to work effectively, staff must be consistent in their approaches. Staff can feel confused by a child's difficult behaviour and it is tempting to try one approach and then switch to another when it does not work immediately. They will need your support to draw up a plan and to stick to it for at least three weeks. If a child hits, kicks or bites, then the same thing must happen every single time, whoever the person supervising and whatever the situation. Otherwise, the children will learn that they can behave in a certain way if they make enough fuss or if they choose their audience or the situation.

Reward when the child is not doing the inappropriate behaviour

As well as focusing on the behaviour to be changed, staff will need your encouragement to think of a list of behaviours that the child would be showing when behaving appropriately instead. These behaviours should be both noticed and rewarded by staff. For example, if staff are planning an approach to stop Kieran from biting, then they might note that whenever Kieran was sitting at a table activity or whenever he was sharing the water play, he did not bite. They should then give attention and praise Kieran for playing well at these times. When praising the appropriate behaviour, they should focus on the positive behaviour – 'Well done for sharing' – and not on the negative – 'Well done for not biting'.

Useful tip
Never remove a sticker once given, whatever the child does next. Stickers are a concrete sign that the child behaved in an appropriate way at that particular moment, and helps them to learn that you have praised them because they did something, not because you decided to be pleased with them.

Ignore attention-seeking behaviour where safe to do so

If a child is constantly using swearing as a means of gaining a reaction from staff, this can be embarrassing and difficult to manage. Experience informs us that the problem of swearing responds best to an ignoring approach, yet staff feel they must be seen to respond and correct it.

Make it fun to behave appropriately

So often, children who show difficult behaviour have become used to gaining attention and reaction for behaving inappropriately rather than appropriately. Staff need to understand that they are in the business of changing the balance of attention so that it becomes more attention-getting and fun for the child to behave appropriately than to misbehave.

Using star charts and stickers

These are usually most effective when a child is about four years old, but they can also be used with younger children if they help. They serve the purpose of letting the child know that they are behaving appropriately at this moment in time and serve as a concrete recognition of their efforts. Therefore they should never be removed because in the next moment the child was behaving differently. Stickers should not be overused and can be faded out gradually as new patterns of behaviour become established. Here is an example of the kind of sticker chart you can design.

My sticker chart
My target:
I was given a sticker each time I managed this

Chapter 8 Special educational needs procedures

- ➤ **SEN Code of Practice**
- ➤ **Planning Early Years Action**
- ➤ **Individual behaviour plans**
- ➤ **Target setting**
- ➤ **Analysis and formulation**
- ➤ **Review meetings**
- ➤ **Involving parents in reviews**
- ➤ **Keeping children central**
- ➤ **Early Years Action Plus**
- ➤ **Statemented provision**

Sometimes you will find that a child's behaviour does not respond to your usual range of approaches and that something additional and different is needed in order for the child to make progress. This is tantamount to saying that the child has special educational needs (SEN) on account of their emotional and behavioural difficulties. Sometimes this will be because the child has a condition that affects behaviour and concentration (see Chapter 9) or sometimes there is no known condition, it is simply that the behaviour has become a significant and long-standing problem because of fixation, regression, failure to display or exaggeration (see page 50). Where this is the case, then you should be guided by the SEN *Code of Practice* (DfES 2001).

SEN Code of Practice

This is a guide for registered early years providers and Local Education Authorities about the practical help they can give to children with SEN. It recommends that early years providers should identify children's needs and take action to meet those needs as early as possible, working with parents and carers. The aim is to enable all children with SEN to reach their full potential, to be included fully in their school communities and make a successful transition to adulthood. The Code gives guidance to early years providers, but it does not tell them what they must do in every case. What are the underlying principles of the Code for early years settings?

- ➤ All children have a right to a broad and balanced curriculum that enables them to make the best possible progress towards the Early Learning Goals.
- ➤ Early years workers must recognise, identify and meet SEN within their setting.

Useful tip
The individual behaviour plan should only include that which is additional to or different from the differentiated early years curriculum that is in place for all the children.

A photocopiable example of an IBP is shown on page 81. There is also the photocopiable sheet 'Individual behaviour plan' that you can adapt for your situation on pages 130 and 131. This plan should be reviewed regularly with the parents. The plan should be seen as an integrated aspect of the curriculum planning for the whole group.

Target setting

There are some helpful training materials to use with staff in the 'Toolkit' that accompanies the DfES SEN *Code of Practice*. In it, staff are advised to write individual education plans for children with SEN containing three or four key teaching targets. The suggestion is that the targets should be 'SMART':

- Specific: written in terms of what the child will actually do at the end of the intervention.
- Measurable: so that you can observe and record change.
- Achievable: so that the child can experience success despite their SEN.
- Relevant: to the Foundation Stage curriculum.
- Time bound: usually within a half-term or a term in early years settings.

Staff find the writing of SMART targets hard to do because they often confuse targets for themselves ('We will all keep an eye on Jason and distract him when he starts to fight') with targets for the child ('Jason will be able to play for ten minutes without starting to fight'). It is helpful to remind them that teaching targets (and this includes behaviour targets) should always begin with the child's name and be followed by an action that can be observed clearly. If the targets they set answer these three questions, they should be specific enough:

- Who is going to do the behaviour? (This will always be the child.)
- What is the child going to do? (This should be in clear, observable language.)
- Under what conditions? (This should make it clear whether the child will be supported and supervised, or whether you are now expecting self-control. This would also cover the particular situation in which you are setting the target.)

You will find that you can help staff cover most conditions in their target by using a phrase starting with 'When...':

- 'When playing independently.'
- 'When Susie is supporting him in a small group.'
- 'When reminded to say sorry.'

Analysis and formulation

In Chapter 7, you considered how you can use behaviour management approaches to help staff work out what might be maintaining a child's difficult behaviour and what you might do to intervene and change it. In these situations you may find it helpful to use the 'Behaviour planning' sheet (see pages 128 and 129). This leads staff through the questions and observations they need to make in order to collect enough information to draw up an individual behaviour plan. It asks them to consider:

Case study

These examples of behaviour targets could be used as a discussion point in a staff meeting. Talk about whether they are specific enough.

- Ali will stop being naughty at snack time.
- We will make sure that Sara and George are not left alone together.
- Darren will ask for the truck when he wants to play with it when we remind him to.
- Edward will stop swearing.
- Ella will sit quietly for five minutes at story time when placed next to the leader and shown the pictures.
- Harry will play less aggressively for ten minutes.

Things to consider:

- Do these targets use clear, unambiguous language?
- Do they say who will do what under what conditions?
- Are they written in terms of what the child will do?
- Would it be clear to you all when each target had been reached?
- Could you make these targets more specific and smarter?
- Does this child need approaches and support that are additional and different to what you already offer in the setting?
- How will you plan next steps for this child?
- Can this kind of assessment be used for all the children?
- Who would do it, when and how?

- What is the difficult behaviour they wish to change (in unambiguous words)?
- What new behaviour do they wish to see instead?
- How will they observe the difficult behaviour to obtain their 'ABC'?
- What antecedents tend to lead up to the difficult behaviour?
- What are the consequences of this behaviour for the child?
- What rewards seem to work for the child?
- What are the child's strengths and interests?

This will help them to analyse what they feel is contributing to or maintaining the behaviour and help them formulate a plan. They will then be in a better position to write a clear individual behaviour plan (see pages 130 and 131) showing how they will change the antecedents, the behaviour and the consequences in order to change the behaviour.

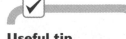

Useful tip
Remind staff that behaviour targets should always begin with the child's name. They state what the child will be able to do at the end of the intervention and not what the adults will do to get there.

Review meetings

When you have an individual behaviour plan in place, you need to meet regularly with parents or carers to review progress. At the stage of Early Years Action these reviews will usually be arranged and chaired by the SENCO of the setting. You will find a possible format for recording these meetings on the photocopiable sheet 'Progress review' on pages 132 and 133, which can be adapted. The SENCO should record:

Useful tip
Remember that behaviour management is just one of many tools you have at your disposal. Remember other ways of looking at children's vulnerability (Chapter 4) and interventions you can plan to support them.

- who was present
- whether anyone else has sent reports
- the progress in the behaviour made since the last review including both good news and bad news (which can be rephrased as 'challenges and opportunities')
- any special support or approaches that have been arranged
- how helpful these have been
- whether there are any recent changes in the situation either in the setting or at home
- whether the targets on the previous IBP have been achieved.

SENCO, key staff and parents or carers then need to negotiate and write out a new IBP to cover the next review period (usually half-a-term to a term). It is best to plan the date of next review meeting at this stage. It is also helpful to agree a list of people to whom the review report will be circulated. This would include any other professional involved or likely to become involved with the child's behaviour or the parents' support, such as Social Services or a Child and Family Service. If you are going to circulate the review report to voluntary organisations or community workers, then this must be because parents or carers think it will be helpful and have given their agreement.

Involving parents in reviews

You can ask staff to involve parents or carers more fully in the reviews by using the photocopiable sheet 'Parents' contribution to review meeting' on pages 134 and 135, perhaps by meeting with parents to take them through it verbally. Encourage staff to keep the language simple and friendly, tapping into the areas of expertise that only parents can have. Staff can find out from parents:

- when their child behaves best at home
- what their child enjoys doing most
- what the biggest problems with behaviour are at home and what seems to help
- whether their child is happy to come to the group
- whether they are worried about anything to do with the group
- whether their child's health has been good lately
- whether they have any worries about their child's development
- what behaviour they would like to see their child doing next
- whether parents have any worries about their child in the future.

They can also help parents plan the questions they would like to ask at the next review meeting.

Keeping children central

There are also ways of involving children in the review by asking parents, carers or a key worker to talk to the child before the review meeting. They could find out what the child likes doing best in the group and anything that worries the child. Sentence completion can be a helpful approach – 'I don't like it when...' or 'I like it when...'. You will find the photocopiable sheet 'Child's contribution to review meeting' for staff to adapt on page 136. It always helps to keep children central to the discussion if there are examples of the child's work, photographs and creations present for everyone to admire and celebrate. Otherwise, they can seem to be rather dry occasions which focus significantly on the special educational needs of the child. Where appropriate and where the right mix of informality and respect can be struck, children could be present and playing happily as you all talk. The exception to this would be where things are being discussed that might upset the child or might upset parents in front of their child, or where it would be hard for you to focus if the child were distracting you. Choose the right situation for you, your setting, the parents or carers and the child, but hold on to the principle of working in full partnership with parents and keeping the child central to all the planning.

Useful tip
Make sure you have provided childcare for young family members if you are holding a review with a family in your setting.

Early Years Action Plus

When reviewing the child's progress and the help they are receiving, the provider might decide to seek alternative approaches to learning through the support of the outside professional services. You might have been able to tap into general advice from support professionals when planning your Early Years Action, but most require an actual referral to be made if they are to become involved directly or individually with the child. When you plan interventions that work with outside professionals so that the outside advice actually contributes to the individual behaviour plan, this is known as taking Early Years Action Plus.

Early Years Action Plus is characterised by the involvement of specialists from outside the setting. The SENCO continues to take a leading role, working closely with the member of staff responsible for the child, and:

- draws on the advice from outside professionals and specialists, for example, early years support teachers, educational psychologists, Portage workers (see page 93) or behaviour support teachers
- ensures that the child and his or her parents and carers are consulted and kept informed
- ensures that an individual behaviour plan is drawn up, incorporating the specialist advice, and that it is incorporated within the curriculum planning for the whole setting
- monitors and reviews the child's progress with outside specialists
- keeps the head or manager of the setting informed.

Nobody knows the child's behaviour as well as parents or carers and yourselves. If you are going to involve an outside professional, you need to think of the best way of transferring what you know to them. The professionals may have certain specialist knowledge about behaviour and development but they do not know the child as well as you do. It will be helpful if you collect together your observations, assessments, behaviour planning and IBPs in order to pass on information about the difficult behaviour and what has been done to change it. Behaviour cannot be assessed by a professional in isolation – it has to be explored in terms of the contexts in which it happens and the approaches that seem to help.

Statemented provision

For a very few children, the help provided by Early Years Action Plus will still not be sufficient to ensure satisfactory progress, even when it has run over several review periods. The provider, external professional and parents or carers may then decide to ask the LEA to consider carrying out a statutory assessment of the child's SEN.

The LEA must decide quickly whether or not it has the evidence to indicate that a statutory assessment is necessary for a child. It is then responsible for co-ordinating a statutory assessment and will call for the various reports that it requires, from the early years teacher (usually a support teacher, early years practitioner or LEA nursery teacher), an educational psychologist, a doctor, and the Social Services department if involved, and will ask parents or carers to submit their own views and evidence. Once it has collected in the evidence, the LEA might decide to issue a 'statement of SEN' for the child. Only children with severe and long-standing SEN receive a statement; about one to two per cent of children.

Because of the findings of the Audit Commission it is possible that the number of statements nationally might be reduced further as more SEN funding gets delegated to schools. It is likely in the future that the bulk of the responsibility and funding for managing SEN will pass to providers, unless a child needs a very high level of funded support because of complex and multiple needs. In the meantime, there are various rights of appeal in the cases of disagreement about statementing and your local LEA can provide information about these.

Chapter 9 When behaviour is 'different'

- ➤ **Behaviour difficulties and SEN**
- ➤ **Autistic difficulties**
- ➤ **Asperger syndrome**
- ➤ **Attention deficit/hyperactivity disorder**
- ➤ **Learning difficulties**

Behaviour difficulties and SEN

Chapter 8 outlined the approaches that should be followed if a child's behaviour difficulty is significant enough for it to prevent that child or others accessing the Foundation Stage curriculum. There are four main ways in which behaviour might be seen as 'abnormal' (see page 50):

➤ Fixation: where a behaviour becomes 'stuck' and the child does not seem able to learn how to change or move on.
➤ Regression: where a child reverts to patterns of behaviour that they had already grown out of.
➤ Failure to display: where a child fails to make progress in behaviour, social and emotional skills perhaps due to general developmental difficulties or specific events in their lives.
➤ Exaggeration: where a child shows the kind of behaviour typical of the age and stage but this becomes magnified, as in the case of extreme temper tantrums.

Most of this book concerns the management of these four kinds of behaviour difficulties. There is also a smaller group of children whose behaviour is sufficiently unusual or 'different' that they might go on to be diagnosed with a particular condition such as autism, Asperger syndrome or Attention deficit/hyperactivity disorder (AD/HD). This chapter describes these children, what staff might observe and what they can do to help and support them.

These children's names will probably be on your SEN register because you have already decided that additional or different approaches to managing their behaviour are necessary. However, they will not necessarily have been referred for statutory assessment or have a statement of special educational needs. The fact that a child has been diagnosed with a certain condition rarely in itself means that a

Useful tip
Staff will need your support to understand that they can assess and plan interventions for a child's behaviour with or without a diagnosis. Find out what general advice and support might be available to you so that you do not lose time waiting for any specialist referral.

statement is necessary. Sometimes staff will need your help to understand this. A diagnosis does not change what you do in the setting, but it can add useful information and perhaps introduce other outside professionals and support. With the right training and understanding, staff should be implementing helpful approaches long before anyone else decides that a child's behaviour falls within the autistic spectrum or constitutes AD/HD, oppositional-defiant disorder (ODD) or conduct disorder (CD). The graduated response to SEN outlined in Chapter 8 makes this clearer.

Autistic difficulties

Some children appear indifferent to other people and behave as if they are 'in a world of their own'. They might have been diagnosed as having autism, autistic features or Asperger syndrome (see page 89). All these conditions have some overlap. Children with semantic pragmatic language difficulties can also behave in similar ways.

What staff might observe

➤ These children may not play with other children and join into activities only if an adult insists and assists.

➤ They might indicate their needs by taking an adult's hand and leading it to want they want, almost as if the adult were a tool or a means to an end, rather than a social being.

➤ They might have very little language, they might echo what is said to them or they might talk a lot about topics of great interest to them.

➤ Sometimes, these children might become absorbed in arranging toys in a certain way, collecting certain objects, or spinning or turning toys repeatedly to watch them move.

➤ Their eye contact might be very poor and they might be unable to play imaginatively, unless it is in a very stereotyped way.

➤ Their behaviour might be bizarre or very fearful, especially if familiar routines are disturbed.

➤ They might be extremely good at some things, such as doing puzzles, identifying numbers, making music or drawing.

Useful strategies

If you know or suspect that a child has difficulties within the autistic spectrum then there are general strategies that you and your colleagues should find helpful:

➤ Start by helping the child feel settled when playing one-to-one with a key worker. Gradually involve one or more other children in the play but stay close to support and assist. If the child understands language, use this time to talk about sharing, taking turns and understanding what other children might be thinking.

➤ For children who are severely affected, spend ten minutes a session playing alongside the child, playing with another of the same toy or piece of equipment. Copy what the child is doing. When the child begins to notice what you are doing, move in and play together with the child, sharing the same toy. Again, copy the child's actions. The idea is to encourage the child to see that their behaviour is resulting in the adult's behaviour. It is then possible to move on to begin to play turn-taking games with the child.
➤ Encourage staff to plan turn-taking games, for example, blowing bubbles for the child to burst, shaking a 'slinky toy' and holding it between you and the child so you can each feel its movement, rolling a musical ball to and fro, or setting up and knocking down skittles. The idea here is that the child will begin to see the adult's company as useful and fun.
➤ Try to keep to a familiar and structured routine. Ask staff to take a series of photographs of the typical session and show the child these to illustrate what is happening next.
➤ Provide a simple commentary about what the child is doing, 'Jake is painting' so that the child links words to actions.
➤ Provide plenty of encouragement whenever the child communicates with them, whether by voice or through actions.
➤ Show interest in the child's intense hobbies but introduce new things too. Support the child's choice of activities, but distract the child if he or she becomes too absorbed or obsessed with them.
➤ Give very clear and simple messages, showing the child as well as telling.
➤ Provide a quiet 'safe base' where the child can go to if he or she feels 'overloaded' or stressed. Provide some favourite music or an activity there for relaxing.

Asperger syndrome

Hans Asperger (1906–1980) was a paediatric doctor who lived and worked in Vienna. He identified a cluster of children who had similar patterns of behaviour and development. These behaviours were similar to autism although many of the children were highly intelligent and, unlike the autistic children, had good language skills. He wrote about this syndrome of behaviours and it became named after him. Children with Asperger syndrome have difficulties and needs that lie within the autistic spectrum. Each child with this syndrome is an individual, yet there are certain behaviours and mannerisms that apply to many of them.

What staff might observe

➤ Children with Asperger syndrome find it difficult to cope with social situations and do not always understand what is expected of them. They may appear 'naughty' to people who do not understand their needs but in fact they have genuine difficulties.
➤ They find it hard to hold a two-way conversation or to take turns with other children, tending to see the world from their own viewpoint alone.
➤ Their speech might be well developed, yet have an odd or pedantic feel to it as if it does not 'flow' easily. There might be a strange intonation, or it might be full of learned phrases of passages from favourite videos.

Useful tip
Most Local Education Authorities now have a specialist advisory service for children with autism and Asperger syndrome. Contact your local Education Department or Early Years Partnership for details. You will also find contact details for the National Autistic Society on page 143.

➤ Children with Asperger syndrome find it hard to interpret non-verbal signals. They may stand too close to you when talking, not understand when you are annoyed or fail to understand your gestures.
➤ They find it very difficult to cope with any changes from their usual routines. A new helper in the setting or a new activity might unsettle their behaviour badly.
➤ They often have intense interests that they pursue to the exclusion of everything else. They might talk non-stop about their favourite topic and fail to see when you are not interested or are not following their meaning.
➤ They may have an excellent memory for facts or things that they have seen, especially when these fit in with their area of interest.
➤ They are often a little clumsy, may walk in a rather odd manner or have actions or behaviours that they repeat over and over.

Useful strategies for you and your staff

➤ Follow a set routine each session. Display the order of this routine visually to the child using a series of pictures or symbols. Within this, you will be able to make small flexible changes.
➤ Give warnings about changes of activity, 'When we have had drinks we will go outside'.
➤ Use the child's name and establish eye contact before speaking. Ask the child to look at the speaker when listening.
➤ Arrange for a key worker to play alongside the child with one or two other children to encourage sharing and turn-taking. Ask the key worker to explain social rules clearly and demonstrate them too.
➤ Plan activities that encourage the children to talk about feelings and to practise social skills: what it means to be friendly, how to ask for a toy, what being friendly means and so on.
➤ Teach the child 'reciprocity' (my turn – your turn) using board games, ball play, bubble play, puppet and small-world play.

Case study

Below is a case study that could be used as a discussion point in a staff meeting. Talk about what you would do and why you would do it.

Dilip is just four years old. He has recently joined your setting and has not attended any kind of group before. His mother explained that he had not been happy separating from her and she felt he was too young until now. Before he joined, the manager gathered information about Dilip by talking to the family. Parents said that there were no behaviour difficulties at home, his development appeared to be fine and he had been a bit slow in his language but his family was bilingual.

When Dilip first joined you, he was very quiet. He did not appear to be interested in the other children but was happy as long as he could play with the train set undisturbed. You gave him a few weeks to settle in but were surprised to see that this did not change. Dilip appeared to play in a world of his own, and there was little eye contact with the other children or with the adults. He hardly spoke to anyone in the group, although you have all heard him chattering to himself in the home corner. If there was anyone new in the group he did not seem to notice. However, if his routine changed at all, he would become quickly distressed and make high-pitched screaming sounds. These quickly settled as soon as he returned to his train set.

Things to consider:

- What skills and behaviours does Dilip need to learn?
- Do you think he might have autistic difficulties?
- What other explanations might there be for Dilip's behaviour?
- What observations would you carry out to find out more about his needs?
- How would you help him?
- What further information do you need from other people?

- Build on the child's interests to encourage writing and drawing tasks in order to develop hand control. For example, perhaps the child has an intense interest in wheeled toys and will add the wheels to pictures of cars even if he or she will not copy circles.
- Use circle time and music time to encourage sharing and communicating in a larger group.

Attention deficit/hyperactivity disorder

Some children have attention difficulties that are greater than for other children their age. They may or may not have been diagnosed as having Attention deficit/hyperactivity disorder (AD/HD). At this age and stage of development the most important way to help them is to build up their attention skills through their play and early learning.

What staff might observe

- They are likely to find themselves very busy! They have perhaps found themselves reacting more and more frequently to calamities, spills, tumbles

Useful tip
Reassure staff that the first approach for helping a child with AD/HD is behaviour management. Most health authorities do not prescribe medication such as Ritalin until the child is older because of the possible side effects.

or clashes of will, and are now finding that they need to make active plans for 'getting one step ahead'.

➤ Staff members might have been tempted to see the child as constantly misbehaving, although, on reflection, have realised that the child cannot always help this behaviour. Either way, they will probably be feeling that it is time to apply some structured interventions.

Useful strategies for you and your staff

➤ Children with short attention spans benefit from clear routines and structures so that they know what is going to happen and when.

➤ 'Sandwich' short periods of sustained concentration and effort with periods of time when the child can be more active or have a free choice in his or her play.

➤ Give very strong encouragement and praise to keep play fun, attention-getting and motivating for the child.

➤ Break tasks down into simpler steps so that the child with a short attention span can still play and learn from them.

➤ Keep demands on the child short and simple to begin with.

➤ Children with attention difficulties benefit greatly from the chance to talk with a member of staff ahead of any activity, to plan it together and then to review what he or she has done afterwards.

➤ These children often find it easiest to concentrate when playing in pairs rather than a large group, so allow for this when planning activities that need careful thought and attention.

➤ Find a distraction-free space to work in for activities that require sustained concentration, looking or listening. Encourage staff to plan ahead for how to make best use of this.

Case study

Below is a case study that could be used as a discussion point in a staff meeting. Talk about what you would do and why you would do it.

Rory is three years old. He has been in your setting since he was two-and-a-half and is described by many of you as a 'whirlwind'. He rarely sits still, he rushes into everything without pausing to think and he flits from one activity to the next. At story time he can quickly become disruptive, pulling other children to the ground and rolling around the floor with them. He has a delightful smile and never seems to bear a grudge or want to upset anyone. His dad says he rarely sleeps through the night and seems for ever 'on the go'.

Things to consider:

- What skills and behaviours does Rory need to learn?
- Do you think he might have AD/HD?
- What other explanations might there be for Rory's behaviour?
- What observations would you do to find out more about his needs?
- How would you help him?
- What further information do you need from other people?

- Try to have a quiet area that staff can withdraw to with a small group of children and use this before difficulties with behaviour arise rather than as a reaction to them.
- Make sure you have eye contact before speaking to the child and use his or her name and a touch to gain attention.
- Give very clear, short and concrete directions, showing the child what to do as well as telling.
- Be prepared to give reminders constantly since the child might forget their instructions readily.
- Provide a running commentary as the child plays to hold his or her attention on what he or she is doing and to show that staff value, and are interested in, what the child is doing.

Learning difficulties

Some children's development appears to be progressing normally, but more slowly, than most children their age. These children might be classed as having 'learning difficulties'. Just because a child has learning or developmental difficulties, it does not follow that there will also be behaviour difficulties. However, their behaviour might be unusual because it seems so immature. Knowing that the development is generally immature might help staff understand why the behaviour also seems to be at a younger stage.

Sometimes a child with general developmental difficulties might be receiving help and support through a local Portage service. Portage is a home-based teaching programme in which parents are helped to teach their child's development step by small step. If you hear that the Portage service has been involved, then it is helpful to contact the Portage Home Visitor and arrange to share information and approaches. There will also be a detailed developmental check-list that staff will be able to use as part of their observations and planning.

What staff might observe

- These children often find it difficult to understand instructions that contain more than one or two pieces of information.
- These children might play very fleetingly with the toys and activities and so might be more prone to distraction and disrupting others.
- Some of these children enjoy feeling and manipulating the toys and equipment rather than playing with them constructively or imaginatively.
- Some of these children will still be at the stage of playing alone, or in parallel to, other children and have not yet reached the stage of playing socially.
- Some children find it difficult to control their fingers in fine movements or to climb, balance and run smoothly.
- These children's skills might appear to be out of line with their age. It could be that they are mildly delayed in their development and this might be influencing both their learning and their behaviour.

Useful tip

The National Portage Association provides useful training on providing 'quality play' for children with developmental difficulties. You will find the address on page 144.

Useful strategies for you and your staff

➤ Keep language used in managing behaviour short and clear.

➤ Encourage the key worker to observe the child carefully using an observational check-list, or using your own setting's early years curriculum. Work out what the child can already do and make a note of all their strengths, interests and areas of difficulty.

➤ Arrange for the findings to be discussed with parents or carers, explaining that you are all keen to encourage the child's learning and behaviour. Find out how the child is managing with simple skills at home: getting dressed, eating their food, playing, talking and so on.

➤ Work out together what you would really like the child to be able to do in the next term. Use your existing knowledge and experience of the child to select a few developmental steps that you feel could reasonably be achieved in that time. Again, use your early years curriculum and planning as a 'coat hanger' to hang these steps on.

➤ If you are monitoring the child's needs as Early Years Action (see page 80), use these developmental steps as the targets you will write into an individual education plan, stating what the child's difficulties are, what action you will take to help, what targets you aim to reach, how parents will help and how you will monitor progress.

➤ Once you have decided on a reasonable long-term goal, break this down into manageable steps that the child can achieve week by week. Plan how you will achieve each step, perhaps working alongside the child in a small group or using some individual time. Ask staff to use strong praise, help and encouragement to make sure each step is achieved.

➤ Plan with parents how you will keep closely in touch with each other, so that each of you can be supporting the work the other is doing.

➤ Keep records of your achievements, examples of work and creations, and diary notes of the child's learning so that you can share this at another review session in a term's time.

➤ Encourage your staff not to isolate the behaviour difficulty from the general learning difficulty – teaching one will encourage the other. For example, a child needs to learn to play with another child when being supervised before that child can then learn how to take turns and to share.

Chapter 10 Supporting parents and carers

- **Talking with parents**
- **Useful approaches**
- **Behaviour plans**
- **Keeping in touch**
- **Seeking further support**

Talking with parents

It is not always easy to talk with a parent or carer about their child's behaviour as a variety of emotions can be aroused. You can help your staff by explaining how to 'tune in' to some of the emotional reactions that they might be picking up from a parent.

Guilt

Parents might be wondering what they did wrong, or feeling that staff are blaming them in some way for the fact that their child has a behaviour problem. You and your staff need to emphasise how much you value parents or carers help and advice in helping you manage the difficulty for their child. Start with an introduction along the lines of, 'Thank you so much for coming to talk. We are having some difficulties in managing Tara's temper tantrums. It's clear that she gets quite upset with us all and we are keen to make her sessions happier for her. You know her better than anyone, so it will be really useful to talk'.

Blame

Parents may want to blame other people for the problem, perhaps even suggesting, for example, that their child learned to swear or become aggressive from the setting. They may report that there are no such difficulties at home and so the problem must lie in the way staff are managing their child. It might help to comment, 'That's interesting that there are no problems like this at home. I wonder if she only behaves like this when she has to do something she doesn't want to or when there are lots of other children around – such as when she is expected to share the toys here'. Parents and carers may also have rigid ideas about discipline and blame you for not having the same rules ('All he needs is a good...!'). It helps if you make clear what you are allowed to do and what not and explain why, 'The law does not allow us to smack your child. This is because we now know that smacking encourages children to hurt others and we have to treat children with the same respect as we would anyone else. It is also our policy to use positive approaches that will help your child's emotional development in the long term'.

Protectiveness

They may feel protective of their child and jump to their child's defence. They may also feel that they have made a mistake in sending their child to you and may doubt that you can cope with their child as well as they have. They may also find it hard to share the responsibility of their child's behaviour with you in the setting and therefore lose control of what is happening. A 'no blame' problem-solving approach works best in which staff make it clear that it is the behaviour that is the problem and not the child, 'We would like to work with you to change Kerry's behaviour. What do you think will work best?'.

Anger

People whose self-esteem is low, who feel threatened in some way or who have had negative experiences of professional power may quickly become angry. Encourage staff to take precautions for their own safety (there is more information in Chapter 11). It also helps to have established a working relationship with parents long before you are in the position of having to share any 'bad news'. In this way, you cease to become a threat because you are someone who is already accepted and trusted.

Grief

Sometimes staff raise a fairly minor behaviour problem with parents or carers only to be taken by surprise by an outpouring of grief. Remind staff that they can never know where someone's emotions come from and there may be good reasons why this is happening. Other parents may avoid even meeting you because they are not sure how they will cope. Allow plenty of time to work through any emotion and address all concerns in a practical and helpful way.

Anxiety

Some parents and carers may appear 'over anxious' about their child. They may have their own difficulties in separating from their child and find it very hard to trust you.

Rejection of the problem

Parents and carers may feel that they cannot accept that they have this sort of child and so they act as if it is not happening. Sometimes this coincides with rejection of any kind of label and an expressed wish that their child should not be treated any differently from the other children. It helps if staff can make it clear that they are not keen to label the child but that they are very keen to help the child become a happy, socially-adjusted individual.

Helplessness and denial

Sometimes when family members are stressed or depressed, staff may find avoidance or denial from parents and carers. Typical responses to your attempts to talk may be, 'I'm rushing off and can't talk'; 'He's just like Uncle Dennis was'; 'It's just the way she is' and so on. Other parents and carers may be out of tune with their child's difficulties, perhaps because child and parent are 'unconnected' or have attachment difficulties. In this situation, it can appear to staff as if they simply do not care. Again, it helps if staff can have an understanding of what attachment and connection mean for families so that they can put the reaction into context. The following case study should be helpful.

Case study

This scenario could be used as a discussion point at a staff meeting. Talk about the behaviours you would observe.

Imagine you are sitting in a restaurant. In one corner, there is a couple who are obviously deeply in love. We will call them 'the lovers'. How do you know that they are in love – what behaviours do you actually observe? Make a list of these on a large sheet of paper.

Now imagine you are in the same restaurant and in another corner is a couple who are clearly not getting on very well. We will call them 'the glums'. What do you actually see or hear this time? Make another list.

Things to consider:

➤ Think about parents or carers and children who are 'attached' or 'connected' to each other – do you observe similar behaviours as 'the lovers' and 'the glums'?
➤ You now know what a connected child and carer look like. Can you also recognise when such a connection is not there?
➤ Think of ways you can support attachments/connections by helping parents and carers 'tune in' to their children and to share pleasure in each other.

From an activity by Karen Bibbings, Health Visitor (with permission).

Useful approaches

➤ Help staff to understand why a parent or carer might be saying something. What does this tell you all about their emotional state and how might you be able to help?
➤ If there is avoidance of the issue, encourage staff to take time to share the good news of progress before you need to share the challenges. Give clear information about your expectations in order to inform a parent about what you hope to achieve at each age and stage. This will lead on to what you are going to plan together for those areas that are showing a weakness.
➤ Involve parents and carers in the sessions wherever possible so they can see what staff are trying to achieve. Ask staff not just to share the activities, but to share the reasoning behind them and an idea of how children typically progress. Try to share some of the staff members' enthusiasm in the way children play and learn and to pass on skills.

Useful tip
It is well worthwhile brain-storming approaches with colleagues when you appear to have an intractable problem in communication with parents and carers. With your guidance, this can help everyone develop skills for positively framing their comments and questions.

➤ For helpless or troubled parents, try to give practical workable advice, but try not to give the impression that you are successful and parents are failing; parents with low self-esteem are quick to pick up the fact that they are 'not doing it right'. This leads to resentfulness and avoidance. Instead, negotiate any home-setting activities (see under 'Behaviour plans' on page 99) and be encouraging by asking questions such as, 'What seems to keep his attention at home?'; 'What do you find works best when she behaves like this?'; 'When do you find he behaves best?'; 'What help do you need from us?' and so on.

➤ If a parent or carer denies there is anything wrong, start with where they are 'at' in terms of their understanding, but make it clear what might happen next. A typical response may be, 'I'm glad you're not worried about her. But we must teach her to sit and listen in the group, even if she's fine at home, because she needs to be able to do this by the time she starts school. So perhaps we can talk about what seems to work at home and we'll put together a plan to teach her to concentrate here. As you say, she may settle very quickly. If not, we'll talk again next term and plan what to do next'. Be firm, stick to your plan, and continue to involve parents and carers with every sign of progress or need, making it clear that you are doing this in order to keep them in touch.

➤ If a parent will not stop to talk, negotiate a home visit to meet on their territory. Start by establishing their views and feelings as this will give you important information about their value judgements that will help you decide how to introduce your own concerns. Listen first, talk later, find the common ground last. The common ground is usually your mutual like of their child that is special to both of you.

➤ If parents appear 'over anxious', encourage staff to take their views seriously. Address every point they have made and reassure them with concrete evidence that all is well.

➤ Wherever possible, ask staff to give parents a 'job to do'. Behaviour plans (see page 99) are an excellent starting point.

➤ Some parents or carers might realise there is a problem but refuse any kind of outside help, even though you are sure that things have come to that stage. Use your SEN *Code of Practice* graduated response to prepare the way for this before you reach the point of needing outside professional help, 'I know you are keen for us to meet his needs here in the group and you do not want anyone else involved at this stage. What we'll need to do is plan our approaches with you for the next term or so. We will set some targets between us that will show whether or not we are being successful. If we are not, then we will need further advice in order to do the best for your child. We need to talk again on...'. If you feel really 'stuck', ask the health visitor for advice; he or she might be able to home-visit or check the child's development as part of the routine surveillance.

- You may come up against discrimination from other parents, 'If that child continues to attend, I'll take mine away...'. This is a direct challenge to your Special Needs and Equal Opportunities policy and goes against the spirit of the SEN Disability Act. Explain that it is your policy to welcome all children regardless of special need. State clearly what steps you are taking (in general terms rather than personal details) to make sure that the other children's needs are not compromised.
- Consider arranging a session for everyone on 'managing difficult behaviour' or 'rising to the challenge' – usually every parent, carer (and professional!) has their challenging moments at some stage and this can be a very levelling and unifying experience for everyone.

Case study

Below is a case study that could be used as a discussion point in a staff meeting. Talk about what you would do and why you would do it.

Suppose that Dean has been with you two terms in your setting and his behaviour has been very difficult to manage; he gets very excitable and can lash out at other children if he feels at all thwarted. You have already monitored his needs as Early Years Action and his mother has joined in all your reviews but said very little. You would now like to seek outside help. Dean's mother looks doubtful and says she will have to talk to her partner. Dean's father comes in very angrily and tells you that all Dean needs is sound disciplining. He states that 'there's no way he's going to see a psychologist as there's nothing wrong with his head'.

Things to consider:

- What do you do?
- What emotions might be underlying Dad's reaction?
- How could you work towards bringing parents 'on board'?
- How can you move towards seeking outside help?
- When would it be appropriate to involve an outside agency without parental consent?

Behaviour plans

When you begin to communicate, you will usually find that there are some aspects of the behaviour difficulty at home as well as in the setting. Even if this is not the case, it should be possible to involve parents or carers in your efforts to improve the situation in the setting. One way of doing this is to use a behaviour plan that can be negotiated with parents and used to follow through ideas at home. You will find the photocopiable sheet 'Home behaviour plan' on page 137 and an example on page 100. You will see that a member of staff has filled in the first part while talking with parents and carers. They have then tried out the suggestions and filled in the second part. Parents and a staff member meet once a week to keep in touch and review the plan. This sort of approach can serve as part of your Early Years Action or it can simply be used to work together on developing a child's personal, social and emotional development.

Behaviour plan for: George

This is the behaviour we want to see more of

➤ George will sit with his dad for five minutes to share a picture book.
➤ George will do as he is asked after a count of '1, 2, 3' at least once a day.

This is the behaviour we want to see less of

➤ George tears his books and breaks his toys.
➤ George never does what he is asked to.

Activities to do at home

➤ Just after tea, sit George down with his dad on the sofa and get out the latest picture book lent from nursery. Make sure the baby is with his mum in another room. Let George turn the pages as his dad reads the words and talks about the pictures. Encourage George to lift the flaps and to join in with familiar bits. Let him choose another book if there is time. Continue for five minutes or longer if he wants to.

➤ Choose a few things each day that you really need George to do – perhaps putting his seat-belt on in the car or coming to sit at the table. Make him look at you and tell him what to do. Then count '1, 2, 3' slowly to give him time to do it.

What to do when your child plays well

➤ Make the story sessions fun and praise him for joining in. Do not criticise him or correct him when he pretends to 'read'.

➤ Give him a sticker and praise him enthusiastically if he does what you ask after the '1, 2, 3' count.

What to do when your child shows the problem behaviour

➤ Remove the toys and books. Distract him with just one thing to play with at a time.

➤ If George does not comply after a '1, 2, 3' count, gently lead him through what you wish him to do – fasten his seat-belt for him or lead him to the table.

➤ Patiently repeat if he rejects the help.

How to help your child improve

➤ Keep most of the toys and books out of circulation. Give him a few at a time and play with him for five or ten minutes making it more fun and interesting. This should stop him breaking his toys eventually! Don't expect him to play on his own until he is a little older and can concentrate better.

How did George get on?

George enjoyed the stories – especially when they drove his dad mad! He soon started to ask for more books – we got it up to 20 minutes one day.

He's not good at the '1, 2, 3' warning – he thinks it's a game. We're going to try giving him easier things to do first – like passing the baby's nappy at changing time – and then ask him to do harder things once he's started to enjoy the stickers. Do you think this will work?

He's only broken one toy this week, but it was a special present from his nan so we're a bit upset about it.

Useful tip

Ask parents to rate from 1 to 10 how bad their child's behaviour was at its very worst. Then ask how bad it is now. Ask what they think happened to move things along? This helps them to develop insight into how their child is responding to their behaviour management and also to dwell on the positives.

Case study

Below is a case study that could be used as a discussion point in a staff meeting. Talk about what you would do and why you would do it.

Antra is three years old and strikes you as a very determined little character. She has a loud voice and tends to scream and shout when she cannot have her own way. Occasionally she has hit out at other children, usually those smaller than herself. Her development is advanced for her age and she has excellent language skills. She is an only child and her parents feel that there are no problems at home, but this is possibly because she never has to do anything she does not want to there. They do admit that they feel she is in charge rather than themselves! She has not had much experience of mixing with other children.

Things to consider:

- How might you tap into Antra's strengths?
- What would you say to parents to bring them on board?
- Draw up a behaviour plan (see page 137) that you could use with parents in order to work on her behaviour at home.

Keeping in touch

In a busy setting it can be hard to keep in touch with parents and carers. Someone else may bring or collect the child, especially when parents are at work. Tackle this issue right from the beginning. Make it clear that it is your policy to work closely with parents and carers, and to keep in touch regularly about their children's progress and needs. As part of gathering information on a child who is just starting, make sure you find out:

- who will bring and collect the child
- contact numbers
- what method parents or carers would prefer to keep in touch with you (home-setting diary, termly get-together, weekly chat and so on)
- whether there is a regular time to meet should the need ever arise.

Make it clear that you regard this as a two-way process. Explain that you are available to meet when parents feel the need, just as you hope you can be in touch when you need to talk. This gives you the chance to share all the good news about their child's progress, happiness and achievements before you might find yourself in the position of having to discuss behaviour issues.

Useful tip

Delegate the home-school diary or weekly chat to the key worker and try to make sure that there is continuity so that this staff member gets to know the child and family well.

Useful tip
Collect a resource library of useful handouts and pamphlets on behaviour for parents and carers. You will find some ideas on pages 141–144.

Seeking further support

Sometimes parents or carers will come to you asking for your support or advice on their child's behaviour at home. You may find this surprising if the child's behaviour in the setting is entirely appropriate. It is often the case that children learn to behave very differently in different situations and that, on balance, children reserve their most challenging behaviours for the home. You will be able to reassure them about their child's behaviour with you ('You must have taught her how to behave well because she's so good here – so it's clear that there is nothing seriously wrong. Let's see if we can help you at home by sharing some of the approaches we use here...'). Try setting a regular behaviour plan for a while, based on all the ideas contained in this book and meet regularly to share success.

There may come a point when your support and advice is not enough. Suggest that parents or carers discuss their child with the local health visitor. If he or she cannot help directly, then a referral by the health visitor or GP to the local Child and Family Service might be a possibility. Some of you will also have access to an Early Years Support Service through your LEA or Early Years Partnership, although these services are usually more directed to supporting behaviour in the setting rather than at home. You may also be able to call on the local Social Services Family Support team, a voluntary organisation with a local project, a Sure Start service or a local Portage service. Your Early Years Partnership should be able to put you in touch with agencies which can help.

Chapter 11 Supporting staff

- ➤ **Effects of challenging behaviour on staff**
- ➤ **Stress at work**
- ➤ **Assessing risk**
- ➤ **Sharing information**
- ➤ **Stress management**
- ➤ **Anger management**
- ➤ **Emotional intelligence**
- ➤ **Personal safety**

Effects of challenging behaviour on staff

One of the most stressful aspects of working with young children is having to manage very difficult behaviour, day in and day out. All sorts of emotions are aroused in us. Children's behaviour can make us feel angry, confused, distressed and, above all, guilty for the fact that we have not been able to manage it better. Some research has suggested that children elicit in us the feelings that they have inside. Children who behave in such a way to make us feel angry are probably dealing with a lot of anger in their own lives. Children who leave us feeling distressed and miserable are probably unhappy themselves. Children who leave us feeling confused and bewildered because we cannot work them out are probably very confused children themselves. This insight can be reassuring and comforting to staff who might be wondering why a child's behaviour is not responding to all their usual approaches.

All the principles that relate to children's self-esteem and confidence outlined in this book can be applied equally to managers and other staff members. Knowledge of these principles will help you to plan the appropriate working environment to enhance their well-being. If life is quite stressful in the setting, you may need to carry out a risk assessment of stress levels in your staff. The following ideas should help.

Stress at work

There are general management principles that are helpful in dealing with stress in a working organisation:

➤ Make it clear that stress is a normal part of working life and challenge the prejudice that being under stress is a reflection of personal vulnerability.

➤ Talk about stress openly as a regular part of staff meetings. You might plan a regular circle time for staff or appoint a competent key person with particular knowledge of how to deal with stress and who regularly liaises with management.

➤ Make sure that your policy for stress management is inclusive and that all staff including temporary, part-time and supply are included.

➤ Include a range of techniques for stress management in the professional development programme.

There are also certain Conditions of Service that are more likely to protect staff from stress. This is an issue that is likely to become more important in the future as litigation becomes more frequent. These are the areas that it would be helpful for Conditions of Service to address:

➤ Induction as a right for all staff.
➤ Professional development (including training in how to manage yourself and others).
➤ An identified support or mentor.
➤ The flexible use of compassionate leave.
➤ A system of open references (that is, allowing staff to see their own references) regular and protected non-contact time.
➤ Negotiated job descriptions and specifications reviewed on a regular basis.

Assessing risk

Nowadays it is expected that managers will undertake a risk assessment of stress and an action plan should follow with progress reviewed annually. If the staff in your setting are having to manage very challenging or unusual behaviour in some of the children, then this would be advisable. It is helpful to have a framework for doing this.

Decide whether there is cause for concern

You might decide to use a check-list to help you identify whether there is a prima facie cause for concern. If this showed up an area for concern, then it would be expected that an action plan would follow. A well-being questionnaire is quick to complete and will provide the information you need to initiate an action plan. It will be of use in settings where it is perceived that concerns about well-being are not a major issue, but nonetheless an effective action plan should be put in place. When questionnaire information is collected it is recommended that it is used with strict confidentiality. The data collected should be fed back to all staff and the summary data used to form a back-cloth to open discussion in order to define the difficult areas in more detail. It will lead to a suitable action plan that is fed into, shared and understood by all. You will find an example to use or adapt on pages 138–139.

Make an action plan for reducing stress

Any action plan that you put together as a result of the staff well-being questionnaires should focus on four areas:

- Identify issues that are causing stress (the 'stressors'). For example, staff might feel that the children's behaviour is uncontrollable or that they are not supported as they try to handle it.
- Decide why you think the stressor is there. For example, it might be that not enough children have been placed on your SEN register or there has been insufficient support, training or information for staff members.
- Make a plan for reducing the stressors as far as you are able to.
- Decide how you will evaluate change. For example, staff could complete the same questionnaire at a later date.

Useful tip

It is helpful if all the staff acknowledge that stress exists for everyone – it is a normal reaction to daily life. There will be times for all of us when we feel more stressed than usual. This does not mean that we are weak, but it does mean we need more support from others.

Sharing information

When these kinds of questionnaires are given to staff members, there are certain themes that often emerge. Often, staff members lack confidence and feel insecure (and sometimes unsafe) in having to manage particularly challenging behaviour. They may feel that they lack the specialist skills. They may also be highly anxious about the situation as they feel responsible yet powerless to effect change. Added to this, there may be a strong emotional response from a parent and carer that can leave staff members feeling de-skilled or intimidated. Regular consultation and mentor support are invaluable methods of supporting staff through a difficult situation. Above all, staff need clear information about the child and the approaches to be followed, and also some method of controlling their own levels of stress.

One useful way of sharing information is holding a joint planning meeting either when a child known to have special needs because of their behaviour or emotional development is about to join your setting, or when such a problem arises and other agencies are involved. You need not wait for this to be called by another agency, although it makes sense to combine with other meetings that are going on, thus using a 'joined-up' approach.

Send a letter to other professionals involved and make sure that you invite parents or carers as well, having taken time to explain what the meeting is about. Explain that you need to meet together in order to plan the best approaches for managing the child's behaviour so that the child can benefit fully from the curriculum and opportunities in your setting. Give a clear and unambiguous description of what the difficulty in the behaviour is, and provide details of where and when the meeting will be. Invite professionals to send a brief report or telephone if they cannot make it. Explain that the purposes of the meeting will be:

- to gather and share all relevant information
- to find out which professionals are involved
- to help plan the approaches for managing the behaviour
- to learn about what approaches have helped in the past
- to learn who can be called upon to help in the future
- to set up good communication for the future
- to reassure and support staff who will be in direct contact with the child
- to address potential difficulties early on
- to detail the need for any specific resources from outside the setting.

Useful tip
Support professionals have many demands on their time. Do not let this put you off seeking the information you require, but give plenty of notice and plan well ahead.

You could end with a positive statement about how keen you are to make sure that the child receives the best help and support. You will find a photocopiable pro-forma for this kind of letter on page 140.

Stress management

Stress and anger are closely linked because they both have the same physiological reaction in our bodies. This reaction is sometimes called the 'fight or flight response'. When you are faced with a potential threat, adrenaline is released into your body that places you in a better position to deal with that threat. For early cave dwellers, this literally meant fighting and eating the wild animal or beating a rapid retreat! The blood supply is increased to body and brain, decisions can be taken rapidly and behaviour can be carried out almost automatically for a while. You spend much of your thinking life using the frontal and logical parts of your brain, however during 'fight or flight', the lower and more primitive part of the brain is called into action. The gateway between the two is the part of the brain called the 'limbic system' that deals with emotions. This explanation is extremely simplified, but provides a useful model for explaining to staff what is happening when they feel stressed.

A certain amount of physiological stress is essential for everyday functioning. Without it we might fall asleep! However, prolonged stress and anger can build up so that you become sensitized to certain stressors and over-react to them. Fortunately, there are methods that can be used to reduce the stress reaction if you can be helped to recognise what is causing it and how your body and brain are responding to them. This is called 'stress management'.

Top tips for stress management

These ideas will be useful for sharing with staff members:

- whom you have identified as being at risk through the 'Staff well-being questionnaire' on pages 138–139, or through your regular day-to-day supervision or appraisal
- who have asked you for support and advice
- as part of a staff training activity for everyone, so as not to single anyone out.

Adapt the ideas flexibly for use in your situation with your staff members or use them as a 'wish list' to reduce stress at work:

- Have a work-free zone somewhere in the setting where staff can relax when appropriate and necessary – even if it is an armchair in a quiet corner!
- If a staff member is feeling extremely stressed, try to arrange relief so that they can take a 'five minute breather'.
- Use careful planning to make sure that staff know what to do in certain difficult situations – for example when a certain child has a big temper tantrum.

- Hold regular get-togethers after difficult sessions to debrief and unwind.
- Encourage staff not to compare themselves with others, but to compare themselves with themselves. So what if they handled something not as they would have wished one day – this will help them to do it better the next.
- Remind staff that nobody has to be perfect – just professional and good enough.
- Make sensitive use of humour to lighten things, helping staff still to remain professional and discrete.
- Encourage staff to avoid 'avoiding' – help them set themselves simple targets day by day to make a stressful period less demanding on their confidence.
- Use praise and encouragement to each other regularly – not just from management to staff but between staff members as well.
- Remind staff of all the positive reasons why they chose their job – and make sure there are plenty of chances to play and enjoy the children each session.
- Help staff to recognise and acknowledge areas of weakness in their professional practice. Make these palatable by linking them to a need for training. You will find some useful exercises for increasing staff skills in behaviour management in Chapter 12.
- Plan regular get-togethers outside work to motivate staff and celebrate achievements.
- Develop an ethos in which staff feel that it is alright to ask for support.

Useful tip
How would you eat a dinosaur? One chunk at a time! Help staff break down big challenges into small steps, rewarding themselves each step of the way.

Case study

Below is a case study that could be used as a discussion point in a staff meeting. Talk about what you would do and why you would do it.

Hilary was in a major multiple car crash. Many people were killed or seriously injured but she had walked away relatively unscathed. She was determined that it would not affect her life and after a couple of weeks recovering from the bruises and whiplash she returned to work, which was in fact a new post working in a large community nursery. She found that her colleagues were kind and welcoming, and she decided not to share her recent experiences with them because she did not want to be seen as 'the one who was in that car crash'.

Everything went fine and she enjoyed her new job very much. She felt valued and supported. About a year after the crash, she had to work with a particularly demanding little girl who would lash out at the staff and shout obscenities. This little girl had been taken into care following a turbulent home life and was emotionally disturbed. At first, Hilary did not understand what was happening to herself. She found that her mind went blank and she could not think of what to do. She found herself crying easily and one day burst into tears in front of the children. Her manager offered to sit down with her and sort things out.

Things to consider:

- Was Hilary's reaction understandable – perhaps this was the first stress she had met since the accident?
- What should Hilary tell the manager?
- What could the manager say to Hilary in order to explain how the stress might be affecting her work?
- What does Hilary need to help her move forward?

➤ Encourage staff to live in the present – each session is a fresh start.
➤ Remember that exercise, a good diet and plenty of fluids all contribute towards good stress management.

Anger management

The method of dealing with prolonged anger is similar and known as 'anger management'. During an episode of extreme anger, an event usually takes place that places your 'fight or flight' system on alert – for example, a certain child might refuse to do what he is told and challenges you to do something to make him. You are then hyper-aroused – all your senses are alert to what is going on. As the event unfurls – perhaps you notice that other children are laughing and that a parent is watching too – adrenaline is released in large quantities. You stop thinking clearly and you react emotionally. The adrenaline remains high for many minutes afterwards as your body readies itself for further trouble. After a while, your physiological state returns to normal. Some people liken this reaction to a spark igniting a fuse, the fuse smouldering for a while and then the firework exploding.

The trick to anger management is:

➤ to be aware of the sparks that light your fuse (certain children perhaps, certain behaviours such as cheekiness, or certain situations in which you feel insecure or threatened)
➤ to develop methods of putting out the smouldering fuse before it ignites the firework (asking someone else to take over, placing distance between you and the stressor, breathing fully and slowly, talking yourself through the problem, 'I've coped before – I can cope again!').

Useful tip
Encourage staff to worry only about things at work that they have control over. Other things (such as very challenging child behaviour) should be referred to the manager or SENCO – several heads may be better than one.

Emotional intelligence

In Chapter 1, the term 'emotional intelligence' was introduced to describe the way children handle and understand their own feelings and the feelings of other people. Learning to manage emotional stress and anger are aspects of an adult's emotional intelligence, and you will have recognised many parallels in how you help children manage their emotions and how you can support staff and carers. The exercise on page 109 is enjoyable to do and helps staff members to focus on what is meant by their own emotional intelligence and what they might do to strengthen certain aspects of it.

Group exercise

Below is an exercise that could be used as a discussion point at a staff meeting. Talk about each statement and what it means to you.

- I don't just react to things – I like to take control.
- I know which things from my past influence the way I react to things today.
- I avoid putting things off, I like to consider my options and then take decisive action.
- If I think another adult is behaving badly, I give respectful and direct feedback to them.
- I make sure I praise colleagues and encourage them.
- I try to listen carefully so that I understand other people's points of view.
- I'm not just the way I am – I can change if I want.
- I see problems in my work as challenges.
- I am good at asking for support when I need it.
- I try to manage anger by keeping things in perspective and staying calm.
- I can keep hostile and angry thoughts to myself.
- I am good at seeking compromises.
- I try to be optimistic in the face of disappointment.

Things to consider:

- Are these statements easier said than done?
- What would help you to develop these abilities?
- How do you deal with stress and anger?

This activity can also be done confidentially as an individual exercise or in pairs, with everyone joining in for the 'Things to consider'.

Personal safety

In very simple terms, when you are stressed, you are using your emotional brain more than your logical brain. That is why you may find yourself doing or saying things that you later regret. In the same way, when a member of staff or a parent or carer is very upset, there is no point in appealing to logic – they first have to calm down if they are to be in a position where they can take in information and handle it in a logical and reasoned way. There are certain basic approaches for ensuring your own safety and not making the situation worse:

- Give respectful eye contact but stand diagonally so that you are not face-on and not glaring.
- Keep a distance between you that is more than an arm's length.
- Present an outward demeanour of calmness (however you feel inside). Watch your voice especially and try to keep this calm and level.
- Make yourself less threatening by not challenging their statements at this stage.
- Listen and use statements that affirm the way the other person is feeling. For example, 'I see that you are very upset about this'; 'What a shame this had to happen to you'; 'I hear what you say' and so on.

➤ Make sure that the exit is clear for both of you to move away quickly.
➤ Let the feelings run their course and watch for them to die down. Then change the situation altogether by suggesting that you need to talk about this and to see how you can help.
➤ Move to a calm area away from an audience, offer a warm drink and begin to engage logical brain again by talking rationally about how you can move things forward.
➤ If you are making a home visit that might involve any angry exchange, follow all the usual precautions for ensuring your safety. For example, go in pairs, leave a contact address with colleagues, say when you will be back, keep your mobile telephone to hand and carry a personal alarm.

Case study

Below is a case study that could be used as a discussion point in a staff meeting. Talk about what you would do and why you would do it.

Deline was the home-setting link worker for a busy day nursery. She had been asked to gather more information from home about a little boy whose behaviour was very difficult in the setting. For the past month, this little boy had been hitting and scratching a lot and he appeared to be very angry with himself and everyone else. When she rang up the home, his dad answered and appeared to be very angry. He said he had a bone to pick with the nursery and she 'had better have some answers' for him. He said he'd be at home that afternoon after three o'clock and then slammed the telephone down.

Things to consider:

- ➤ What should Deline do next?
- ➤ Was it a reasonable request that Deline should home-visit?
- ➤ What were the alternatives?
- ➤ Draw up a simple policy for home visits that would help to keep Deline safe.

Chapter 12 Training others

- **Using the right words**
- **Whose problem?**
- **Keeping an eye**
- **Hatching solutions**
- **Easy as ABC**
- **Check-list for staff**

Each manager or SENCO has a responsibility to pass on information about behaviour management to staff members through training and ongoing support. This chapter will help you plan some introductory sessions. The activities do not focus on quick-fix solutions but on helping staff to make their own observations and interpretations about difficult behaviours and to think reflectively when planning interventions. You will be able to supplement or adapt these five training activities by using the many case examples and discussion points throughout the book. You will find the book *Staff Training Activities*, also in this series, very useful for more general training on topics such as SEN, equal opportunities and inclusion.

Using the right words

The activity on page 112 aims to help staff develop clear and positive language when they are talking about behaviour. Staff are shown how to use the same clear language when communicating with parents and carers.

Whose problem?

This activity on page 114 aims to help staff to develop an idea of ages and stages when looking at young children's behaviour. Staff members are helped to decide when behavioural problems might lead to a child's name being placed on the SEN register because additional or different approaches are required.

Keeping an eye

The third activity on page 116 aims to help staff to develop observation and recording approaches when looking at young children's behaviour. They are introduced to the main methods for observing and assessing behaviour and have the opportunity to try these out between the two sessions involved.

Hatching solutions

The activity on page 118 aims to help staff to make hypotheses about behaviour difficulties that will lead to planning an intervention. They are helped to understand the monitoring and review cycle and how to plan the best observations and assessments of behaviour.

Easy as ABC

The final activity on page 120 aims to help staff prepare their own individual behaviour plans for children who have SEN. With your support, their planning will become part of the SEN documentation for that child and form evidence of the child's needs and what seems to help.

Using the right words

Use this activity to help staff members develop clear and positive language for talking about behaviour and talking to parents.

Number of staff: all.

Timing: two sessions of approximately 45 minutes.

What you need: a flip chart and pens; a photocopy of the list of behaviours from 'Talking about behaviour' on page 25 (starting with Jake and ending with Abdul) for each staff member.

Preparation: write out the following flip-chart sheets in advance. Leave the **first two sheets blank.**

On sheet 3 write: When managing behaviour we need to use clear language:

- so that we all know exactly where we started from
- so that we will all know when we have improved things
- so that we will all know when to intervene and when not to
- so that we share what we are doing with others, including parents and carers
- so that the child will understand the rules and boundaries.

On sheet 4 write: 'Cloudy' statements are vague statements about behaviour that are open to many interpretations:

good naughty understand behave settle sensible kind

On sheet 5 write: 'Clear' statements are statements about behaviour that are open to few interpretations and can be seen or heard:

kick say copy run shout throw hold touch bite

On sheet 6 write: Are these 'clear' or 'cloudy' statements?

know sit think appreciate grab recognise swear

On sheet 7 write: Spot the 'cloudy' statements (Is the verb observable?):

- Oliver will sit on the story mat without hitting Jamie. Clear / Cloudy
- Amy likes a lot of individual attention. Clear / Cloudy
- Gita will ask Fay for the car. Clear / Cloudy
- Ben listens quietly to stories. Clear / Cloudy
- Jo will stop being naughty at snack time. Clear / Cloudy

On sheet 8 write: When using clear language with parents and carers:

- start with a positive
- state clearly what the difficulty is
- state what positive behaviour you wish to encourage
- give parents a role – providing advice, information or trying things at home.

What you do

Session 1

➤ Explain that the aim of the session is to raise awareness of the language we use when talking about children's behaviour and to make this clearer.

➤ Write this at the top of the first sheet of the flip chart, 'Sam is being naughty'. Now ask each staff member to pretend that they are looking through a keyhole and seeing Sam, who is four years old, being naughty. What might he be doing? Make a list of their suggestions underneath.

➤ Point out that there are many words that we use frequently to describe children's behaviour that could mean many different things to different people. On sheet 2 of the flip chart, invite people to suggest other words that are used loosely – for example, 'aggressive', 'hyper', 'good', 'silly' and so on.

➤ Put up sheet 3 and spend a few minutes discussing the importance of using clear language when talking about behaviour. Does 'please be good' or 'don't be naughty' answer these requirements?

➤ Provide the definition of 'cloudy' and 'clear' statements on sheets 4 and 5. Explain that this terminology is borrowed from the Portage teaching approach. The words used need to be observable, which means that the verb or action word should be seen, heard or felt. Talk through the example words and see if you all agree. For each word ask, 'Can you see it? Can you hear it?'.

➤ Go through sheet 6 together, inviting comments from everyone.

➤ Now give staff members five minutes to discuss sheet 7 in groups of three to four. In a following plenary session, go through the statements together.

➤ Hand out the photocopies of the list of behaviours from 'Talking about behaviour' on page 25. Allow five minutes for each staff member to complete their own answers and then discuss these as a group.

➤ Arrange groups of three to four and ask each group to consider one of the children in the setting whose behaviour can be difficult to manage. Ask them to think of three clear statements about the appropriate behaviour they would wish to see in its place. Come together as a whole group and go through these.

➤ Finish the session by asking for general suggestions about how staff might actually encourage these behaviours for the children in question.

Session 2

➤ Remind staff of the need to use clear language when talking about behaviour by putting up sheets 4 and 5 again. Add that using clear and positive language also makes it much easier to talk with parents and carers about their child's behaviour.

➤ Divide staff members into small groups of three to four. Give each group a sheet of flip-chart paper and a pen. Describe the following true and familiar story. Ask them to imagine that they are the parents of a little boy who has just started in an early years setting. After the first fortnight, the person in charge meets you with the comment, 'Your child has a behaviour problem'. Ask them to talk about all the thoughts and feelings that might be going round their heads. After ten minutes, look at everyone's work together. Ask the plenary group for ideas on how the words could have been phrased differently.

➤ Show them sheet 8. Ask for suggestions of phrases that could be used when informing parents that their child has different kinds of behaviour problem.

Further action

Keep a record of helpful phrases to act as an *aide-mémoire* for future good communication.

Whose problem?

Use this activity to help staff members develop an idea of ages, stages and expectations.

Number of staff: all.

Timing: approximately one hour.

What you need: a selection of early years toys; a flip chart and pens; a photocopy of 'Behaviour: what is normal?' on page 23; 'Criteria for problem behaviour' on page 50.

Preparation: photocopy 'Behaviour: what is normal?' on page 23 for each person. Leave the **first two pages of the flip chart blank**. Prepare sheets 3 and 4 in the following way:

On sheet 3 write:

Behaviour	Percentage of all children who display this at age:		
	2	3	4
Fights or quarrels			
Hits others or takes things			
Stubborn			
'Talks back' cheekily			
Disobedient			
Tells 'fibs'			
Constantly seeks attention			
Cries easily			
Temper outbursts			
Active, hardly ever still			
Wets self during the day			

On sheet 4 write:

Criteria for problem behaviour

There are four main criteria for helping you to decide whether a behaviour is 'abnormal' or problematical:

- Fixation.
- Regression.
- Failure to display.
- Exaggeration.

What you do

- Explain that the purpose of the session is to talk about developmental stages and expectations about behaviour – in other words what is typical for each age and stage. Add that if their expectations about how a child should behave are wrong, then that child will find it hard to succeed.
- Give an example of a two-year-old who is tall and well-built for his age. If you did not know his age, what would you be thinking about his toddler-like behaviour? What problems is this likely to lead to?
- Ask why it is important to expect the best in children. Tell the story about Mrs Johnson from the 'Case study' on page 13.
- Divide the group into three. Let each group choose a selection of toys. Explain that in ten minutes they are going to pretend to be a certain age and demonstrate this to the whole group.
- Ask one group (without the other groups hearing) to be two-year-olds, the next group to be three-year-olds and the next, four-year-olds. Prompt them if necessary – two-year-olds might be placing one brick on top of another or lining

them up as a train. Three-year-olds might be building more constructively and four-year-olds might be playing more imaginatively and making patterns.

➤ Encourage the groups to demonstrate their play to the others who should guess their age. Challenge them to explain why they think the children are that age and discuss typical ages and stages together.

➤ Write this heading on the first sheet of flip-chart paper, 'Typical behaviour problems in three- to five-year-olds'. Now invite staff to brain-storm typical behaviours that children in their early years show – temper tantrums, snatching, throwing, being naughty and so on. Write all these down in a non-judgemental way whether the comments are 'clear' or 'cloudy'.

➤ Now ask each member to talk with their neighbour and decide when a behaviour actually becomes a problem. For example, if almost all two-year-olds have temper tantrums, does that mean that all two-year-olds have behaviour problems? Allow five minutes for this and then gather in thoughts, writing them onto the second sheet of flip-chart paper.

➤ One of the responses is likely to be that a behaviour becomes a problem if it is not what you would expect from the age of a child. This leads into discussion about expectations, ages and stages.

➤ Put up sheet 3 and ask staff to guess what percentage of all children at age two, three or four might show that problem. Share some humour as you run this almost as an auction, 'Higher? Lower? Are we there yet?'.

➤ Now hand out the photocopy 'Behaviour: what is normal?' on page 23 and compare your guesses.

➤ Put up sheet 4 and use the examples from 'Criteria for problem behaviour' on page 50 to provide examples of each category. Ask staff members to contribute examples of their own from difficult behaviours that you have worked with in the setting.

➤ Revisit the first sheet of flip-chart and go through it deciding when each of the behaviours really becomes a 'problem'. For example, regular temper tantrums in a two-year-old might be considered part of the norm, but at age four they might be seen as a problem. Or temper tantrums that involve toys being broken and placing other children at risk of being hurt would be seen as a problem whatever the age. This usually takes approximately twenty minutes.

➤ Explain that just because a behaviour is typical for an age does not mean that we do not have to manage it in some way. We teach sharing, turn-taking and friendly behaviour as part of the Personal, social and emotional Area of Learning in any early years setting. Explain that the vast majority of behaviour management that goes on will be the day-to-day encouragement and teaching that should be going on anyway.

➤ If behaviour management is working effectively, there will be very few children who need approaches that are additional or different to this. These are the children who need individual behaviour plans and whose names may be placed on the SEN register.

Further action

➤ Try using 'A consultative approach' on page 24 as a way of talking through a real case example.

➤ Discuss how you might best share expectations on behaviour and development with parents and carers in your setting.

Keeping an eye

Use this activity to help staff to develop observation and recording approaches.

Number of staff: all.

Timing: first session of one hour and a second session of 45 minutes.

What you need: photocopies for each person of the 'Five minute behaviour observation sheet' on page 127, the 'ABC behaviour chart' on page 53, and the 'Case study' on page 54; a flip chart or overhead projector with acetates and pens.

Preparation: give out the photocopies of the 'ABC behaviour chart' and the 'Five minute behaviour observation sheet' on pages 53 and 127 for each staff member. Prepare these flip-chart sheets or overheads:

On sheet 1 write: Ways of collecting 'baseline' information:

- Talk to other people.
- Counting or measuring the behaviour.
- Spot observations.
- ABC Diary.
- Behaviour charts.
- 'Fly on the wall' observation.
- The use of check-lists.

On sheet 2 write: The 'ABC' of behaviour management:

- A – the antecedent.
- B – the behaviour.
- C – the consequences of the behaviour.

Remember to gather information about the positives too!

What you do

Session 1

- Explain that the purpose of these sessions is to help staff members to gather information about a child's behaviour in order to plan what to do about it. Add that this is a good way of standing back from the problem and giving themselves thinking time.
- Put up sheet 1 and talk about different ways of gathering information. Explain that the starting point in behaviour management is called 'the baseline behaviour'. Go through each method in turn. Emphasise the importance of gathering information from other people and remind them of what you covered in the training session on using the right words with parents. Ask whether it would be possible for a child's behaviour to be a problem with one staff member but not another. Spend a few minutes talking about why this could be so.
- Next, move on to methods of counting and measuring behaviours. Explain that this is easy when a behaviour is obvious and observable (such as kicking another child) but not so easy when it is more complex (such as 'being unhappy'). Ask staff to think of some examples of behaviours that would be easy to count.

➤ Now challenge their assumption. Choose one behaviour problem such as hitting. Explain that you are going to role-play a child who has SEN and sometimes hurts herself by hitting her face. Should this be easy to observe? Most will answer positively. Ask one person with a second-hand on their watch to say 'go' and to stop you after 30 seconds. Ask the others to make a tally count of how often you hit your face. Make this difficult – start with a few straight hits (be careful not to hurt yourself!) and then start to blur them together and to add rubs and gentle scratches.
➤ Ask everyone to report their tally count and point out how behaviours are often very difficult to measure because we all interpret them differently. It is far more useful to collect information about the context in which behaviours take place.
➤ Now ask for examples of behaviours that would be easy to measure in terms of time – perhaps how long a child plays in the sand, or how long one child plays alongside another. Explain that this is another method of measuring behaviour. However, it can be time-consuming and so spot observations are usually used instead. Hand out the 'Five-minute behaviour observation sheet' on page 127 and explain its use.
➤ Introduce the idea of an ABC diary as a method of gathering information about the whole context of a behaviour. Show the group sheet 2 and explain what 'ABC' means. Explain that the advantage of this is that it gathers information about many kinds of behaviour and gives you a fuller picture. It can also be used to collect information about positive behaviour that will be even more use when planning an intervention.
➤ Return to your list on sheet 1. Give staff members the 'ABC behaviour chart' on page 53 and explain how it can be used, sharing the 'Case study' on page 54 as an example. Talk through a 'fly on the wall' observation and explain how to set this up by arranging for an extra helper, and making sure that others manage the behaviour as you observe and direct the children to the other helper.
➤ Ask staff to divide into groups of three. Invite them to plan how they will carry out one of three kinds of observation before the next training session:

- an ABC behaviour chart over three sessions flagging up three difficult and three successful incidents of behaviour each session
- a 'fly on the wall' observation for 30 minutes
- a five minute behaviour observation sheet during one hour.

Within each group, all three members should plan how to observe the same child but each individual will select a different method of doing so.

Session 2

➤ When you are all ready, meet again. First, ask staff members to go into their same groups to share their findings. Give each group a flip-chart sheet or acetate and ask them to write brief notes about what they did and a pen picture of the child, maintaining confidentiality where possible. Then ask them to note the strengths and weaknesses of the particular observation method they used.
➤ Share your findings. Talk about how to build in the use of behaviour observation to your regular practice.

Further action

➤ Arrange rotas during the training period to make the observations possible.
➤ Build up a resource bank of observation and record sheets.

Hatching solutions

Use this activity to help staff members make hypotheses about behaviour difficulties leading to planning.

Number of staff: all.

Timing: two sessions of approximately one hour.

What you need: photocopies of the 'Behaviour consultation' sheet on pages 123–124, the 'Consultation follow-up' sheet on page 125, and the 'Monitoring and review cycle' on page 80; a flip chart or overhead projector (OHP) with acetates and pens.

Preparation: arrange photocopies of the 'Behaviour consultation' sheet on pages 123–124, the 'Consultation follow-up' sheet on page 125 and the 'Monitoring and review cycle' on page 80 for each staff member. Prepare the following flip-chart sheets:

On sheet 1: make a copy of the 'Monitoring and review cycle' on page 80.

On sheet 2 write: Select a child whose behaviour concerns you. Go through the questions on the 'Behaviour consultation' sheet together.

On sheet 3 write: Behaviour planning:

- What is the difficult behaviour you wish to change (in 'clear' words)?
- What new behaviour do you wish to teach instead?
- What antecedents tend to lead up to the difficult behaviour?
- What are the consequences of this behaviour for the child?
- What rewards seem to work for the child?
- What are the child's strengths and interests?
- When does the child behave 'best'?

On sheet 4 write: A 'get together' to monitor progress:

- What was the original cause for concern?
- Progress made since we last met?
- How did our approaches work?
- What are our current concerns?
- What will we do next?
- Do we need to meet again?

What you do

Session 1

- Explain that the aim of these sessions is to help staff members use their observation techniques to gather information and then decide why a difficult behaviour might be happening. This will help them plan interventions for changing that behaviour.
- Put up sheet 1 to show staff members the copy of the 'Monitoring and review cycle' and talk through it together. Then give them each a photocopy of this to keep.

➤ Now put staff members into groups of two to six. Everyone in a group should already regularly work together, perhaps in the same room. Therefore each group will know the same children and share common challenges in managing any difficult behaviours. If any group claims that they do not work with any behaviour problems, either make suggestions or join them up with another group. You should end up with several small groups, each one able to visualise a particular child and their behaviour.
➤ Emphasise the need for discretion and confidentiality – this is a training exercise and not a part of the regular SEN procedures at this point in time.
➤ Put up sheet 2 and give out the photocopies of the 'Behaviour consultation' sheet for staff members to record their conclusions. Ask each group to decide on a particular child and a particular behaviour that they think it would be helpful to work on.
➤ Tell the groups that the 'action' they decide on should be an observation by each of them and that you will meet together at the second training session to discuss the results of this observation.
➤ Allow half-an-hour for this. Make sure that each group is clear about who and what they are going to observe and what method/s of observation they are going to use. Ask each staff member to contribute to the observation and decide how this will be done, just as you did in the 'Keeping an eye' training sessions (see page 116).
➤ Ask staff to bring back their consultation sheets and all their observations to the next session.

Session 2
➤ Explain that the aim of this session is for staff to analyse their observations and decide why a difficult behaviour might be happening. Explain that you can never be certain about this but it gives you a starting point for planning an intervention that you can then evaluate.
➤ Put up sheet 3 and go through the questions that they can ask each other. Put staff members into the same groups of two to six. Allow half-an-hour for groups to share their findings and begin to look for patterns in the child's behaviour.
➤ Ask each group to prepare a case study to present to the whole group, describing their observations, their analysis and why they think the child might be behaving in this way.
➤ Listen together to each group's case study and encourage constructive and supportive feedback from the others. Allow five to ten minutes per group.
➤ Finish by demonstrating how a monitoring and review cycle is beginning to fit together. Show them sheet 1 once again. Point out that they have now looked at 'formulation'. In the next session, they will begin to look at 'implementation', which means planning an intervention.
➤ Show staff sheet 4 as an illustration of how they can now hatch possible solutions and meet regularly with each other or with the SENCO/manager to monitor progress. Give out the copy of the 'Consultation follow-up' sheet and discuss how this might be built in to the framework for behaviour management in your setting.

Further action

Plan a regular consultation slot so that staff who are concerned about a particular child's behaviour can meet regularly with SENCO or manager to hatch solutions and plan interventions that should help.

Easy as ABC

Use this activity to help staff members prepare their own individual behaviour plans.

Number of staff: all.

Timing: two 1 hour sessions.

What you need: a flip chart; felt-tipped pens; photocopies of 'Behaviour planning' on pages 128–129, 'Individual behaviour plan (for Holly)' on page 81, and 'Individual behaviour plan' on pages 130–131; pens or pencils.

Preparation: make photocopies of 'Behaviour planning' on pages 128–129, 'Individual behaviour plan (for Holly)' on page 81, and 'Individual behaviour plan' on pages 130–131 for each person.

What you do

Session 1

➤ Remind staff of the need to use clear language when talking about behaviour. Put up a flip chart and divide it into two lengthwise. Ask the staff for a list of all the behaviours in the setting that can be difficult to manage. Avoid words such as 'naughty' or 'aggressive' and ask staff to state clearly what the child might actually be doing. Write the list on the left-hand side of the flip-chart sheet.

➤ Now go back to the list and invite staff to suggest a new behaviour that you would see once the difficult behaviour has gone – for example, instead of a child 'hitting other children', she would be 'playing happily with other children' and instead of 'biting', he would be 'asking for a toy'. Write these on the right-hand side of the flip-chart sheet.

➤ Explain to staff that these positive statements about behaviour can become 'targets' for a child with a behaviour difficulty. In other words, it is not sufficient to make a difficult behaviour disappear without teaching another appropriate behaviour in its place.

➤ Invite the staff to move into groups of three or four. Each group should think of a child whose behaviour has been challenging to manage. It could be that one member of staff can picture a child she used to work with and can describe a pen picture to the others. It could be that the whole group is familiar with a child in the group already. Stress the need for confidentiality and respect during the discussion and ask staff to choose an anonymous name for the child being discussed.

➤ Give the staff a photocopy of 'Behaviour planning' on pages 128–129.

➤ Remind staff of the 'ABC' analysis covered in their earlier session and of the methods they learned for observing and measuring behaviour. Invite each group to discuss the child's behaviour together and to complete parts 1 to 6 of the 'Behaviour planning' sheet. Allow 20 minutes for this activity.

➤ Ask staff to put their own names on their sheets. Collect these in and keep them safe for the second session, along with the flip chart.

Session 2

➤ Go over the first session, reminding the staff of how they could balance each difficult behaviour with a new behaviour they would wish to teach instead. Show them the flip chart and remind them of the 'targets' that they chose. Explain that

they are now going to practise writing targets for particular children's behaviour.
➤ Invite the staff to go back into their previous groups. Hand out their behaviour planning sheets and give them a few minutes to refresh themselves of the child being discussed.
➤ Now hand out the photocopies of the 'Individual behaviour plan' on pages 130–131. Explain that if a child's behaviour is so difficult to manage that it is interfering with their early learning, then staff should talk to the SENCO and draw up an individual behaviour plan. Refer to the photocopiable sheet to explain what such a plan looks like.
➤ Go through the different sections. Explain that when the staff are putting together a plan with the help of the group's SENCO, this is called taking Early Years Action. When they are doing so with the advice of an outside professional, such as a support teacher or psychologist, then this is called taking Early Years Action Plus.
➤ Give out copies of the 'Individual behaviour plan (for Holly)' and talk it through. Add that individual behaviour plans should always be discussed with parents and carers.
➤ Explain that the purpose of an individual behaviour plan is not necessarily to 'cure' a particular behaviour difficulty, but to show that you are taking reasonable steps towards managing it. There will be aspects of the child's behaviour you can easily change, and other areas of needs that may be beyond your ability to change. If the latter is true, then an individual behaviour plan provides clear evidence that further support and advice is needed.

➤ Invite groups to work together to complete an individual behaviour plan for the child being discussed. Emphasise the need to describe the behaviour clearly, to decide on a new behaviour to replace the old and then to set the whole thing up so that the child is likely to succeed. Remind staff again of the 'ABC' approach, which will help them design an individual approach for the child's behaviour. Ask them to choose three clear targets for the child to achieve in one term's time.
➤ Allow staff half-an-hour for this activity, visiting each group to help them complete the plan. You will find the information you need in Chapter 8.
➤ Ask groups to discuss their work as a plenary group, each one giving a brief and anonymous pen picture of the child and then sharing their individual behaviour plan.

Further action

➤ Arrange for a regular support session when staff can work on individual behaviour plans for certain children and can then report back on how effective they are.
➤ If possible and if helpful, invite the Area SENCO or support teacher to play a consultative role.

Check-list for staff

Here is a check-list for your staff concerning the issues raised in Chapter 12:

- Do staff members use clear and positive language when talking about behaviour?
- Do they avoid 'cloudy' blanket terms such as 'naughty'?
- Do staff think in terms of problem behaviour rather than problem children?
- Do staff see the need for ongoing contact with parents and carers?
- Do staff feel more confident when talking to parents about their child's behaviour?
- Are staff members able to use positive and supportive language when giving feedback to each other?
- Are staff members able to use positive and supportive language when giving feedback to the children?
- Do staff have an approximate idea of which behaviours are typical of which ages and the wide range of children's development?
- Do they understand that each child is an individual with individual needs?
- Do they recognise that behaviour happens within a context and that it is the context that must be changed rather than the child?
- Do they understand that children come to them from many different contexts and cultures?
- Do they see behaviour as something to be taught, just as the other aspects of the Personal, social and emotional curriculum?
- Do staff members have a range of interventions and approaches they can use in day-to-day behaviour management?
- Can staff decide when a child's behaviour has become a 'problem' that needs additional or different approaches?
- Has each member of staff practised using more than one method of observing behaviour?
- Can staff select the best method of observation for each behaviour or situation?
- Can staff members lift useful information from observations and begin to see patterns in children's behaviour?
- Can staff members make good use of a consultation meeting with you to plan approaches for managing behaviour?
- Can they plan and monitor a simple behavioural intervention?
- Can each staff member write an individual behaviour plan?
- Do they know whom to turn to in the setting for advice on behaviour management?
- Do you have a behaviour policy that covers all you need to?
- Even if you only have a few children showing behaviour difficulties, would all staff feel confident in working with these children?
- Do staff members feel supported in their work with behaviour difficulties?
- Do you have a system for making sure that staff are consistent in their approaches?
- Do you have a system for dealing with sensitive issues?
- How do you carry out Early Years Action for the children who have behavioural and emotional difficulties?
- What is involved in Early Years Action Plus for these children in our setting?
- When do we need to top up this training programme?
- What other topics should be included?

Behaviour consultation

Name of child: ____

Date of consultation: ______________

➤ Who was present?

➤ What is the behaviour you are worried about?

➤ What concerns you about this child's behaviour?

➤ What approaches have you tried so far?

➤ What effects have you noticed?

➤ How would you like things to change?

- Are there other factors you think might be important?

- How are parents or carers involved?

- What do parents or carers feel about the problem?

- Is any other agency involved?

- What will we do about the problem?

Actions	**To be carried out by**

When will we talk about this again? ______________________________

Consultation follow-up

Name of child: ______________________________

Date of follow-up: ______________________________

- Who was present?

- What was the original cause for concern?

- Progress made since we last met:

- How did our approaches work?

- What are our current concerns?

- What will we do next?

Do we need to meet again? ______________________________

Our behaviour policy

Name of setting: ______________________________

Our aims: ______________________________

____

____

➤ How we do this:

➤ How we respond to children who have emotional or behaviour difficulties:

➤ How we involve parents and carers:

➤ Our SENCO who advises on children with behavioural and emotional difficulties is: ______________________________

➤ These staff have had training in behaviour management: ______________

____

____

➤ We measure whether our behaviour policy has been effective by:

Date this behaviour policy will be reviewed: ______________________________

Five minute behaviour observation sheet

Child's name: ____________________

Date: ____________________

Adult observer: ____________________

Time started: ____________________

➤ What behaviour is being observed?

➤ Make a point of watching the child briefly every five minutes: **tick** if behaviour was observed, **cross** if behaviour was not observed. Under '**Activity**', give brief details of where the child was playing or what/who with, for example, 'In the sand tray with Jon'.

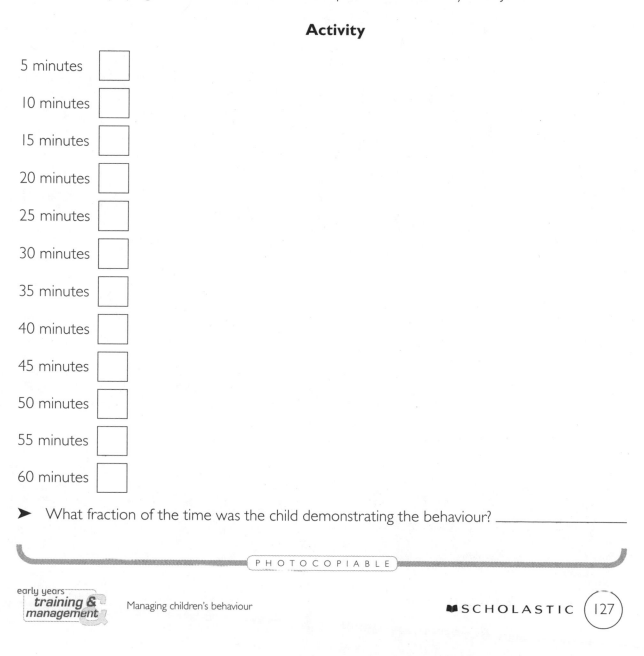

		Activity
5 minutes	☐	
10 minutes	☐	
15 minutes	☐	
20 minutes	☐	
25 minutes	☐	
30 minutes	☐	
35 minutes	☐	
40 minutes	☐	
45 minutes	☐	
50 minutes	☐	
55 minutes	☐	
60 minutes	☐	

➤ What fraction of the time was the child demonstrating the behaviour? ____________________

Behaviour planning

Name of child: ______________________________

Name of staff member: ______________________________

Preparation

➤ What is the difficult behaviour you wish to change (in 'clear' words)?

➤ What new behaviour do you wish to teach instead?

➤ How will you observe the difficult behaviour to obtain your 'ABC'?

Analysis

➤ What **antecedents** tend to lead up to the difficult behaviour?

➤ What are the **consequences** of this behaviour for the child?

➤ What rewards seem to work for the child?

➤ What are the child's strengths and interests?

➤ Now write on the 'Individual behaviour plan' (pages 130–131) showing how you will change the antecedents and the consequences in order to change the behaviour.

Individual behaviour plan

Name: ______________________ Early Years Action/Plus (delete if appropriate)

Behaviour difficulty:

Action

1. Seeking further information — Who will do what?

2. Seeking training or support

3. Observations and assessments

4. Managing the behaviour

What new behaviour do we wish to encourage instead?

What will we do whenever the difficult behaviour happens?

What will we do whenever the new behaviour happens instead?

Help from parents

Three targets for this term

1.

2.

3.

How will we measure whether we have achieved these?

Review meeting with parents/carers: ______________________________

Who else to invite

Progress review
Early Years Action/Early Years Action Plus

Name of child: ______________________________

Date of review meeting: ______________________

➤ Who was present?

➤ Who has sent reports (attached)?

➤ Progress since the last review:

Good news:

Challenges:

Opportunities:

➤ Any special support or approaches arranged:

➤ How helpful has this been?

➤ Any recent changes in the situation?

In the setting:

At home:

➤ Have the targets on the previous IBP been achieved?

➤ Negotiate and attach the current IBP.

➤ Date of next review meeting: ______________________________

➤ Copies of this will be sent to:

Parents' contribution to review meeting

Name of your child: ____________________

At home

➤ When does your child behave best at home?

➤ What does your child enjoy most at home?

➤ What are the biggest problems with behaviour at home?

➤ What seems to help?

About the group

➤ Is your child happy to come to the group?

➤ Are you worried about anything to do with the group?

➤ How do you feel about your child's behaviour there?

➤ Do you feel your child's needs are being met?

Health

➤ How has your child's health been lately?

➤ Are there any changes in medication or treatment?

➤ Are you worried about your child's development?

The future

➤ What behaviour would you like to see your child doing next?

➤ Are you worried about anything in the future?

➤ What questions would you like to ask at the review?

➤ What changes would you like to see following the review?

PHOTOCOPIABLE

Child's contribution to review meeting

Dear Parents – please talk to your child or fill this in as you think they would like to:

My name: ______________________________

➤ This is what I like doing best in the group:

➤ These are things that worry me:

➤ I don't like it when:

➤ I like it when:

PHOTOCOPIABLE

Home behaviour plan

Name: ____________________________________

➤ This is the behaviour we want to see more of:

➤ This is the behaviour we want to see less of:

➤ Activities to do at home:

➤ What to do when your child plays well:

➤ What to do when your child shows the problem behaviour:

➤ How to help your child improve:

➤ How did ____________________ get on?

Staff well-being questionnaire

There is a responsibility for us to carry out a risk assessment for stress. We have decided to use this questionnaire as a route to help understand our staff well-being. Please complete this confidentially. The whole staff will be given feedback of the overall findings.

Circle **4** if you strongly agree
3 if you generally agree
2 if you do not agree
1 if you strongly disagree

➤ I find the environment in the setting extremely pleasant:

4 3 2 1

Any further comments about physical spaces and comforts:

➤ I really enjoy working with the children:

4 3 2 1

➤ I have a number of colleagues with whom I have an excellent working relationship:

4 3 2 1

➤ Generally, relationships among staff are very good:

4 3 2 1

Any further comments? Do you generally feel heard, seen, understood, appreciated and listened to?

➤ My professional development is given a high priority by the setting, for example, in-service training, courses, career planning, further qualifications and study:

4 3 2 1

➤ I feel actively engaged in the shaping of the learning aims of the setting:

4 3 2 1

➤ There is an excellent relationship between me and my line manager:

4 3 2 1

➤ It is fine to share problems concerning children's difficult behaviour with the management or SENCO:

4 3 2 1

➤ There are commonly agreed procedures for dealing with challenging behaviour:

4 3 2 1

➤ The setting has a strong ethos with which I am very sympathetic:

4 3 2 1

➤ I am generally clear and happy with the direction in which the setting is going:

4 3 2 1

Any general comments you might like to add?

➤ Please think of two changes at work that would help you and improve your well-being:

1.

2.

Thank you for your help.

Planning meeting

Dear colleague

Name of child: ____________________ **Date of birth:**________________

Address:

Setting: _________________________

As you may know, this child is currently attending our setting and we need to plan the best approaches for managing the difficult behaviour.

Nature of difficulty:

We are holding a planning meeting to help us plan the best approaches.

Date: ______________ **Time:** ______________

Venue: ______________________________________

The purposes of this meeting will be:

- to gather and share all relevant information
- to find out which professionals are involved
- to help us to plan our approaches for managing the behaviour
- to learn about what approaches have helped in the past
- to learn who can be called upon to help in the future
- to set up good communication for the future
- to reassure and support staff who are in direct contact with the child
- to address potential difficulties early on
- to detail the need for any specific resources from outside the setting.

We do hope you can attend or perhaps send us any information that will be helpful. We are looking forward to meeting you and planning the best support we can.

Yours faithfully

cc. Parents and professionals already involved.

Useful resources and contacts

Useful books for staff to read

➤ *Circle Time for the Very Young* by Margaret Collins (Lucky Duck Publishing).
➤ *Asperger Syndrome: A Practical Guide for Teachers* by Val Cumine, Julia Leach and Gill Stevenson (David Fulton Publishers).
➤ *Spotlight on Special Educational Needs: Emotional and Behavioural Difficulties* by Jonathan Fogell and Rob Long (National Association for Special Educational Needs – NASEN) (see page 143 for contact details).
➤ *Behaviour in Pre-school Groups* by Ann Henderson (Pre-school Learning Alliance) (see page 144 for contact details).
➤ *Developing Individual Behaviour Plans in Early Years* by Dr Hannah Mortimer, (NASEN).
➤ *Supporting Children with AD/HD and Attention Difficulties in the Early Years* by Dr Hannah Mortimer (QEd).
➤ *Emotional Literacy and Mental Health in the Early Years* by Dr Hannah Mortimer (QEd).
➤ *Personal, Social and Emotional Development of Children in the Early Years* by Dr Hannah Mortimer (QEd).
➤ *The Music Makers Approach: Inclusive Activities for Young Children with Special Educational Needs* by Dr Hannah Mortimer (NASEN).
➤ *Learning Through Play: Circle Time* by Hannah Mortimer (Scholastic).
➤ *Turn Your School Around* by Jenny Mosley (Cambridge/LDA).
➤ *More Quality Circle Time* by Jenny Mosley (Cambridge/LDA).
➤ *Here We Go Round: Quality Circle Time for 3–5 year olds* by Jenny Mosley and Helen Sonnet (Positive Press Ltd).
➤ *Effective Teaching and Learning in the Classroom – A Practical Guide to Brain Compatible Learning* by Sara Shaw and Trevor Hawes (The Services Ltd) (see page 144 for contact details).
➤ *Ring of Confidence – A Quality Circle Time Programme to Support Personal Safety for the Foundation Stage* by Penny Vine and Teresa Todd (Positive Press Ltd).

Books that are useful to share with parents

➤ *New Toddler Taming: A Parent's Guide to the First Four Years* by Dr Christopher Green (Vermilion).
➤ *Positive Parenting* by Frank Merrett (QEd).
➤ *From Pram to Primary – Parenting Small Children from Birth to Age Six or Seven* by Mickey and Teri Quinn (Family Caring Trust) (see page 144 for details).
➤ *Confident Children: Developing your Child's Self-esteem* by Glen Stenhouse (Oxford University Press).

Useful resources

➤ 'Being Yourself' (a subsidiary of Smallwood Publishing Ltd) provides hand puppets and therapeutic games for professionals working to improve mental well-being and emotional literacy in children – send for a catalogue from The Old Bakery, Charlton House, Dour Street, Dover CT16 1ED (visit www.smallwood.co.uk).
➤ The *Understanding Childhood* leaflets (available from The Child Psychotherapy Trust, Star House, 104–108 Grafton Road, London NW5 4BD).
➤ *Jenny Mosley Circle Time Kit* includes puppets, rainstick, magician's cloak and many props for making circle time motivating (LDA).

Books that are useful to have in the setting

➤ DfEE *Full Day Care – National Standards for Under Eights Day Care and Childminding* (ref: DfEE 0488/2001).
➤ DfES SEN *Code of Practice* (ref: DfES 581/2001).
➤ DfES *Promoting Children's Mental Health within Early Years and School Settings* (ref: DfES 0112/2001).
➤ *Manager's Handbook* by June O'Sullivan, *Early Years Training and Management* series (Scholastic).
➤ *Staff Training Activities* by Pauline Kenyon, *Early Years Training and Management* series (Scholastic).
➤ *Behavioural and Emotional Difficulties, Autistic Spectrum Difficulties, Sensory Difficulties, Physical and Co-ordination Difficulties, Medical Difficulties, Speech and Language Difficulties, Special Needs Handbook and Learning Difficulties* all by Dr Hannah Mortimer in the *Special Needs in the Early Years* series (Scholastic).

National organisations concerned with young children and their families

➤ **Alliance for Inclusive Education**

Unit 2, 70 South Lambeth Road, London SW8 1RL, tel: 020 7735 5277.
(Campaigns to end compulsory segregation of children with special educational needs within the education system.)

➤ **Barnardo's**

Tanners Lane, Barkingside, Ilford, Essex, IG6 1QG, tel: 020 8550 8822, fax: 020 8551 6870, website: www.barnardos.org.uk Send for their publication list – Barnado's Child Care Publications, Barnado's Trading Estate, Paycocke Road, Basildon, Essex SS14 3DR.
(Provides care and support for children in need and their families, with projects throughout the UK.)

➤ **Children's Rights Alliance for England**

94 White Lion Street, London N1 9PF, tel: 020 7278 8222, fax: 020 7278 9552, e-mail: info@crights.org.uk website: www.crights.org.uk
(Working towards the creation of the office of Children's Rights Commissioner. Seeks to promote the fullest possible implementation of the UN Convention on the Rights of the Child.)

➤ **Children's Society**

Edward Rudolf House, Margery Street, London WC1X 0JL, tel: 0845 300 1128 e-mail: supporteraction@childrenssociety.org.uk website: www.the-childrens-society.org.uk
(Works with children in need and their families, for example in independent living projects for children leaving care and home-finding projects for children with special needs. Runs several family centres and parenting projects.)

➤ **Child Poverty Action Group**

94 White Lion Street, London N1 9PF, tel: 020 7837 7979, fax: 020 7837 6414 e-mail: staff@cpag.org.uk website: www.cpag.org.uk
(Acts on behalf of all poor and distressed families.)

➤ **Cruse Bereavement Care**

Cruse House, 126 Sheen Road, Richmond, Surrey TW9 1UR, tel: 0870 167 1677 (helpline), fax: 020 8940 7638, e-mail: info@crusebereavementcare.org.uk website: www.crusebereavementcare.org.uk
(Support and information for the widowed and their children.)

➤ **Families Need Fathers**

134 Curtain Road, London EC2A 3AR, tel: 020 7613 5060, e-mail: fnf@fnf.org.uk website: www.fnf.org.uk
(A UK charity that provides information and support to parents, including unmarried parents of either sex, and is chiefly concerned with the problems of maintaining a child's relationship with both parents during and after family breakdown.)

➤ **Family Service Units**

207 Old Marylebone Road, London NW1 5QP, tel: 020 7402 5175, fax: 020 7724 1829, e-mail: centraloffice@fsu.org.uk website: www.fsu.org.uk
(Services and supports disadvantaged families and communities. Aims to prevent family and community breakdown.)

➤ **Gingerbread**

7 Sovereign Close, Sovereign Court, London E1W 2HW, tel: 0800 018 4318 (freephone advice line, 9am–5pm Mon to Fri), fax: 020 7488 9333, e-mail: office@gingerbread.org.uk website: www.gingerbread.org.uk
(Supports lone parents and their children with financial, social and legal advice,

and through social and practical activities. There are more than 300 local self-help groups.)

➤ **Home-Start UK**
2 Salisbury Road, Leicester LE1 7QR, tel: 0116 233 9955, fax: 0116 233 0232 e-mail: info@home-start.org.uk website: www.home-start.org.uk
(National organisation supporting Home-Start schemes that provide trained parent volunteers to help any parent of pre-school children who is finding it hard to cope. Volunteers visit parents in their own homes. Home-Start is established in more than 300 communities across the UK and with British Forces abroad.)

➤ **Hyperactive Childrens Support Group**
71 Whyke Lane, Chichester, West Sussex PO19 7PD, tel: 01243 551 313 e-mail: web@hacsg.org.uk website: www.hacsg.org.uk
(Support and advice for carers and professionals for children who have hyperactivity/ADH.)

➤ **The National Autistic Society**
393 City Road, London EC1V 1NG, tel: 020 7833 2299 or Autism Helpline: 0870 600 85 85, fax: 020 7833 9666, e-mail: nas@nas.org.uk website: www.nas.org.uk
(Support and advice for carers and professionals working with children who have difficulties within the autistic spectrum.)

➤ **National Association For Special Educational Needs (NASEN)**
NASEN House, 4/5 Amber Business Village, Amber Close, Amington, Tamworth, Staffordshire B77 4RP, tel: 01827 311 500, fax: 01827 313 005, e-mail: welcome@nasen.org.uk website: www.nasen.org.uk
(Professional association with a database of relevant courses for those wishing to train in SEN; also runs training courses itself.)

➤ **National Children's Bureau**
8 Wakley Street, London EC1V 7QE, tel: 020 7843 6000 or 020 7843 6008 (library enquiry line, 10–12pm and 2–4pm), fax: 020 7278 9512, e-mail: library@ncb.org.uk website: www.ncb.org.uk
(A multi-disciplinary organisation concerned with the promotion and identification of the interests of all children and young people. Involved in research, policy and practice development, and consultancy.)

➤ **National Council For One Parent Families**
255 Kentish Town Road, London NW5 2LX, tel: 020 7428 5400 or 0800 018 5026 (freephone information and maintenance/money helpline), fax: 020 7482 4851, e-mail: info@oneparentfamilies.org.uk website: www.oneparentfamilies.org.uk
(Seeks to improve the economic legal and social status of one-parent families.)

➤ **National Council of Voluntary Child Care Organisations**
Unit 4, Pride Court, 80–82 White Lion Street, London N1 9PF, tel: 020 7833 3319, fax: 020 7833 8637, e-mail: office@ncvcco.org website: www.ncvcco.org
(Umbrella group for voluntary organisations dealing with children. Ensuring the well-being and safeguarding of children and families, and maximising the voluntary sector's contribution to the provision of services. Runs a freephone helpline and courses for parents and foster parents, and has a range of downloadable information on the website.)

➤ **National Newpin**
Sutherland House, 35 Sutherland Square, London SE17 3EE, tel: 020 7358 5900, fax: 020 7701 2660, e-mail: info@newpin.org.uk website: www.newpin.org.uk
(Offers parents and children an opportunity to achieve positive changes in their relationships and break the cycle of destructive family behaviour. Newpin offers

parenting skills training programmes and includes a Fathers' project.)

➤ **National Portage Association**

Administrator, 127 Monks Dale, Yeovil, Somerset BA21 3JE, tel: 01935 471 641. (For Portage parents and workers, and for training in Portage and for information on 'Quality play' training.)

➤ **One Parent Families in Scotland**

13 Gayfield Square, Edinburgh EH1 3NX, tel: 0131 556 3899 or 0800 018 5026 (helpline), fax: 0131 557 7899, e-mail: info@opfs.org.uk website: www.opfs.org.uk

(A national voluntary organisation whose aim is to enable lone parents to achieve their full potential, as individuals and as parents.)

➤ **Parent Network (Scotland)**

15 Smith Place, Edinburgh EH6 8NT, tel: 0131 555 6780, e-mail: parent.network.scotland@care4free.net

(A programme of information, education and support run by trained parents for parents.)

➤ **Parentline Plus**

520 Highgate Studios, 53-79 Highgate Road, London NW5 1TL, tel: 0808 800 2222 (helpline), website: www.parentlineplus.org.uk

(Formed following the merger of Parentline and the National Stepfamily Association. Supports anyone parenting a child including grandparents.)

➤ **PIPPIN Parents in Partnership – Parent Infant Network**

Birch Centre Annex, Highfield Park, Hill End Lane, St Albans, Herts AL4 0RB, tel: 01727 899 099, website: www.pippin.org.uk

(Promotes positive early family and parent–infant relationships. Aims to maintain and improve the emotional health of families during the period surrounding the birth of a new baby. Offers parentcraft classes, and a range of projects that includes work with fathers.)

➤ **Stepfamily Scotland**

5 Coates Place, Edinburgh EH3 7AA, tel: 0131 225 5800 (helpline), fax: 0131 225 3514, e-mail: info@stepfamilyscotland.org.uk website: www.stepfamilyscotland.org.uk

(Support and information for members of stepfamilies and those who work with them.)

Other useful contacts

➤ The Magination Press specialises in books that help young children deal with personal or psychological concerns. Send for a catalogue from The Eurospan Group, 3 Henrietta Street, Covent Garden, London WC2E 8LU.

➤ For helpful information on learning styles, contact The Services Ltd, PO Box 12, Leicester, LE2 5AE, tel: 0116 279 1111.

➤ Pre-school Learning Alliance, 69 Kings Cross Road, London WC1X 9LL, tel: 020 7833 0991.

➤ Family Caring Trust, Unit 8, Ashtree Enterprise Park, Rathfriland Road, Newry, Co Down BT34 1BY.

➤ Lucky Duck Publishing has a catalogue of videos, books and resources. Contact Lucky Duck Publishing Ltd, 3 Thorndale Mews, Clifton, Bristol BS8 2HX, tel: 0117 973 2881, e-mail: publishing@luckyduck.co.uk website www.luckyduck.co.uk

➤ nfer Nelson, Unit 28, Bramble Road, Techno Trading Centre, Swindon, Wiltshire SN2 8EZ, tel: 0845 602 1937, e-mail: information@nfer-nelson.co.uk website: www.nfer-nelson.co.uk

The Complete Paintings of

Cézanne

Introduction by **Ian Dunlop**

Notes and catalogue by **Sandra Orienti**

Penguin Books

Penguin Books Ltd, Harmondsworth, Middlesex, England
Viking Penguin Inc., 40 West 23rd Street, New York, New York 10010, U.S.A.
Penguin Books Australia Ltd, Ringwood, Victoria, Australia
Penguin Books Canada Ltd, 2801 John Street, Markham, Ontario, Canada L3R 1B4
Penguin Books (N.Z.) Ltd, 182–190 Wairau Road, Auckland 10, New Zealand

First published by Rizzoli Editore 1970
This translation first published in Great Britain by Weidenfeld & Nicolson 1972
Published in Penguin Books 1985

Printed in Italy

Photographic sources

Colour Plates : Carrieri, Milan ; Courtauld Institute, London ; Held, Ecublens ; Hinz, Basle ; Mandel, Milan ; Nimatallah, Milan ; Scala, Antella.
Black and white illustrations : Glasgow Museum and Art Gallery, Glasgow ; Indianapolis Museum of Art, Indianapolis (Ind.) ; Metropolitan Museum of Art, New York ; Museum of Fine Arts, Boston (Mass.) ; Národní Galerie, Prague ; National Gallery of Art, Washington, D.C. ; Rizzoli Archives, Milan ; Städelsches Kunstinstitut, Frankfurt ; Tate Gallery, London ; Vallotton, Lausanne.

Introduction

It is perhaps difficult today to appreciate the excitement which Cézanne's work aroused in painters, writers and critics at the turn of the century. He had been struggling at his art for over thirty years and yet people thought of him as a discovery, a new talent and an overlooked master. Gustave Geoffroy, one of the first historians of Impressionism met Cézanne in 1894 and wrote: "All the little known facts about his life, his almost secret productivity, the rare canvases which seem to follow none of the accepted rules of publicity, all these give him a strange renown, already distant; a mystery surrounds his person and his work. Those in search of the unfamiliar, who like to discover things which have not been seen, speak of Cézanne's canvases with a knowing air, giving information like a password."

Even painters who had known Cézanne for most of their working lives were surprised by his work. No one had been closer to him than Pissarro and no one had done more to encourage and help him through the many difficult patches of his career. Yet the first Cézanne exhibition, organised by Vollard in 1895, overwhelmed him and he spoke of Cézanne's "astonishing subtlety, truth and classicism". He was particularly impressed by the large figure paintings, which were in many ways the most difficult to appreciate. "Curiously enough," he wrote to his son, "while I was admiring this strange disconcerting aspect of Cézanne, familiar to me for many years, Renoir arrived. But my enthusiasm was nothing compared to Renoir's. Degas himself is seduced by the charm of this refined savage. Monet, all of us. Are we mistaken? I don't think so."

Younger artists began to seek out his work and in the early 1900s Picasso and Braque saw their first Cézannes. At the Salon d'Automne of 1904 and 1905 Cézanne's contribution made a strong impression and in the winter of 1904 those two remarkable American collectors, Leo and Gertrude Stein, bought their first major Cézanne, a portrait of the artist's wife. Two English critics, Roger Fry and Clive Bell, joined the growing number of admirers and their enthusiasm, expressed through writings and the famous Grafton Gallery exhibition of 1910–11, helped change the course of British art. "Those artists among us whose formation took place before the war," wrote Fry, "recognise Cézanne as their tribal deity . . ."

There is a good reason why Cézanne appealed so strongly to painters in the early years of this century, and continues to do so today: few artists have left such a clear record of the process by which a painting is constructed. Cézanne's method is visibly imbedded into the surface of his canvases. You can see the dabs of paint building up to form the contours and planes of an object. You can sense the picture forming with each mark. According to Vollard, Cézanne used very pliable brushes made of sable or polecat hair. After each touch he washed them in his medium-cup filled with turpentine. Painting, for Cézanne, was a laborious, protracted business. He followed the Impressionist method of working straight onto the canvas, first studying the motif, then looking at the paint on his palette, dipping his brush into the paint and finally applying the dab to the canvas. The difference in Cézanne's case was that each step in this chain of events was a drawn-out effort of will, requiring immense concentration and perseverance. Pictures took months to advance: they could never be said to have been completed. His apples and oranges would rot while he painted them and he was forced to use artificial flowers in some of his still-lifes. His sitters suffered as much as the artist. At any moment he was liable to fly into a tantrum and hack a portrait to pieces. Vollard says that when he sat for his portrait he was careful to avoid all controversial subjects. After 115 sessions Cézanne abruptly abandoned the project saying: "The front of the shirt is not bad."

In the last years of his life Cézanne mellowed and endeavoured to pass on his views about art and painting to young admirers like Charles Camoin and Émile Bernard. Cézanne became the painters' painter, the forerunner of Cubism, the artist who attempted to "redo Poussin after nature" and advised young painters "to treat nature by the cylinder, the sphere, the cone, everything in proper perspective so that each side of an object is directed towards a central point".

There is a dark side to Cézanne, like the dark side to the moon. It is rarely seen and often conveniently forgotten. It is the Romantic, the follower of Delacroix, the student who copied Rubens and Veronese in the Louvre and drew Baroque sculpture, the young man who was anti-classical and anti-Ingres. Cézanne, as has been pointed out, was the first "wild-man of modern art", a precursor of Expressionism. In the 1860s there were many artists who questioned the dominance of the Academy over the art schools and Salons, but Cézanne appeared to be the most bitterly opposed to the system. He transported his canvases to the Salon in a wheelbarrow, works which he knew would be rejected. The polite, well-dressed Manet, who had been rejected himself on more than one occasion, once asked Cézanne what he was intending to send to the forthcoming Salon. "A pot of shit", was the short reply.

Cézanne's explosive temper, his over-sensitivity and suspiciousness were well-known to his friends. His coarse language was matched by an unkempt, dirty appearance. His big black beard, and rugged peasant countenance must have terrified those who did not know him. It was this man who, people said, painted with a "pistol loaded with paint". One work, *A Modern Olympia* (no. 250), reproduced here on the cover, became Cézanne's chief contribution to the first Impressionist exhibition of 1874, where it must have seemed far removed in spirit and technique from the landscapes of the Impressionists. In *A Modern Olympia* and other works of this period, the prematurely balding figure of the artist is seen seated in the foreground. Before him are a series of bleary, overblown, naked females, hideously distorted, who hide their femininity by appearing to crouch or squat on their haunches, or by turning their backs to the spectator and the painter, lying front-down on the grass, their buttocks perched on vast thighs like substitute breasts. The drawing in these paintings is on the level of graffiti, but the colour is strong and sensual. In the last hundred years there have been few works, either by the Expressionists or by a modern painter like Francis Bacon to equal the unrestrained emotionalism of these dark paintings.

Cézanne had something to say, but to his mortification he felt that he had not the means to say it. He lacked the gift of illustration, the sort of talent which any commercial artist can pick up at art school. In vain Zola tried to encourage his former school companion: "One sentence in your letter made a bad impression upon me," he wrote. "It was this: 'Painting which I love, even though I am not successful, etc., etc.' You, not successful, I think you deceive yourself! I have already told you: in the artist there are two men, the poet and the workman. One is born a poet, one becomes a workman. And you, who have the spark, who possess what cannot be acquired, you complain when all you need to succeed is to exercise your fingers, to become a workman!"

Both men agreed that skill alone was not enough to make an artist. In 1866 Zola defined his and Cézanne's belief, explaining, "a work of art is a corner of nature seen through a temperament", and on the title page of a pamphlet reprinting his Salon reviews are the words, "that which I seek above all is a man and not a picture". All who came in contact with Cézanne agreed he had "temperament". His examiner for the École des Beaux-Arts, M. Mottez, explained the reason for his rejection: "Cézanne has the proper temperament for a colourist; unfortunately his work is extreme."

Cézanne never seems to have doubted that he had "temperament", and he used to divide other painters into those who possessed this quality and those who did not: "Manet hits off the right tone – but his work lacks unity – and temperament too", he said to Vollard. And to the painter Guillemet he remarked: "Don't you think your Corot is a little short on temperament?" The painting he admired was "*couillarde*" or "husky", and the rest he considered more or less "emasculated".

It is that very "temperament" which, in a sense, saved Cézanne. He never lapsed into mechanical repetition. Every painting, even if it was based on a motif he had studied a hundred times over, required all his concentration. Every brushstroke was a positive effort; every moment spent before the canvas was a positive affirmation of his "temperament". It is this emotional aspect of Cézanne, the barely concealed rage which lies behind every dab of paint, which supports the Classicist, the painter of spheres, cones, and cylinders, and the forerunner of Cubism.

IAN DUNLOP

An outline of the artist's critical history

The usual documentation, compiled from first-hand knowledge of the man and his development as an artist, is almost entirely lacking as far as Cézanne is concerned. Yet this very dearth turns to a kind of advantage, in that it gives him a charisma all his own.

There are various explanations as to how it happened. First, the nature of the artist himself. His range of sensitivity makes him emerge as a man both proud and despondent, shy and assured. It began in his young days, when the options were open on a literary career too. His preference, in becoming an artist, may be read as an inkling of perennial awareness, and this amounts to so much more than the hint of precocious talent.

As time went by, he was always on the move. Tempestuous moods and feelings drove him from one place to another, each for a little while where he could live and work. This chronic unrest seldom comes across in his paintings, which breathe the same air of search and research, in profound need of perfection. Then there is the difficulty he experienced in making firm friends, after the early period, in itself significant. And again, his generosity in later years when young artists – Camoin and Bernard among them – found a ready welcome at his Provençal home. They wanted his advice, for different motives, either in so many words or direct from his work.

The upshot has been that – apart from some heart-warming declarations of support, like Rivière's now famous piece of 1877, followed by others at irregular intervals – an approach could best be made through Cézanne's letters, and his friends'. In trying to ascertain the course of his artistic and spiritual progress by this means, the first batch concerns his relationship with Zola. It marked a turning-point. In some ways, Zola can be credited with having encouraged Cézanne to go against the wishes of his father. For it was Zola who first saw his possibilities as an artist.

"God help me if I am a bad influence on you, if art and dreaming are not good for you. . . . Come on then, pick up your brushes and make a fresh start. . . . I have faith in you. . . . I think I speak for you, at least I feel able to." (25 June 1860).

Their correspondence over the years is revealing, to a far greater extent than Zola's panegyrics whenever the Impressionists were exhibiting. At the same time it is obvious that what ended the relationship was Zola's inability to understand the precise value of Cézanne's contribution to contemporary art. Indeed, the artist was engaged in conducting unique investigations.

Matters came to a head in 1886, when *L'Oeuvre* was published. Some of the writer's notes for the book make clear his intentions. The thumb-nail sketch of the leading character, Claude Lantier, reads: "He is a flawed genius, short of fulfilment. Very little is missing, a bit of balance in this direction or that. In addition, he has produced some absolute marvels. A Manet, a Cézanne – dramatised. More of a Cézanne."

Contemporary evidence may therefore be deemed to be of relative value only, and no vital import. It is mostly episodic: Vollard, or Gasquet, or the *Souvenirs* of Bernard. When his work is admired, and this goes for later publications as well, evaluation is seldom properly grounded. The monograph of Fry (1927) is the first to be rigorously appreciative.

Expert opinion since then has gradually begun to delve. Over the last forty to fifty years, progress has been made, especially with regard to the origins of Cubism. But the letters remain a prime source for discerning what the artist was thinking or feeling; his motivations, his ideas, his results are recorded with the same honesty which went into his work.

Cézanne has come in for more abusive treatment – at the hands of both press and public, over the last fifteen years – than any other artist you care to name. Hardly a harsh word that has not been said of him at one time or another. And his reputation, for that matter, is still notorious . . .

What he most closely resembles is a Greek of the golden age. That imperturbable calm, in all of his canvases is also found alike in ancient Greek painting or vases. Those who ridicule his *Bathers*, for example, are just like the Barbarians who find fault with the Parthenon.

Cézanne is a great painter. It has been alleged that he did not know how to draw, by people who have never held crayon or brush. "Not right", they cry, failing to discern so tremendously refined and talented an achievement for what it is.

I am well aware that, all things considered, Cézanne cannot have the success of fashionable painters . . . but his work has the inexpressibly compelling quality of Biblical times or ancient Greece. The movements of his figures are simple but on a grand scale, like statuary; his landscapes are majestic and impressive; his still-lifes fine, and with tonal values so near reality that there is something awesome about them. His painting never fails of impact. This is because of his ability which enables him to endow the canvas with the full force of feeling which nature moves in him. G. RIVIÈRE, in *L'Impressionniste*, 14 April 1877

A revelation as a colourist ... who contributed more than Manet to the Impressionist movement. An artist whose retina is diseased, and his visual perception so far from the normal that he found a new art over the horizon. In these terms may be summarised Cézanne, the all-too-forgotten. J.-K. HUYSMANS, *Certains*, 1889

... and then it suddenly appears that Zola's friend, this mystery man from Provence, a painter full of ideas if not whole, subtle and yet crude, is a great man. A great man? Not a bit of it; more a case of turn and turn about. But undoubtedly a temperament to watch; the new school owes him a good deal, perhaps more than they realise. A. ALEXANDRE, in *Le Figaro*, 9 December 1895

He commits the blunders and errors of a true primitive. G. LECOMTE, in *La Revue d'Art*, 1899

There are a dozen works, landscapes and portraits signed by an ultra-Impressionist named Cézanne, enough to make Brisson merry. It is all very funny, especially the bronzed and bearded head whose cheeks must have been laid on with a trowel and looking mighty eczematous ...

The experts, who are at their wits' end about how to list such vagaries, have simply described each one as: Juvenile Period ...

Had Cézanne been in the nursery when such a sickening mess was made, it would be no laughing matter ... but when the keeper of Médan [Zola] actually supports such folly, what is one to think? ...

Admit Cézanne ... and you might as well set fire to the Louvre ... H. ROCHEFORT, "L'Amour du Laid", in *L'Intransigeant*, 9 March 1903

His Estaque landscapes transform a lovely land of sapphire and gold into a leaden bog where the light never smiles.

The name of Cézanne is going to remain linked with the daftest art of the last fifteen years. C. MAUCLAIR, in *La Revue Bleue*, 21 October 1904

Being a good workman and doing a decent job was for him the key to everything. Good painting meant good living. He gave himself entirely, his whole strength behind each stroke of the brush. You need only have seen him at work, painfully tense, his face as if in prayer, to realise how much spirit went to the task. He was shaking all over. Hesitant, his forehead carked with unseen thought, chest sunken, shoulders hunched and hands all a-trembling until the moment came. Then firm and fast, they started to work gently and always from right to left, with a will of their own. He would step back a couple of paces, then let his eyes return to the objects. R. M. RILKE, Letter to Clara, 9 October 1907

It was amusing to watch the public at a loss. They had been spoiled for work of such burning sincerity by run-of-the-mill painters who in turn felt themselves outraged. People's values are supposed to have improved but it was like being back in the days of Duret. Visitors to the little Impressionist exhibitions used to laugh out loud on the staircase, before they even set foot inside. Now young people's enthusiasm has more than made up for such silly behaviour. They realise what a boon it is, a self-improving occasion given them this year by Cézanne, and last year by Gauguin. C. MORICE, in *Le Mercure de France*, 1 November 1907

Not to have seen him painting makes it hard to appreciate how slow and burdensome work was to him sometimes. In my portrait, the canvas is bare in two places. I mentioned this to Cézanne. He replied: "If all goes well at the Louvre by-and-by, perhaps tomorrow I shall know what to do about it. Try and understand ... if I fill in anyhow, I shall have to start the picture all over again from that point." A. VOLLARD, *Paul Cézanne*, 1914

He was so entirely unimaginative as to be quite unable to choose those forms most suitable to convey the idea of harmony which he wished to express. He never made choice of one among a large number of objects, in order to present the median element and thus embody all. Instead he would pick any object whatsoever, regardless of whether it was ugly or beautiful, and make his choice from there. The object acquired such unity of character and force of expression that it came across like the law ...

He was a painter. Nothing interested him in reality outside the juxtaposition of colour and form imparted by light and shade to objects. The laws thus revealed were so unsparing that a lofty spirit might take them as governing the life of body or mind. E. FAURE, *P. Cézanne*, 1926

To give Paul Cézanne his true parentage, Michelangelo and Æschylus are names to conjure with. Like the Tuscan, he knew the mystic force which mute objects release, whether rocks or trees. Like the Greek, he sensed the untamed power implicit in the heart of unstudied people. His landscapes and figures are infused with this two-fold strength. It makes his work rough going – as flinty, fierce and fought-over as theirs is – and yet a ground where flower and herbage can lift a modest head with the simplicity and spontaneity of nature.

For Cézanne to contrive to depict material of this solemnity meant cutting through a lot of imaginative undergrowth so that the style alone might convey the sacred drama. Indeed, his colour and drawing are pared down, not to say poor and brutal. In his painting, there recurs the chromatic conflict which Masaccio was the first to evoke with any realism, in the Brancacci chapel of the Carmine church; the vigorous twist and turn are those of Tintoretto.

Unhampered by rule or reservation, his style comes across with the harshness of outline seen in living things, and in surroundings. A. SOFFICI, *Scoperte e massacri*, 1929[2]

The Provençal's great merit was to return painting to a mainstream course. As a result, the art of a whole epoch may be held to stem from his initiative and effort. The Positivist period left a backwash of experiment *a priori* (luminist, divisionist, complementarist). These were all cast aside and the return made to painting nature in the soul's magic looking-glass. The standpoint was no longer emotive or perceptual (as it had been with the Impressionists). Instead, it meant a profound religious commitment on a grand scale. In the light of history, we may call it essentially Italian . . .

Cézanne never paints according to a plan that is more or less revolutionary. He works under pressure; in a mystical way, it directs and devours him. His palette sings or cries, screaming as the drama unfolds. His art has nothing of the hedonist, descriptive or phenomenal. In his canvases, painting as understood by Manet and Monet is outclassed. It is no longer a question of what is "temperamentally true" as Zola saw it. Indeed, there is an ethical and transcendental element in his work, of which Zola's approach contains no inkling. This is the connecting link between Cézanne and the great Italians: Giotto, Masaccio, Michelangelo, Tintoretto, Caravaggio . . .

The spiritual aspect of Cézanne's Italianism is herein comprised, not like Poussin, after the Italian fashion, but in essence. His feeling finds outward expression in a manner, also characteristically Italian.

The crux of his style concerns volume, the interplay of light and shade. The possible variations (intensity, position, thrusting or static) represent his syntax. This is shaped and coloured relative to the degree of chiaroscuro.

It all goes to make him an heir of the Venetians, and of that sculptural tradition founded on the towering personality of Giotto and the polyhedral mass, and on Masaccio, hewing his figures from great chiaroscuro columns. M. TINTI, "Italianismo di Cézanne", in *Pinacotheca*, March-June 1929

No one in the history of art ever clung to the unchanging more inexorably than Cézanne. The great dream of stability went out with classical thinking, science having contributed instead the idea that everything is always changing. The Impressionist movement accepts this. . . . Cézanne resists. A last flicker of Latinity, trying to recreate the security which went up in smoke in the seventeenth century. With patience and passionate devotion, in search of what is solid and will endure: form and structure, the eternal bases of reality and thought, the outward life and that of the mind. R. HUYGUE, *Cézanne*, 1936

The greatness of Cézanne, contemporary with the Impressionists, their friend and sympathiser, lies in the immediate recognition of his own task as that of going further, using their analytical results for a synthesis on his own account. L. VAUXCELLES, "Cézanne au musée de l'Orangerie", in *Le Monde Illustré*, 9 May 1936

A Latin temperament of an exceptionally stormy nature; tremendous powers of concentration, in many ways prone to extremes and full of contrasts; a prey to unrest, yet a firm believer in prodigious dreams; refined, delicate and careful to the point of shyness; imbued with all the formidable logic of a Kant, yet under severe emotional strain: Cézanne is an exceptional man, in the Romantic and decadent sense of the term. He could have just stopped short of full expression. Instead, he tried for many years to bring his unruly being under firm control. It was a desperate struggle and went deep enough to leave his character permanently scarred. C. L. RAGGHIANTI, *Impressionismo*, 1944

Undoubtedly, there are several Cézannes in Cézanne. Imaginative and practical, sensual and intellectual, the southerner and the mediterranean; one is baroque while the other is classical; one is a lover of reality, instinctive and constantly renewed, a painter who handles material like a sculptor his clay, a pastrycook his dough, a farmer his plot of land. The other is a great traveller in the realms where all is a phantasy of love and delight. The great Romantics had all made brief excursions into that territory; Nerval and Baudelaire were most familiar with its haunts. One is overjoyed with the look of the world and corresponding artistic creation, another disappointed with nature as something man must impress. The baroque southerner loves movement and effect at its most lyrical. The classical mediterranean type favours style and reserve, the old unchanging order. If ever Racine's words about that cruel war when a man is up against himself, applied to a living person, it is to the painter, Paul Cézanne. B. DORIVAL, *Cézanne*, 1948

Cézanne is alone, desperately so. He does not make followers. He does not try to conquer or convince. He only wants to express himself. To say what he has to say. It means an effort, a pressure which is inevitably painful. It is a moving sight. Cézanne brings forth in sorrow. His best paintings are serene because they are most meaningful. But they cannot entirely mask the anguish suffered in order to achieve, the patience and persistence of the work; the anguish is never quite gone. For Cézanne knows nothing of the open-heartedness, optimism, cheery sensuality of a Renoir. Cézanne withdraws and concentrates his forces. He cannot abide a lyrical outburst. He does not trust eloquent speech any more than he trusts nature not to lay traps for him, either now or later. Nature he respects and worships, but never expects to find it agreeable. A hard second look is all he can give nature's charms. What he wants to know is just the essential, which lasts. F. JOURDAIN, *Cézanne*, 1950

It is a superficial judgment that finds subjects of scant interest from the human point of view in the works of Cézanne's last period. Colour and composition lodge an immediate appeal. The old masters treated the most important subjects with the same seriousness Cézanne reserves for the form and tonal values of apples, trees or faces. There is great strength in the way he paints. Minute strokes build up until stillness and movement, consonance and contrast are perfectly balanced. His works express man's best qualities: sensitivity, power to reflect, vigour from strong conviction and integrity. M. SCHAPIRO, *Cézanne*, 1952

. . . from the artist in him, Cézanne received the impetus to reject any kind of mainstay that was conventional or conformist. In the struggle between man and painter, it was the painter that won. And then the contour-line is broken and begins to stretch out beyond the natural limit of objects. It takes a headlong plunge, then back it comes with too little or too much. . . . The phenomenon has been described as a blunder or a piece of baroque by those whose only discernment is academic. In fact, it corresponds to his ability to penetrate beyond appearances. His aim, to discover the *genuine relationships* of which he was so passionately in search. M. RAYNAL, *Cézanne*, 1954

. . . In fact, Cézanne was not intent on renouncing Impressionist language for a return to plastic form, obtained by traditional chiaroscuro drawing and modelling. Nor had he in mind, like the Cubists, an integral analysis of the various planes of objects and their simultaneous and abstract surface projection. His declared aim, to "solidify". To subject visual appearances to a geometric norm. This meant nothing else than a longing to recreate – on the exclusive colour base which the Impressionists with Pissarro foremost amongst them had shown him – a pictorial universe. It would be the result of much thought, each step requiring patient application. To recover, in other words, the simplificatory values of flesh and bones which Monet and his circle had felt bound to reject in favour of expressing the more immediate fluctuating aspects which things wore. G. A. DELL'ACQUA, *Gli impressionisti francesi*, 1956

He did the same motif countless times over. . . . And he took away anything that was accessory or episodic, in order to reduce it to the bare essentials. Then he gave each element the same emphasis, the most that was evident. His backgrounds come to the fore, making an urgent appeal from between foreground objects, and become inwoven with them. Instead of receding, distant outlines seem to make a move forward and stand out. Foregrounds are usually cut, so that the eye travels straight back, there to focus. . . . Object resemblance and descriptive reproduction are unwanted. A few bare essentials and Cézanne can make a still-life like a primitive dwelling, stone upon stone. There are no plans and no allowance for extras. His figures have the same kind of look, stiff-jointed and above all, motionless. A. M. BRIZIO, *Ottocento-Novecento*, I, 1962[3]

A rare specimen indeed, this sophisticated painter who knew how to preserve purity of feeling. Preconceived systems are not allowed to lend their comfortable support; he wants no help from the old-fashioned armoury of classical perspective, which gives a composition spatial balance *a priori*. He is openly undergoing each experience, as if no man before had ever been through them. L. BRION-GUERRY, *Cézanne et l'expression de l'espace*, 1966

It would not be possible to trace the line of development of modern art without direct and constant reference made to Cézanne. The teaching of the master from Aix-en-Provence has been of fundamental importance for all that came after. The heritage he left is still with us today. He was no restorer of a classical order, a counterpoise to presumed Impressionist disorder, as has been maintained. How much less was he an abortive genius, unable to realise his great potential, as Zola at one point felt. He belonged to the Impressionists' civilisation, unthinkable without it, but he does more, he makes a personal statement about the world as he sees it. It is a vision born of solitude and a desire to build, which began in close touch with nature but attains a dimension of its own. The style relies on pureness of volume and image, and on vibrant colouring – fantastic and structural. N. PONENTE, *Cézanne*, 1966

Letters of Cézanne

TO CAMILLE PISSARRO

You are perfectly right, grey is the only colour dominant in nature. But it's fearfully hard to get.

TO HIS MOTHER

I must be working the whole time. Not to have something ready for the gawpers, you understand. People usually value finished work but all it wants is a workman's skill and then it's common and artless. When I try and finish something, it's only to do much better next time and get more meaning. Of course, people do come into the picture at some stage. It makes one's admirers so much more stalwart than just going by the appearance of the thing.

Paris, 26 September 1874

TO AMBROISE VOLLARD

Hard at work and in sight of the Promised Land. I wonder if it will be like it was with the Children of Israel's leader, or will I be allowed to enter?

There is some progress to report. But why so long in coming and so hard won? Is art really a sacred calling with no room except for devotees, who must be of one mind?

Aix-en-Provence, 9 January 1903

TO CHARLES CAMOIN

Couture used to tell his pupils, "Good company is what you need" and "Go to the Louvre". But when you have made the rounds, hurry up and leave the great men to themselves. Get your second wind out there, in touch with nature, instincts and those inner impressions of art we all have.

Aix-en-Provence, 13 September 1903

TO CHARLES CAMOIN

The artist sometimes takes a while to get on terms with the model. You must not let your pet master, whoever he is, be more than a guide. Or else we are imitators. The meaning of nature as you take it and your own good gifts are all you need to be free. Do not let the advice or approach of anybody make you change your own way of feeling. Someone older can be a strong influence. But once you start "feeling", your own reaction will out into the light of day and emerge on top assuredly. That is the best way to go about things. Drawing is only giving form to what you see.

Michelangelo is a maker and Raphael a doer, always. Raphael is great but the model is master. He stops to think and then he is no match at all for that great rival.

Aix-en-Provence, 9 December 1904

TO ROGER MARX

Age and ill-health are catching up with me, before I can make that dream of art I have been pursuing all my life come true ever. But I am indebted to those admirers who somehow got the idea of what I wanted to do, even when I was not quite sure myself how to go about making art that was new. I really don't think you can take over from the past, just add one more link to the chain. What it calls for is a painter's temperament and an artistic ideal, meaning an outlook on nature. Then, with adequate powers of expression to get across to the average viewer, you will have got yourself a decent place in art history.

[*Aix-en-Provence*] *23 January 1905*

TO ÉMILE BERNARD

The main line to follow is just to put down what you see. Never mind your temperament or your ability in respect of nature. And you can forget all about what happened before. This is the way for an artist to express his whole personality, in my view, be it great or small.

I am an old man now, near seventy and "colour awareness" from light gives me an awful lot to think about. I can't seem to cover a canvas or put edges on objects, so difficult and delicate have these matters become to me. It makes the image or painting incomplete. Yet one plane falls on top of another, which is where neo-Impressionism came in. Those outlines done in black are quite mistaken and we must do everything to fight back. The answer lies in consulting nature, that is where to find the means.

Aix-en-Provence, 23 October 1905

TO ÉMILE BERNARD

. . . I do believe I have made some small progress in those studies you last had of me. But it pains me to relate that understanding nature better for purposes of paint and extending the expressive range go hand-in-hand with age and failing strength.

Official exhibitions are so dull because the only procedures on display are those already explored, some to a greater and some to a lesser extent. A bit more character, emotive content and comment would be a good thing.

The Louvre is the ABC where we learn to read. It is not enough to get the sayings of famous forbears off by heart. When the museum is left behind, nature is what concerns us. We have to try and get the spirit of the thing right, then record it each man in his own fashion. Time and thinking work to modify the way in which we see. Thus, we eventually arrive at understanding.

[*Aix-en-Provence, 1905*], *Friday*

The paintings in colour

List of plates

PLATE I LOUIS-AUGUSTE CÉZANNE London, National Gallery
Whole (168×114 cm.)

PLATE II SORROW Paris, Louvre
Whole (165×125 cm.)

PLATE III CUTTING WITH THE MONTAGNE SAINTE-VICTOIRE Munich, Neue Staatsgalerie
Whole (80×129 cm.)

PLATES IV-V A MODERN OLYMPIA Paris, Louvre
Whole (46×55 cm.)

PLATE VI JAR, COFFEE-POT AND FRUIT Paris, Louvre
Whole (63×80 cm.)

PLATE VII GLASS, CUP AND APPLES
Whole (41.5×55 cm.)

PLATE VIII THE ROBBERS AND THE DONKEY Milan, Civica Galleria d'Arte Moderna
Whole (41×55 cm.)

PLATE IX SELF-PORTRAIT IN A HAT Berne, Kunstmuseum
Whole (65×51 cm.)

PLATE X SMALL DELFT VASE Paris, Louvre
Whole (41×27 cm.)

PLATE XI MADAME CÉZANNE LEANING ON A TABLE
Whole (61×50 cm.)

PLATES XII-XIII

THE HOUSE OF THE HANGED MAN AT AUVERS Paris, Louvre
Whole (55×66 cm.)

PLATE XIV MADAME CÉZANNE WITH A FAN Zurich, Bührle Collection
Whole (92.5×73 cm.)

PLATE XV MADAME CÉZANNE IN A GARDEN Paris, Musées Nationaux
Whole (81×65 cm.)

PLATE XVI

SELF-PORTRAIT Paris, Louvre
Whole (26×15 cm.)

PLATE XVII FARM-YARD Paris, Louvre
Whole (63×52 cm.)

PLATE XVIII AUVERS FROM VAL HARMÉ Zurich, Private collection
Whole (73×92 cm.)

PLATE XIX POPLARS Paris, Louvre
Whole (65×80 cm.)

PLATES XX-XXI ROCKS AT L'ESTAQUE São Paulo, Museu de Arte
Whole (73×91 cm.)

PLATE XXII SMALL BRIDGE Paris, Louvre
Whole (59×72 cm.)

PLATE XXIII VASE, PLATE, INK-WELL AND FRUIT Paris, Louvre
Whole (61×50 cm.)

PLATE XXIV MAN SEATED Basle, Kunstmuseum
Whole (55×46 cm.)

PLATE XXV FIVE WOMEN (BATHERS) Basle, Kunstmuseum
Whole (65.5×65.5 cm.)

PLATE XXVI HOUSE AND FARM AT JAS DE BOUFFAN Prague, Národní Galerie
Whole (60×73 cm.)

PLATE XXVII BRIDGE OVER THE MARNE AT CRÉTEIL Moscow, Pushkin Museum
Whole (71×90 cm.)

PLATE XXX VESSELS, BASKET AND FRUIT Paris, Louvre
Detail (29.5×24 cm.)

PLATE XXXI ROCKS AND HILLS IN PROVENCE London, Tate Gallery
Whole (65×81 cm.)

PLATE XXXII WOMAN WITH A COFFEE-POT Paris, Louvre
Whole (130×97 cm.)

PLATE XXXIII BELLEVUE HOUSES
Whole (60×73 cm.)

PLATE XXXIV MAN WITH A PIPE London, Home House Trustees
Whole (73×60 cm.)

PLATE XXXV TWO CARD-PLAYERS London, Home House Trustees
Whole (58×69 cm.)

PLATES XXXVI-XXXVII

TWO CARD-PLAYERS Paris, Louvre
Whole (45×57 cm.)

PLATE XXXVIII TWO CARD-PLAYERS Paris, Louvre
Detail (life size)

PLATE XXXIX TWO CARD-PLAYERS Paris, Louvre
Detail (life size)

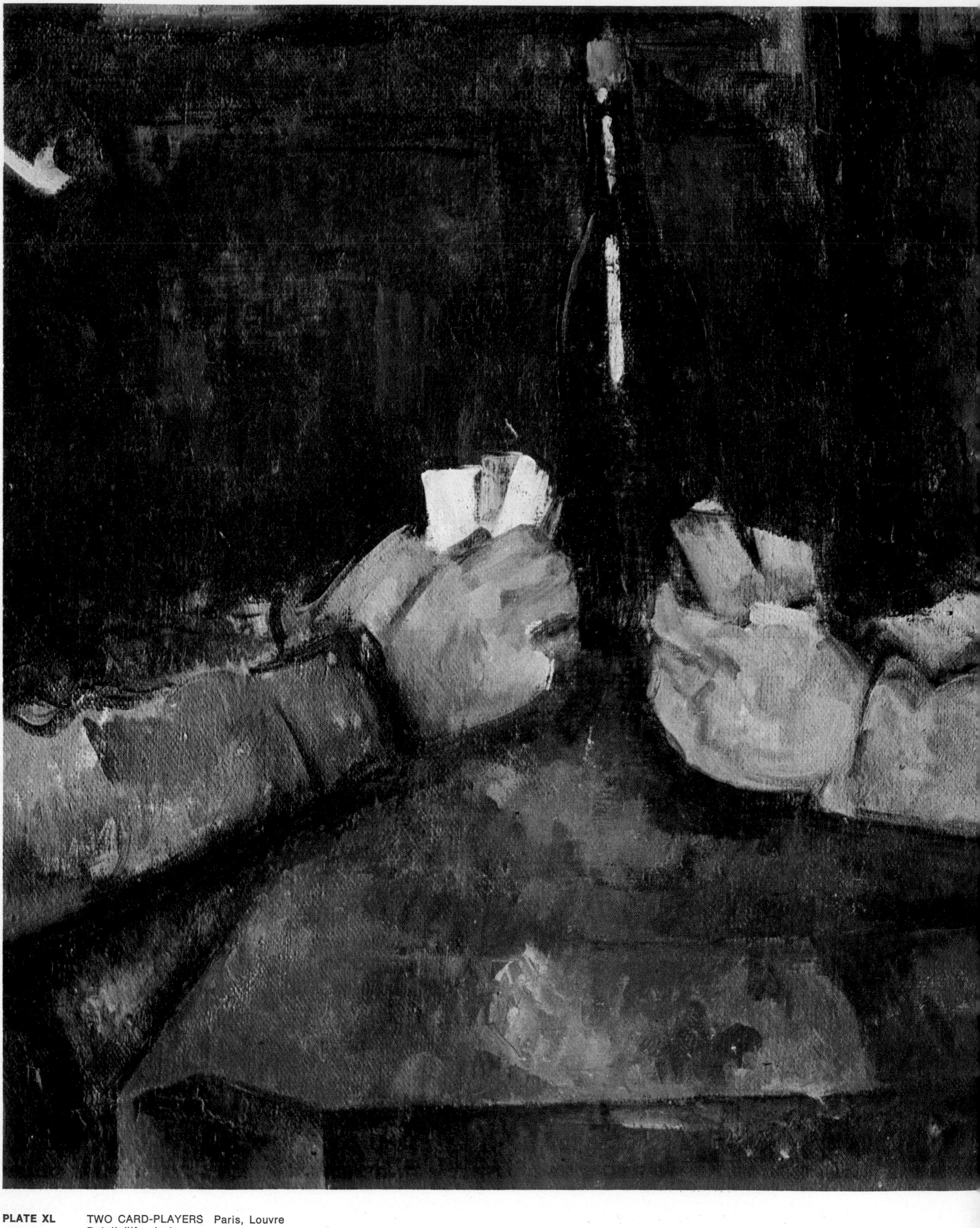

PLATE XL TWO CARD-PLAYERS Paris, Louvre
Detail (life size)

PLATE XLI MADAME CÉZANNE IN RED São Paulo, Museu de Arte
Whole (89×70 cm.)

PLATE XLII FOUR MEN (BATHERS) Paris, Louvre
Whole (22×33 cm.)

PLATE XLIII GROUP OF MEN (BATHERS) Paris, Louvre
Whole (60×81 cm.)

PLATES XLIV-XLV

LAKE ANNECY London, Home House Trustees
Whole (64×81.3 cm.)

PLATE XLVI MADAME CÉZANNE IN A YELLOW CHAIR Chicago (Ill.), Art Institute
Whole (81×65 cm.)

PLATE XLVII THE GREAT PINE São Paulo, Museu de Arte
Whole (84×92 cm.)

PLATE XLVIII ROCKS IN A WOOD Zurich, Kunsthaus
Whole (48.5×59.5 cm.)

✓ waistcoat

PLATE XLIX BOY IN A RED WAISTCOAT LEANING ON HIS ELBOW Zurich, Bührle Collection
Whole (79.5×64 cm.)

PLATE L BOY IN A RED WAISTCOAT LEANING ON HIS ELBOW Zurich, Bührle Collection
Detail (life size)

LATE LI ONIONS, BOTTLE, GLASS AND PLATE Paris, Louvre
Whole (66×81 cm.)

PLATES LII-LIII CURTAIN, FRUIT BOWL, CARAFE AND PLATE WITH FRUIT Paris, Louvre
Whole (73×92 cm.)

PLATE LIV JOACHIM GASQUET Prague, Národní Galerie
Whole (65×54 cm.)

PLATE LV GROUP OF WOMEN ("LES GRANDES BAIGNEUSES" - I) Philadelphia (Pa.), Museum of Art
Whole (208×249 cm.)

PLATE LVI TREES AND ROCKS New York, Museum of Modern Art
Whole (81×65 cm.)

PLATE LVII OLD WOMAN WITH A ROSARY London, National Gallery
Whole (85×65 cm.)

PLATE LVIII OLD WOMAN WITH A ROSARY London, National Gallery
Detail (life size)

PLATE LIX TREES AND ROCKS Paris, Musées Nationaux
Whole (91×66 cm.)

PLATES LX-LXI

GROUP OF WOMEN ("LES GRANDES BAIGNEUSES" - II) London, National Gallery
Whole (130×195 cm.)

PLATE LXII PLAIN WITH HOUSES AND TREES (THE MONTAGNE SAINTE-VICTOIRE) Zurich, Kunsthaus
Whole (65×81 cm.)

PLATE LXIII VALLIER FULL-LENGTH London, Tate Gallery
Whole (63×52 cm.)

PLATE LXIV HOUSE AND TREES Milan, Private collection
Whole (65×81 cm.)

The works

Bibliography

The authority on Cézanne's work remains L. Venturi. First, his descriptive catalogue (*Cézanne, son art, son oeuvre*, Paris 1936); the material was largely updated by him later. ("Cézanne", *Universal Encyclopaedia of Art*, III, 1958). Venturi was at work on a revised edition of the catalogue (unpublished), with additions, when he died. His work was continued by John Rewald, whose catalogue of the oil paintings is soon to be published.

On the date order of paintings, some of the exhibition catalogues will be found helpful, namely: J.-E. Blanche, P. Jamot and C. Sterling (Catalogue of the Orangerie exhibition, Paris 1936); G. Jedlicka (Catalogue of the Zurich Kunsthaus exhibition, 1956); R. Wittkower, M. Schapiro and T. Reff (Catalogue of the Knoedler Gallery exhibition of watercolours, New York 1963); J. Rewald and D. Phillips (*Cézanne*, Museum of Fine Arts, Boston 1971); L. Gowing and R. Ratcliffe (*Watercolour and Pencil Drawings by Cézanne*, London 1973); and W. Rubin (ed.) (*Cézanne. The Late Work*, Museum of Modern Art, New York 1977).

For personal reminiscences, not always to be taken at face value, the following are particularly noteworthy: É. Bernard ("Souvenirs sur Paul Cézanne", *Mercure de France*, October 1907), although he tends to see Cézanne as the source of his own painting; A. Vollard (*Paul Cézanne*, Paris 1914), full of lively information from personal contact with the artist; C. Camoin ("Souvenirs sur Paul Cézanne", *L'Amour de l'Art*, January 1921), singing his praises; J. Gasquet (*Paul Cézanne*, Paris 1921), an articulate portrait if not always quite accurate; G. Geoffroy (*Claude Monet, sa vie, son temps, son oeuvre*, Paris 1924); L. Larguier (*Le dimanche avec Paul Cézanne*, Paris 1925), describing his visits when Cézanne was elderly; R. M. Rilke (*Lettres sur Cézanne*, Paris 1944). But Cézanne's mind comes out most clearly in his letters, edited for publication by J. Rewald (*Correspondence*, Paris 1937).

The best of the biographies are: G. Coquiot (*Cézanne*, Paris 1919); G. Rivière (*Le maître Cézanne*, Paris 1923); G. Mack (*Paul Cézanne*, New York 1935); J. Rewald (*Paul Cézanne, sa vie, son oeuvre, son amitié pour Zola*, Paris 1939; *History of Impressionism*, 3rd edition, New York 1973); H. Perruchot (*La Vie de Cézanne*, Paris 1956). Depicted against the background of contemporary society, by R. W. Murphy (*The World of Cézanne, 1839–1906*, New York 1968).

A very great deal has been written about his work. In particular, see: J. Meier-Graef (*Cézanne und sein Kreis*, Munich 1922); R. Fry (*Cézanne, A Study of his Development*, New York 1927); E. Faure (*Cézanne*, Paris 1936); R. Huygue (*Cézanne*, Paris 1936); F. Novotny (*Cézanne und das Ende der wissenschaftlichten Perspektive*, Vienna 1938); A. C. Barnes and V. de Mazia (*The Art of Cézanne*, New York 1939); B. Dorival (*Cézanne*, Paris 1948); M. Schapiro (*Cézanne*, New York 1952); D. Cooper ("Two Cézanne Exhibitions", *The Burlington Magazine*, 1954); M. Raynal (*Cézanne*, Geneva 1954); K. Badt (*Die Kunst Cézannes*, Munich 1956); L. Gowing ("Notes on the Development of Cézanne", *The Burlington Magazine*, 1956); J. Richardson ("Cézanne et Aix-en-Provence", *The Burlington Magazine*, 1956); T. Reff ("Cézanne and Poussin", *Journal of the Warburg and Courtauld Institutes*, 1960; *The Burlington Magazine*, 1960; *Gazette des Beaux-Arts*, 1960, 1962, and 1963; "Cézanne and Flaubert", *The Art Bulletin*, 1962; *The Art Quarterly*, 1962); B. Barilli ("Gli impressionisti, Cézanne e alcune teorie della percezione", *Palatina*, 1960); M. Waldfogel ("A Problem in Cézanne's Grandes Baigneuses", *The Burlington Magazine*, 1962; *Gazette des Beaux-Arts*, 1965); E. Loran (*Cézanne's Composition. Analysis of his Form with Diagrams and Photographs of his Motifs*, Los Angeles 1963); S. Lichtenstein ("Cézanne and Delacroix", *The Art Bulletin*, 1964); and E. Rossi ("La prospettiva nella pittura moderna", *Il Veltro*, 1964). More recently, in Italy: N. Ponente (*Cézanne*, Milan 1966) and M. de Micheli (*Cézanne*, Florence 1967) survey the artist's main working problems. The most recent work on Cézanne published in English is R. Shiff (*Cézanne and the End of Impressionism*, Chicago and London 1984), which also contains an up-to-date bibliography.

On the watercolours, see especially: L. Venturi (*Cézanne, Water Colours*, London 1943); G. Schmidt (*Aquarelles de Paul Cézanne*, Basle 1952); G. Adriani (*Cézanne Watercolours*, New York 1983); and J. Rewald (*Paul Cézanne: The Watercolours, a Catalogue Raisonné*, London 1983).

On his drawings: J. Rewald (*Paul Cézanne, Carnets de dessin*, Paris 1951); A. Neumeyer (*Cézanne Drawings*, London 1958); A. Chappuis (*Les dessins de Paul Cézanne au Cabinet des Estampes . . . de Bâle*, Olten-Lausanne 1962; *The Drawings of Paul Cézanne – a catalogue raisonné*, New York and London 1973); S. Longstreet (*The Drawings of Cézanne*, Los Angeles 1964); and W. V. Anderson (*Cézanne's Portrait Drawings*, Cambridge (Mass.) and London 1970).

On his engravings: J. Leymarie and M. Melot (*Les Gravures des Impressionnistes: Manet, Pissarro, Renoir, Cézanne, Sisley*, Paris 1971); and J. Cherpin (*Paul Cézanne, l'oeuvre gravé*, Marseille 1973).

Outline biography

1839 19 January Paul Cézanne was born at Aix-en-Provence. The address was no 23 rue de l'Opéra. His father, Louis-Auguste, came from a family engaged in business and craft skills; they were originally from Cesana Torinese and the move to France was made in the eighteenth century. His father set up in Aix in 1825 when he opened a hat factory.
Paul was baptised on 22 February in the church of Sainte-Madeleine.

1841 4 July Birth of his sister Marie.

1844 29 January Louis-Auguste married the children's mother. She worked in his factory and was the daughter of a chair-maker; her name was Anne Élisabeth Honorine Aubert.

1844–9 Paul went to the primary school in rue des Épinaux. In 1849, he started at school of Saint-Joseph as a day-boarder.

1848 Louis-Auguste Cézanne took over a bank, the Barges, which was in trouble and founded a new one with his partner Cabanol. It was called, "Cézanne et Cabanol". The family began to be quite comfortably off.

1852 Paul boarded at the Bourbon college, where he was given a traditional and religious education. He made friends with some of the other boys: Émile Zola and Baptistin Baille.

1854 30 June Birth of his sister Rose.

1856 He attended Gibert's drawing classes at the school of Arts in Aix and became thoroughly versed in the academic style after David.

1858 Cézanne took the second prize for drawing at the school in Aix. He also studied music and played in an orchestra in which Zola played the flute and became a Wagner opera enthusiast. He was often out walking through the countryside round Aix, in the company of Zola and Baille. Then Zola moved to Paris; thus began their correspondence. Cézanne passed the school-leaving examination with a credit in his special subject (literature), and enrolled for a course in law to please his father; but he was already considering whether to become a full-time painter.

1859 Cézanne's father's business flourished. As was the custom thereabouts, Louis-Auguste proceeded to purchase a place a mile or so from Aix. It was called Jas de Bouffan, and had been built originally by a courtier of Louis XIV. Paul spent the summer there, and started a little studio of his own.

1860 His mother and sister Marie lending their support, Paul began to try and persuade his father that he was cut out for the artist's life. He found the work of Loubon, a Provençal painter, interesting and also studied the Aix museum's collection of the Caravaggio school. He made friends with Fortuné Marion who was to become an archaeologist and geologist; also with Numa Coste, the future columnist, the sculptor Philippe Solari, the painter Achille Emperaire and the old painter Villevieille, the journalist Marius Roux, the writer Henri Gasquet and the art critic Anthony Valabrègue.

1861 Parental consent won at last, it was arranged for Paul to go to Paris with his father and sister Marie. As it turned out, he stayed there from April to September only. In Paris he lived in the rue des Feuillantines and attended the Académie Suisse. He met Guillaumin and through him Pissarro and made long visits to the Louvre; he also went to the '61 Salon. He showed some interest in traditional painters such as Cabanel and Meissonier, but the contrast between their work and that of the old masters he found disturbing in the extreme, so he soon lost heart, and neglected his friends including Zola. On his not being accepted for the École des Beaux-Arts, he returned to Aix in September. His first experience of Paris was not a happy one. He agreed to go and work for his father at the bank, but also enrolled for more drawing classes.

1862 Cézanne found work at the bank uncongenial and wrote the following lines on the subject:
"Cézanne le banquier ne voit sans frémir
Derrière son comptoir naître un peintre à venir."
In November he returned to Paris and stayed for a year and a half. Once again, he attended the Académie Suisse. He met Francisco Oller and Guillemet and was often in the company of Guillaumin and Pissarro; also Bazille, Renoir, Sisley and Monet. The Café Guerbois was one of their meeting places.

1863 The year of the Salon des Refusés. Cézanne visited it with Zola. He admired Manet but felt more drawn to Courbet and Delacroix.

1864 Paris found him restless. In July, he returned to Aix. This was to be the pattern from now on; he would live in the north of France and the south by turns.

1865 Publication of Zola's *Confession de Claude*; the book was dedicated to Cézanne and Baille.

1866 At the beginning of the year, Cézanne was in Provence. In July, along with Baille, Solari, Zola, Valabrègue and Chaillou he went to at Bennecourt. (Zola wrote something about this in *L'Oeuvre*.)
Cézanne's paintings were still being rejected for the Salons. He wrote the famous letter to the Beaux-Arts inspector Nieuwerkerke, part of which runs as follows: "I cannot accept the judgment of colleagues as legitimate, for I did not ask them to make it." He was introduced to Manet, who admired his still-lifes. In August he returned to Aix.

1867 Cézanne returned to Paris in January but spent the summer at Aix. In October he returned once more to Paris.

1868 Cézanne passed the year mostly at Aix.

1869 Cézanne was in Paris many months but never long at the same address. Meeting with Hortense Fiquet who may have been a model. They lived together without his father's knowledge.

1870 During the war, he was at Aix and in the Marseilles area where he spent six months at the little village of L'Estaque, away from friends and acquaintances.

1871 At the end of the war, he returned to Paris and went to live in rue de Chevreuse, in the same house as his friend Solari.

1872 On 4 January, his son Paul was born. In the spring, he moved to Pontoise with Hortense and the baby. There he set to work with Pissarro and others, painting in the open air, "sur le motif".
In the autumn, the little household was on the move again, this time to Auvers-sur-Oise. Here, he spent the two happiest years of his life in the house of Dr Gachet, one of the few men to think the new art worth something and a collector of work by young artists.
Cézanne also did some engraving with material and equipment provided by Dr Gachet who was interested in the subject. Pissarro wrote to tell Guillemet that he had a painting of Cézanne, "of remarkable power and force".

1873 Cézanne did a lot of view-painting, at Pontoise and Auvers. Met "Père Tanguy" and Van Gogh.

1874 In Paris, at Pissarro's urgent request, he agreed to show at the first Impressionist exhibition in Nadar's former studio. He sent in the *House of the Hanged Man* (no. 136) and *A Modern Olympia* (no. 250), among other works. The comments were scandalised and ironical. Once again, Cézanne was rejected for the Salon.

1875 He met a future friend, supporter and collector, Chocquet. He lived in rue de Vaugirard in Paris but was often away in the south.

1876 Cézanne spent the summer at L'Estaque. After his lack of success in 1874, he declined to take part in the second Impressionist exhibition.

1877 Back at work in Pontoise and Auvers. Eventually he allowed sixteen of his canvases to be hung at the third Impressionist exhibition. But the reaction was unfavourable once more, from both public and critics, with one exception: the young writer, Georges Rivière. Cézanne saw little of his old friends and lived in rue de l'Ouest, Paris.

Photographs of Cézanne, c. 1860 and 1890.

The artist, from a Pissarro drawing of 1874 and a Renoir pastel of 1880 (see no. 508).

1878 At L'Estaque, Cézanne painted throughout the year. Every so often he went to Aix, as his mother was ill. He had a serious disagreement with his father who found out about young Paul and resolved to cut his allowance.

1879 Cézanne was at Melun, from May to February of the following year. He often went to Médan, to see Zola who had bought a house there and had begun to write his cycle of novels about the Rougon-Macquart family.

1880 In Paris from February to May of the following year. There he saw more of Chocquet, and also his old Impressionist acquaintances. He met Huysmans and the new advocates of Naturalism. He passed the summer with Zola at Médan.

1881 Cézanne returned to Pontoise, where Pissarro was. Late in the year he spent a while at Aix.

1882 Though he had submitted work for the Salon over a good many years, he had always been rejected. At long last, however, the tables were turned. It came about through the good offices of Guillemet, who presented him as a pupil. Cézanne was in Paris from March to September, then went home to Jas de Bouffan (see **1859**).

1883 He worked for a few weeks with Renoir at La Roche-Guyon. He met Monticelli in Marseilles, and the two of them set off together through Provence. Their favourite rendezvous was Gardanne, from the evidence of the paintings.

1884 In February, Cézanne went to L'Estaque to meet up with Monet and Renoir on their return from Italy. He was often over at Aix.

1885 A brief love affair in the spring left him very low. It was stormy while it lasted and there are some letters written to Zola of this time. He did some more work with Renoir at La Roche-Guyon, then went to Gardanne. In late July he joined Zola at Médan.

1886 Publication of Zola's *L'Oeuvre*. The novel was about a painter called Claude Lantier. Both Manet and Cézanne saw bits of themselves in him. The trouble was that it was a tale of flawed genius ending in suicide and Cézanne found this a harsh judgment on his art from the hand of a friend. So he wrote from Gardanne on 4 April; the letter is not bitter but it is final. He and Zola were long-standing friends but that was all over and they were never to meet again.
On 28 April, he married Hortense Fiquet. His father had eventually met both Hortense and little Paul, but on 23 October, his father died. Paul and his two sisters were left a fortune of two million francs.

1887 Cézanne was in Aix most of the year and hard at work. He exhibited at Brussels, with the "Groupe des Vingt".

1888 He returned to Paris and took to visiting the Ile-de-France area. He painted at Chantilly and round about, also on the banks of the Marne. He met Van Gogh again and then Gauguin but did not like his work.

1889 Cézanne took part in the Paris World Exhibition, with the *House of the Hanged Man* (no. 136). The rest of the year he spent most of his time at Jas de Bouffan and Renoir was his guest there for a while.

1890 He sent three paintings to the "Groupe des Vingt" in Brussels and visited Paris briefly, but to painters of the avant-garde and his old cronies he was a master.

Cézanne was in Paris from January to June, then at Aix for the remainder of the year.

1896 He took the waters at Vichy and also stayed at Talloires on lake Annecy. He met an admirer in the poet Joachim Gasquet. He found lodgings in the Paris quarter of Montmartre, where he lived and worked alone.

1897 He rented a small cottage, near Bibémus cave outside Aix and was often at work painting in the locality and the Arc valley.

On 25 October, his mother died. Jas de Bouffan was more painful than he could bear.

1898 Cézanne was at Aix until

1902 Denis persuaded him to show at the Salon des Indépendants. He saw a lot of Gasquet, Léo Larguier and a couple of young painters, Charles Camoin and Émile Bernard, who was later to publish *Souvenirs sur Paul Cézanne*. The Légion d'Honneur for which his name had been put forward by Mirbeau was refused him.

On 29 September Zola died and Cézanne was very upset although they had never met after their friendship ended.

1903 Cézanne spent the whole year at Aix.

1904 At the Salon d'Automne, one room was of works by Cézanne alone. He spent a few weeks in Paris and went, a last time, to Fontainebleau. He sent

deteriorated and they did not arrive in time to see him alive.

He died on 22 October in the house on rue Boulegon and was buried in Aix cemetery.

1907 In October, some 56 works comprised an important retrospective exhibition at the Salon d'Automne.

Granel, now the owner of Jas de Bouffan, offered the Cézanne interiors to the French State. The offer was declined.

1909 Death of Dr Gachet, a friend and collector from the old days in Auvers.

1910 Oils and watercolours, totalling 68 works, were on show at Bernheim-Jeune, Paris.

1911 In the Camondo bequest, the following were acquired by

(*From the left*) *The artist sitting in his friend Pissarro's garden, with Pissarro standing in front of him, on the right, 1877; aged about 30 and carrying his material and equipment for working "sur le motif" (outdoors); portrait of 1894 in his studio, with the* Apotheosis *of* Delacroix *beside him, on which he was apparently engaged (see no. 264).*

1891 The one and only time Cézanne went abroad: he left Provence for the Jura and Switzerland, and on his way back stopped in Paris before going home to Aix. He began to suffer from diabetes, which was to remain with him for the rest of his life.

1892 He spent a while at Fontainebleau.

1894 Cézanne went to Giverny, in order to see Monet. He also met Rodin, Geoffroy and Clemenceau there, but Monet got on his nerves and there were frequent disagreements. At the Duret sale, Monet bought one of his works. There were three more among the Caillebotte bequest which the Louvre declined to accept.

1895 Year of Cézanne's first big one-man show, at the Galerie Vollard in rue Lafitte. He sent in some 150 works, which was too many to display at one time. Public and critics liked him no better than before

the autumn when he went away to Paris.

1899 He sent in three paintings to the Salon des Indépendants. He decided to sell Jas de Bouffan, and took a house in the centre of Aix (no. 23, rue Boulegon) where he lived until his death. It was run by a trusted housekeeper, Madame Brémond. Here he lived very quietly and simply; his wife and son were mostly away in Paris.

1900 Cézanne stayed in Aix, showed at the Paris World Exhibition. A painting by him was bought on behalf of Berlin's Staatliche Museen. Year of Maurice Denis's painting, *Hommage à Cézanne* which was bought by Gide.

1901 Cézanne showed again at the Salon des Indépendants and also at the Salon de la Libre Esthétique in Brussels. He bought some land at Lauves, a few miles outside Aix and had a studio built there.

in some new work to the Salon de la Libre Esthétique in Brussels, but age and his ailment were beginning to affect him and he became harder to get along with.

1905 He showed again at the Salon d'Automne and at the Salon des Indépendants. He at last finished the *"Grandes baigneuses"* (no. 657) on which he had been working for seven years.

1906 Cézanne was represented at the Salon d'Automne with ten works. Denis painted his *Visite à Cézanne*. Friends and well-wishers often called on him but he liked solitude and to consider problems presented by his art.

On 15 October he was out of doors, at work "sur le motif" when he was caught in a sudden squall. He had a seizure and was carried back to the house, unconscious, on a washer-woman's hand-cart. His wife and son were summoned from Paris, but his condition

the Louvre: The *House of the Hanged Man* (no. 136), the *Card-Players* (no. 639) and the *Blue Vase* (no. 493).

1921 Cézanne exhibition at the Kunsthalle in Basle.

In November, exhibition at Cassirer, Berlin. Death of Joachim Gasquet, the author of a book about Cézanne, containing many anecdotes and personal reminiscences.

1923 The Aix municipality named the Chemin des Lauves Avenue Paul Cézanne in his honour.

1926 Important retrospective exhibition at Bernheim-Jeune. It comprised 58 canvases with 99 watercolours.

The "Société Paul Cézanne" founded in Aix.

1927 At Médan in the house of Zola, a painting was discovered: *Paul Alexis Reading a Manuscript to Zola* (see no. 32).

Death of the painter Guillaumin.

1928 Cézanne exhibition at Wildenstein, New York.

Caillebotte bequest to the Louvre included four works by Cézanne.

1930 Death of Zola's widow. Some 80 letters from Cézanne were found among the writer's papers.

1933 Exhibition of Cézanne watercolours at Seligmann, New York.

1934 Important Cézanne retrospective at the Philadelphia Museum of Art.

1936 In April, a major Cézanne exhibition opened at the Orangerie in Paris. Another big exhibition in Basle (Kunsthalle).

1937 The Salon des Indépendants shows 85 works by Cézanne. An important Cézanne exhibition also at the Museum of Art in San Francisco (Calif.).

1939 Centenary of the artist's birth. Exhibitions were held in London, Paris, Lyons and New York.

Death of Vollard the collector, friend and agent of the master.

1941 Death of Émile Bernard, painter and author of *Souvenirs sur Paul Cézanne*.

1947 In January, the Galerie de France in Paris ran an exhibition entitled "L'influence de Cézanne, 1908-11".

Exhibition at the Art Museum, Cincinnati (Ohio).

1951 The Gachet heirs gave the Louvre some tokens of the master and three works: the *House of Dr Gachet* (no. 145), *A Modern Olympia* (no. 250) and the *Delft Vase* (no. 216).

1952 Grand Cézanne exhibition at the Art Institute of Chicago, with 127 works; it was later transferred to the Metropolitan Museum in New York.

1953 Brief Cézanne exhibition at Aix, with 24 oils, 26 watercolours and drawings.

From June to September, 23 works of Cézanne are on show at the Orangerie in Paris, as part of of an Exhibition on "Monticelli et le Baroque provençal".

1954 The United States embassy in France made a donation to the Academy of Aix, of the Lauves studio where the master once worked.

In Paris, exhibition at the Orangerie entitled "Hommage à Cézanne".

At the Tate Gallery in London, 65 canvases by him were shown.

Further gift from the Gachet estate to the French museums.

1956 Fifty years from the death of Cézanne. Exhibition in Zurich (Kunsthaus), comprising 215 works in oils, watercolours and drawings.

1963 Exhibition of watercolours by Cézanne at the Knoedler Gallery, New York.

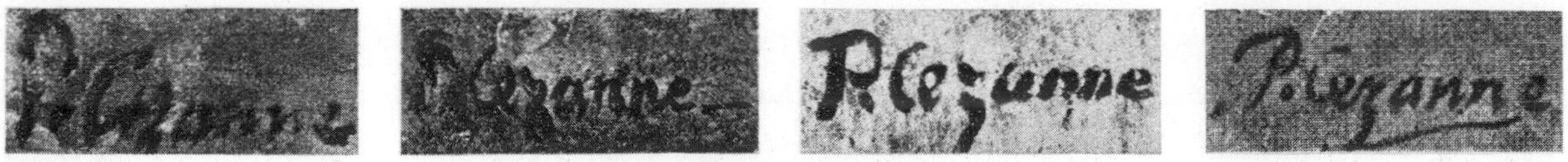

Cézanne's signature on paintings numbered respectively: nos. 195, 216, 243 and 779.

Catalogue of works

Cézanne's artistic language seems a slow growth when traced through his painting, whatever the level of direct contact and awareness. This is because each cycle of investigation confirmed in the artist that base of experience and performance, on which an inimitable style is built. The formal approach to a space/colour relationship became an experience of epic proportions, explored by the mind's eye "sur le motif", in a way both familiar and constantly new.

Over the formative period, knowledge of contemporary Provençal painting counted a good deal with him. A romantic treatment of landscape painting from life is what the work of Loubon and Monticelli gave him. It was in his youth, when he also enjoyed literary associations which took a lot of living down. His school-days, the friendship with Zola and Baille, the long tramps through the Aix countryside were other landmarks at this first stage of his development. During the early days in Paris, when he was not sure of his own path, visits to the Louvre presented him with the accomplishments of Caravaggio and Velasquez, Zurbaran and Rubens, Tintoretto and Veronese. There were other likely influences among his contemporaries: Daumier perhaps, since he was also Provençal-born; more certainly, Delacroix and Courbet.

Courbet's work may have pointed the connection with real landscape painting and the "feel" of the material. The example of Delacroix was fundamental, not only during the formative period but it may be argued throughout his painting life. For Delacroix – over and beyond questions of treatment and interpretation after the Romantic style – taught him about composition. This, in order to present a wider front, not hide-bound in matters of form, where light and colour might be endowed with their due attributes.

Now it may seem that Cézanne's own nature led him to embark on an emotive and romantic plane. As time went by, a balance gradually emerged between classic formal treatment on the one hand and utter freedom of expression on the other. Classic indeed, but not at all idealised. Together with the exercise of restraint, these factors produced an outlook whereby he saw nature and depicted it neither by concentrating the spatial vehicles nor assessing the reactions of his retina. It was more a summation by him of what each object stood for. The process was from within; it was paced by his own reading and the task of restitution.

In the early paintings, up to those datable around 1870, one may discern a headstrong plunge after the reality of objects. The painter tried for his effect by the use of dark outlines, to mark off what objects embodied and denote their position in terms of spatial interrelationship. A romantic sub-stratum, textured by literary references in line with his liking for solitude. The tendency was to dramatise the event, even make it somewhat theatrical in concept. The artist was making a stand, as if involved rather than apart from the event recorded. In the *Black Clock* (no. 126), the formal context already bore direct reference to the life of the objects depicted. Cézanne had begun to wish himself out of the picture.

He sensed the entitlement of painting, in terms of quality, volume, the whole spatial organisation of a work. In this process both of his detachment and of a painting's considered structural entity, he was helped by what he knew of the Impressionists in general and more especially by the company of Pissarro. The components of a work – the *House of the Hanged Man* (no. 136) may serve as an example – no longer vied with each other for the attention of the viewer, according to the predilections of the painter. More of a visual synthesis was achieved here, with light as the guiding feature to determine spatial development planes and call into being the range of living colour.

His quiet work from Pontoise and Auvers strengthened the ground won and indicated the way forward to the days when he was completely self-standing. The ins-and-outs of his dealings with Impressionism, were valuable in helping him learn. For Cézanne, the function of each brushstroke was less to line it up next to the one before, than to overlap it to some extent, as though under need of constant correction from his perceptiveness. The aim, to make form endure by an uninterrupted process of becoming which operated in reality.

Thus, form and volume tend to take on something of solemnity and density. In works from 1877-88 particularly, a marked structural austerity comes across from the image itself. To speak of the abstract may seem absurd, and out of place with the Aix master's inner evolutive process. It was a crucial period. Cézanne was deeply engrossed in the pursuit of the elusive identity of solids, that is to say their inherent structure. His approach was to strip off the layers of sensory appreciation, one by one. The purpose of this was to distil that moment of impact between artist and quality of subject. The result might be a motif or theme, or food for further thought.

The pattern of choice, in art and letters, is clearer in Cézanne than in a good many other painters. And yet, more can be found out from his life style and his sayings, from those who met him or knew him professionally, than from the study of his work. His reactions can be categorised under two headings. First, with regard to the model, he was shaping and re-shaping in order to get away from blind imitation of reality. Next, with regard to the promptings received from external artistic example.

His use of the colour blue makes the point. He started with the value assigned it by Poussin, whose work he loved. Here, it meant distance and spatial depth. He then absorbed some implications, whether of Goethe's colour theory or the Nietzsche definition of Wagner's *Lohengrin* as "blue music". The colour thus came to have a complicated meaning, mainly on account of the literary streams. It then fed back, in decanting the essences of objects and ended up as a kind of key in balancing other chromatic values. His use of blue was compulsive, not that he was unaware of the mazy ground in which it took its origin. But he gave it a genuine value, an identity of its own. It was justified and indeed guaranteed within the terms of meaning of a new reality.

Nevertheless, he usually seemed at something of a loss when starting out to tackle a theme. As time passed, there was a gain in exclusivity until the entire working process was characterised, not to say governed, by this means. The series of *Bathers* and *Montagne Sainte-Victoires* show what happened. The artist repeated the theme and it remained stubborn, not fully conveyed and complete. The central motif thus went through many versions. The erotic and sensual early works apart, the corpus may be summarised as: portraits of his wife, still-lifes, landscapes, self-portraits, card-players and bathers. Now the variants are sometimes very slight, scarcely distinguishable, as telling points in narrative or composition. But seen as style, a depth of elaborative detail and consideration lay behind them. Cézanne tried to exhaust the perceptive range. Then the rendering would equate more closely and convincingly with a mind's eye of the thing.

He was always concerned to make his references to nature faithful. This was ensured by analysing a landscape into components, in terms of innate structure. The ascendency of inner awareness over the everyday reality thus produced a synthesis. In the late period, some of the still-lifes seem to exalt objects within a spatial arrangement that responds to the artist's resolute intentions. Chromatic values are concentrated, in an attempt to heal the contradictions attendant upon intuitive grasp that the work is capable of perfection.

The themes may seem few, considering the span of his working life. Cézanne has been faulted for this, on more than one occasion. There is something here, very meaningful for his painting. The language sets out to shed inessentials and try describing reality from the other side. Cézanne's relationship with things and nature may be summed up in this approach to the inner life. His work records the emotional reality, in complex formal structure and unfettered colour.

"My small feeling", he called it. Relative powers of expression were constantly measured. The attitude of mind and spirit was underlined in the kind of precept which the master gave Bernard. It is taken from a letter of 1904: "Treat nature as cylindriform, spherical or conical, in due perspective." Not that he meant this to be read as a form of extreme geometric faith, or in a categorical way. What he aspired to was a visual order, beyond the physical and objective appearance of reality, and organic to a degree. Indeed, the letter continued: "... for us men, nature is more depth than surface. Whence the need of introducing enough blue tones to let the air into our light vibrations, represented by yellows and reds."

These words almost summarise his painting experience, aimed at rendering form, colour and space in stylistic balance. From the early days through the pro-Impressionist phase to the late period, his artistic language was developing. It spoke of an isolated and autonomous presence. Feeling out of nature remained the vital and irreversible work basis. Skill in handling means of expression was no less indispensable. It required "very long-standing experience". Then and only then could the objective in visual terms and subjective in terms of knowledge meet and mingle.

The master with no school or direct following, the recluse of Aix, yet managed to state the main problems of painting this century and argue a case. After his death, a good many people began to profit by the example. First amongst them, the Cubists. avant-garde splinter movements line up, when placed in chronological order. Picasso's *"Demoiselles d'Avignon"* (1907) came within a year of Cézanne's death. How powerful the example was, may be gauged from Picasso's own words:

"In 1906 the influence of Cézanne, this Harpignies of genius, was everywhere. His art of composition, contrast of form and colour harmony was catching on rapidly. Two problems faced me. I grasped that painting had intrinsic value apart from the life-like representation of things. I wondered whether I ought to give the facts not as seen but rather as they were known."

The date-order of some titles is problematical, for want of precise information. The *Catalogue* therefore follows the arrangement by sub-division of period which was drawn up by Venturi and remains standard procedure. (The Venturi number for each work is preceded by the abbreviation V.).

Within the main groups, succession in kind relies on the known interests of the artist at a given time, and not on some other artificial device. Each group has a heading, which relates to the contents in general or particular. The heading is intended to cover the items so comprised, without further repetition.

The *Catalogue* only concerns oil-paintings on canvas which are safely ascribed. Distinctive symbols may therefore be dispensed with; where the support differs, a note to that effect has been added. Dimensions (in centimetres) will be found on the line after location, if known; otherwise, after the title. Wherever the work is signed and dated by the artist, this is entered: (s) & (d). Sometimes, both: (s d).

Location is something of an open question because of works changing hands. Public collections only have been included and private ones where recently verified.

Museum entries, in shortened form for the *Catalogue* purposes, are presented in full in the *Topographical index* at the end of the volume.

Romantic period up to 1871

Cézanne's education was in the French liberal tradition. His friends, his close relationship to Zola – with its personal and literary overtones; the drive to self-expression when the options were still open on other art forms, such as poetry; his first hesitant attempts at painting, with an eye on contemporary Provençal art, especially the work of Loubon: all these crystallised when he went to Paris, first in 1861 and then in 1863.

To point the difference that these two journeys made, two groups under the heading *Various compositions* describe the course of his development. The first, from his school and early student days; the second, more thoughtful and with a touch of the personal element.

Various compositions

I 1859–62
These are basically academic exercises or occasional products (like the screen for his father's study at no. 1 or the Jas de Bouffan interiors at nos 6 to 9). The subjects are mixed and romantic in taste and are taken from famous works (no. 12) and fashion magazines (no. 14) or else are adorned with strange emblems, like The Visitation *(no. 13), where, beside the two women, is a head of Satan, his black hair on end, rising above flames.*

1. Eighteenth-Century Pastoral
402 × 250 1859–60 V.1–3
Screen painted perhaps with a friendly hand from Zola for the study of his father Louis-Auguste Cézanne. On the back are grotesque decorations. It is usually taken as the artist's first work.

2. Girl with a Parrot
23 × 31 1859–60 V.8
See nos 68 and 69.

3. Two Children
55 × 46 1859–60 V.10

4. The Poet's Dream
82 × 66 1859–60 V.11

5. Country Interior with Three Women and a Baby
46 × 38 1859–60 V.9

6. Spring
Paris, Petit Palais
314 × 97 1859–62 V.4
Wall-painting, transferred to canvas, as nos 7 to 9. These were to decorate a room at Jas de Bouffan. The signature "Ingres" on all four and date "1811" on no. 9, are generally taken as an artist's prank (Venturi). Gasquet wrote, The *Four seasons* make one think of some strange fresco-painter of the fifteenth century working for Épinal . . . the composition is nobly decorative throughout."
About this time or soon after, Cézanne did some more decoration for Jas de Bouffan. They are partly still *in situ*, 1936 (Venturi): nos 12, 16 and 71; partly dispersed: nos 15, 17, 18 and 48.

7. Summer
Paris, Petit Palais
314 × 109 1859–62 V.5
See no. 6.

8. Autumn
Paris, Petit Palais
314 × 104 1859–62 V.6
See no. 6.

9. Winter
Paris, Petit Palais
314 × 104 1859–62 V.7
See no. 6.

10. The Judgment of Paris
15 × 21 1860–1 V.16

11. Chinese Worshipping the Sun
28 × 33 1860–2 V.13

12. Hide-and-Seek
1860–2 V.14
Copy of a noted work by Lancret See also no. 6.

13. The Visitation
27 × 20 1860–2 V.15
Over the door is written: "Père Zorobabel", in token of the Virgin's ancestry (a man of David's line who led the Remnant back to Jerusalem after the Captivity, 537 BC). Below, in red: "La mère des 7 douleurs – Belzébuth". The head rising from the flames may symbolise the power of evil (Venturi).

14. Interior with Two Ladies and a Girl
Moscow, Museum of Modern Western Art
57 × 92 1860–2 V.24
According to Dorival this was inspired by a plate in the *Magasin pittoresque* or the *Illustrateur des Dames*.

II 1863–71
The two Paris visits of 1861 and 1863 gave Cézanne a double opportunity. First, to study the great masters, old and new at the Louvre. Second, to meet the circle of young painters gathered round Manet after the 1863 Salon des Refusés. His work tends either to echo the masters (e.g. a composition after Caravaggio: no. 26; a stylised El Greco: no. 27) or reflect new thinking. The Orgy *(no. 20), a tribute to Delacroix and possibly Couture as well as an obvious influence by the Venetians (Veronese, Tintoretto and Bassano); Geoffroy deemed it a "fundamental point of departure". The subject has been referred (Lichtenstein) to Flaubert's* Tentation de Saint Antoine, *published in book-form in 1874, though* L'Artiste *had carried extracts earlier (no. 29 may also refer to it).*
The realism of Courbet did not pass unnoticed (see nos 15, 16 20, 29, 30 and 41); Venturi remarked on it as "a corrective to romantic excess".

15. Bather by a Rock
166 × 103 1864–6 V.83
The figure is reminiscent of the *Bather* by Courbet at the Louvre. See also no. 6.

16. Contrasts
1864–6 V.87
See also no. 6.

17. Christ in Limbo
170 × 97 * 1866 * V.84
Probably inspired by a work of Sebastiano del Piombo at the Prado. See also no. 6.

18. Sorrow (Mary Magdalen)
Paris, Louvre
165 × 125 * 1866 * V.86
The subject is religious or symbolical in character, and

1

2

3

4

5

6

7

8

9

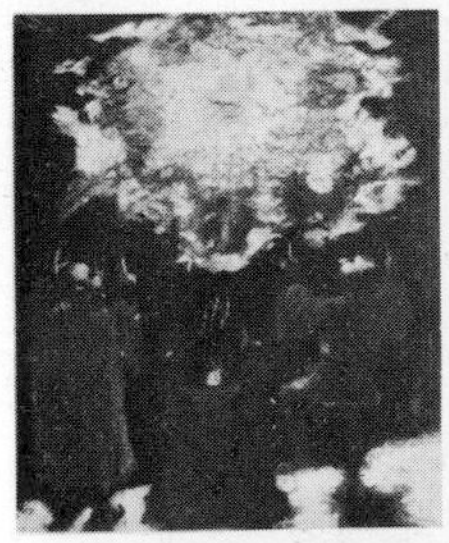
11

10

12

13

14

15

16

17

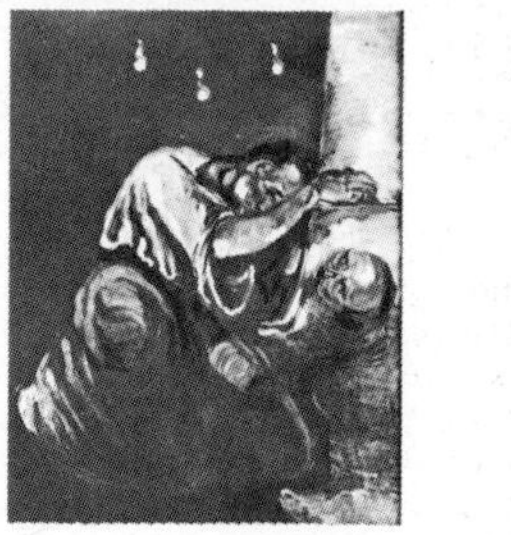
18 (plate II)

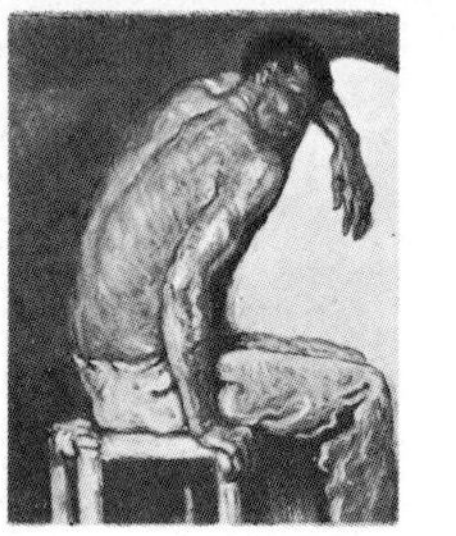
19

20

21

22

23

25

24

26

27

28

29

30

31

32

33

34 (plate VIII)

35

36

there are echoes of Daumier. The dense colour impasto and sweeping brushstrokes heighten the romantic effect, with strong chiaroscuro. See also no. 6, and plate II.

19. The Negro Scipio
São Paulo, Museu de Arte
107 × 83* 1866 * V.100
The model was a well-known character among the artists of the Académie Suisse. The painting shows the influence of Delacroix (Venturi).

20. The Orgy
130 × 81 1864–8 V.92
This shows the influence of Delacroix (Lichtenstein).

21. Women Dressing
22 × 32 1864–8 V.93
Paper glued on canvas.

22. Nymphs and Satyrs
24·5 × 31 1864–8 V.94

23. Stove in a Studio
42 × 30 s 1865–8 V.64
This is inspired by works on a similar subject of Delacroix and Corot, at the Louvre. It is not a mere copy (Venturi).

24. Two Men out Walking
39 × 31 1865–8 V.96
The two figures are of friends, Marion and Valabrègue.

25. The Abduction
90·5 × 117 s d 1867 V.101
The connection with Delacroix's *Hercules and Antæus* has been noticed (Lichtenstein), male force contrasting with female surrender, the expression of violence and love, the fluent line, the brilliant and rich colour. "In the background, in front of a white cloud, is a mountain vaguely reminiscent of the Montagne Sainte-Victoire" (Rewald).

26. Autopsy (The Laying-Out)
49 × 80 1867–9 V.105

27. Figures Outdoors (Riverside)
27 × 36 1867–70 V.115

28. A Murder
64 × 81 1867–70 V.121

29. The Temptations of St Anthony
Zurich, Bührle Collection
54 × 73 1869 V.103
The theme was repeated some years later (nos 268 and 269).

30. Figures Outdoors (Promenade)
28 × 36 1868–70 V.116

31. "Le déjeuner sur l'herbe"
60 × 81 1869–70 V.107
The theme, after Manet, was also repeated subsequently (nos 258 and 536). In the foreground, the figure in rear view is perhaps Cézanne.

32. Paul Alexis Reading a Manuscript to Zola
São Paulo, Museu de Arte
131 × 161 1869–70 V.117
Paul Alexis, an admirer of Zola, arrived in Paris in September 1869; Zola and Cézanne went south in August 1870, so the work may belong to the interval. Zola could have suggested the double portrait to his painter friend but it was unfinished because of the war. It is set in the garden of Zola's Paris house, rue de la Condamine. It was found in an attic of the Médan house by Zola's wife after his death, and assigned to Cézanne (Venturi).

33. Zola Reading
52 × 56 1869–70 V.118
The writer's visitor may be Paul Alexis (see no. 32).

34. The Robbers and the Donkey
Milan, Civica Galleria d'Arte Moderna (Grassi Bequest)
41 × 55 1869–70 V.108
The theme, out of the *Metamorphoses* of Apuleius, was used also by Decamps and Daumier among others. The atmosphere is dramatic, indicative of the grandeur to follow later.
See plate VIII.

35. Idyll (Don Quixote on the Barbary Coast)
65 × 81 d 1870 V.104
The man in the centre, in black, may be the artist himself.

36. A Modern Olympia
56 × 55 1870 V.106
The subject was repeated some years later (see no. 250). The title echoes Manet.

37

38

39

40

41

42

43

44

45

46

37. Two Ladies Outdoors (Promenade)
58 × 46 * 1870 * V.119
This was taken from a fashion plate; the two ladies are the painter's sisters: Marie on the left and Rose on the right.

38. Bathers
Christie's sale 14.4.70
20 × 40 * 1870 * V.113

39. Female Nude Drying her Hair
29 × 13 1869–71 V.114

40. Girl at the Piano
Moscow, Museum of Modern Western Art
57 × 92 1869–71 V.90
This may be a portrait of the painter's sister Marie.

41. Two Ladies and Two Gentlemen Outdoors (Conversation Piece)
92 × 73 1870–1 V.120
After a fashion plate. This features the painter's sisters Rose and Marie, and his two friends Valabrègue and Marion.

42. Two Bathers and a Fisherman
14 × 21 1870–1 V.1520 A

43. Afternoon in Naples (Rum Punch)
14 × 24 1870–2 V.112
See no. 251.

44. Woman Strangled
31 × 25 1870–2 V.123

45. The Boat of Dante
25 × 33 1870–3 V.125
This is a copy of the Delacroix's painting at the Louvre which was in turn inspired by Dante's *Inferno*, Canto VIII.

46. Hamlet and Horatio
35 × 30 1870–3
First published 1956 (Venturi), this belonged to Dr Gachet. The subject is taken from the Delacroix painting at the Louvre.

Portraits

Compared with the above compositions, this group has perhaps more unity – Cézanne is on the road to a personal style, with an eye to Daumier (no. 48) and more to Courbet (nos 53, 67 and 70). Some are still romantic in concept though the technique was being revised. A third dimension is conveyed by the thick impasto, laid on not by brush but formed with a spatula "which makes the colour more intense and conveys some idea of volume although the painter does not adopt contrasting light and indeed no chiaroscuro to give the relief effect" (Venturi). Note this particularly in the "Oncle Dominique" series (nos. 55 to 63).

47. Self-Portrait
44 × 37 1858–61 V.18

48. Louis-Auguste Cézanne
London, National Gallery
168 × 114 1860–3 V.25
In all probability, this portrait of Cézanne's father was painted at Jas de Bouffan, with a good deal of regard for the work of Daumier. Gasquet wrote of it, that "he [Cézanne] painted it in impasto, large, solid and full-bodied as if he wanted good colours to celebrate the tie of parentage".
See also no. 6, and plate I.

49. Man with a Dark Beard
35 × 27 1860–3 V.20

50. Émile Zola
26 × 21 1861–2 V.19

51. Head of an Old Man
Paris, Louvre
51 × 48 1860–5 V.17

52. Self-Portrait
Christie's sale 28.6.68
44 × 32 1862–4 V.1509

53. Study of a Woman
46 × 38 s d 1864 V.22
Thought to be Zola's wife (Adhémar).

54. Bust of a Young Man
60 × 54 *1864* V.95

55. "L'Oncle Dominique"
46 × 33 *1865* V.75
Probably the painter's uncle on his mother's side.

56. Man in a Cotton Cap ("L'Oncle Dominique"; Self-Portrait ?)
New York, Museum of Modern Art
84 × 64 *1865* V.73

57. "L'Oncle Dominique"
39 × 30·5 *1865* V.80

58. "L'Oncle Dominique"
44 × 37 *1865* V.82

59. "L'Oncle Dominique" (The Advocate)
63 × 52 *1865* V.74

60. "L'Oncle Dominique"
46 × 38 *1865* V.79

61. "L'Oncle Dominique"
41 × 33 *1865* V.76

62. "L'Oncle Dominique"
40·5 × 31·5 *1865* V.77

63. Dominican Monk ("L'Oncle Dominique")
New York, Haupt Collection
65 × 54 *1865* V.72
One of the best-known "Oncle Dominique" portraits. Again the painting is fiercely executed, the colour applied sometimes with brush and sometimes with spatula. A distant Gothic inspiration, and the white habit of the Dominican order may identify the uncle's name (Schapiro). Lacordaire had been influential in reshaping the Dominican Order; he had organised a society to encourage religious art which interested the Romantics. This is not a portrait properly speaking (Schapiro) but a mask and symbolic image; it is expressive of a strong personality, with feelings restrained by the religious habit.

64. Self-Portrait
Moscow, Museum of Modern Western Art
45 × 41 s 1865–6 V.81

65. Anthony Valabrègue
New York, Wildenstein Collection
116 × 98 s 1866 ? V.126
Probably the portrait mentioned by Valabrègue in a letter to Zola, of November 1866 (nos 78 and 79, usually taken as of some years later). "Paul made me sit yesterday for a study of the head. . . . I look so vigorous that it reminds me of the curate of Champfleury's statue. . . . Luckily, it was only one day. His uncle ["Oncle Dominique", see nos 55 to 63] is mostly the model. A portrait comes up of an afternoon and Guillemet makes awful jokes about it." (See details on Valabrègue, in *Outline biography*, **1860**.)

66. Bust of a Man
Winterthur, Reinhart Collection
81 × 62 *1866* V.102
This may be "Oncle Dominique" again.

67. Louis-Auguste Cézanne
200 × 120 1866 ? V.91
The artist's father is reading *L'Évènement*, the paper which printed Zola's article about the 1866 Salon which contained a violent attack on Meissonier, Cabanel and other painters of fashion. The title, clear enough to be read, is a tribute to the writer. The painting shows some considerable development on the formal plane, remarked on by Guillemet in a letter to Zola (autumn, 1866).
On the wall in the background is the still-life no. 124.

68. Girl with a Parrot
28 × 20 1864–8 V.99

69. Girl with a Parrot
45 × 37 ? V.98

70. Self-Portrait with Long Hair
41 × 32 1865–8 V.23

71. Achille Emperaire
42 × 40 1864–9 V.85
See also no. 6, and *Outline biography*, **1860**.

72. Achille Emperaire
200 × 122 s 1867 V.88
The sitter's name is written at the top in capitals. The high-backed chair of floral design is also in no. 67; the two works presumably date from about the same time, also on grounds of stylistic affinity. Gasquet describes it as "consumed with hunger for life, a creature of caricature, limp hands and fine, sad face turned aside . . . overhead, his name rather wryly proclaimed, notice-board size: Achille Emperaire".

73. Marie Cézanne
50 × 39 1865–7 V.78

74. Marie Cézanne
St Louis (Mo.), City Art Museum
55 × 38 1867–9 V.89

75. Head of a Man
41 × 33 *1869* V.110

76. Bust of a Boy
58 × 50 1868–70 V.109

77. Young Man with a Dark Beard
1868–70 V.97

78. Anthony Valabrègue
60 × 50 *1870* V.127
See also no. 65.

79. Anthony Valabrègue
1870 V.128
See also no. 65.

80. Man with a Straw Hat (Boyer)
New York, Metropolitan Museum of Art
55 × 39 s 1870–1 V.131
The sitter was a childhood friend of the painter, a notary of Eyguières in later life.

81. Boyer
1870–1 V.130

82. Boyer
Ottawa, National Gallery of Canada
47 × 38 1870–1 V.132

83. Fortuné Marion
43 × 33 1870–1 V.129
See *Outline biography*, **1860**.

47

48 (plate I)

49

50

51

52

53

54

55

56

57

58

59

60

61

62

63

64

65

66

67

68

69

70

71

72

73

74

75

76

77

78

79

80

81

82

83

84

85

86

87

88

89

90

91

92

93

94

95

96

97

99

101

98

100

102

103

104

105

106

107

108

109

110

111

Landscapes

Admiration for Corot is evident in some of the early and delightfully luminous pieces (nos 86 and 88), but Cézanne's interest soon turned to the Provençal painters especially Loubon who was represented at the Aix museum and Monticelli (nos 102, 108, 109), who became a friend and had belonged to the group led by Loubon. To these sources may be attributed the heady colour contrasts; the heightened tonal effect was his own (nos 87, 92–6, 105–6 and 109). About 1870 and only then (no. 107), the treatment of form begins to simplify towards the landscapes characteristic of his prime.

112

113

114

115 (plate III)

116

117

84. Trees and Houses (Romantic Landscape)
26 × 33 1858–60 V.26
Perhaps inspired by a print.

85. Trees and Houses (Romantic Landscape)
26 × 33 1858–60 V.28

86. Path among the Trees
35 × 30 1860–5 V.29

87. Farm-Yard
Parke-Bernet sale 12.2.68
26 × 33 1860–5 V.31

88. Hills with Trees and a Dwelling
19 × 30 1860–5 V.32

89. Woodland Scene
35 × 22 *1864* V.27

90. Woodland Scene
23 × 30 *1864* V.30

91. Hill with Trees and River
22 × 28 *1864* V.1510

92. River in Trees
1865–7 V.33

93. River Bend among Rocks and Trees
33 × 41 1865–7 V.34

94. House in a Clearing
26 × 39 1865–7 V.35

95. Hills with Trees
1865–7 V.37

96. Path by Trees, and a Dwelling
24 × 38 1865–7 V.36

97. Avenue at Jas de Bouffan
1865–7 V.38
His father bought the property in 1859. The house and farm dated from the previous century and had been the home of a governor of Provence. Local people thought the gesture showy, typical of a self-made man. "Jas de Bouffan" means a windy place. Cézanne loved it and did a great deal of painting there during his frequent long stays.

98. Stream among Trees
35 × 116 1865–7 V.46

99. Boulders
22 × 32 1865–70 V.1512

100. River on a Plain
Lausanne, Vallotton Collection
26·7 × 34·7 1866–8 V.41

101. Village Church
Cambridge, Fitzwilliam Museum
64·8 × 54 1866–8 V.49

102. Clearing
1867–9 V.43

103. Rue des Saules, Montmartre
32 × 41 1867–9 V.45

104. Road
33 × 46 1867–9 V.44
Described as a view of the Tour du Télégraphe, Montmartre (Venturi).

105. Winding Road in Provence
Montreal, Museum of Fine Arts
91 × 71 1867–70 V.53

106. Cutting
19 × 33 1867–70 V.42
Scene near Jas de Bouffan.

107. Road with Houses in Provence
59 × 78 1867–70 V.54

108. Garden at Jas de Bouffan
23·5 × 30 1867–70 V.39

109. Pool at Jas de Bouffan
46 × 53 1867–70 V.40
The pool was in the grounds of the Cézannes' home in the country; the painter reproduced the subject on several occasions.

110. Avenue at Jas de Bouffan
36 × 44 1869 V.47

111. L'Estaque under Snow
Zurich, Bührle Collection
73 × 92 *1870* V.51

112. Fishing Village at L'Estaque
42 × 55 *1870* V.55

113. Sunset at L'Estaque
44 × 60 *1870* V.57

114. Works by the Montagne Sainte-Victoire
41 × 55 *1870* V.58

115. Cutting with the Montagne Sainte-Victoire
Munich, Neue Staatsgalerie
80 × 129 * 1870 * V.50
The head of Sainte-Victoire is in the background. This was a motif especially dear to the artist in his prime. See plate III.

116. Fork in a Road
New York, Museum of Modern Art
57 × 70 1871–2 V.52

117. Beside the Seine at Bercy ("La halle au vin")
73 × 92 1871–2 V.56
Painted from the window of the artist's house in Paris.

Still-lifes

In this line of painting as in landscapes, the artist was to make great strides forward later on. Note the oblique-angled knife, inspired by Manet, evoking a new spatial plane (nos 119 and 129), another subsequently-recurrent feature.

118. Peaches on a Plate
18 × 24 1860–4 V.12
Deemed a copy of an item in the Aix museum, attributed to Cuyp or an unknown artist of the late eighteenth century.

119. Jug, Bread, Eggs and Glass
Cincinnati (Ohio), Art Museum
59·2 × 76·2 s d 1865 V.59

120. Glass, Pan and Two Fowl
32 × 40 s 1864–6 V.60

121. Bottle, Glass and Lemons
1864–6 V.63

122. Skull and Carafe
60 × 50 1865–6 V.68
The theme of the skull, treated at this period, later recurs to heightened effect.
A "sombre canvas of impasto warmly-felt and moving as a Rembrandt" (Gasquet). The same writer recalled hearing Cézanne recite one evening by the river Arc, the following lines from Verlaine:
"Car dans ce monde léthargique
Toujours en proie aux vieux remords
Le seul rire encore logique
Est celui des têtes de morts."

123. Skull, Candlestick and Book
47·5 × 62·5 1865–7 V.61
See also no. 67.

124. Mug, Sugar-Bowl and Pears
30 × 41 1865–7 V.62

125. Bread and Leg of Lamb
Zurich, Kunsthaus
27 × 35 1865–7 V.65
The same subject was treated by Claude Monet – perhaps over the same years.

126. Black Clock
Paris, Niarchos Collection
54 × 73 1869–70 V.69

127. Apples and Leaves
1870–2 V.66

128. Relief, Scroll and Ink-Well
Paris, Louvre
1870–2 V.67
The relief may portray Dr Gachet, done by Solari who

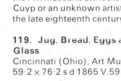

118

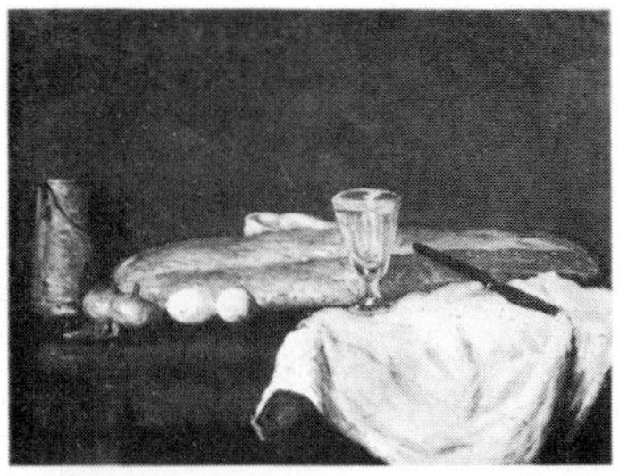

119

120

121

122

123

124

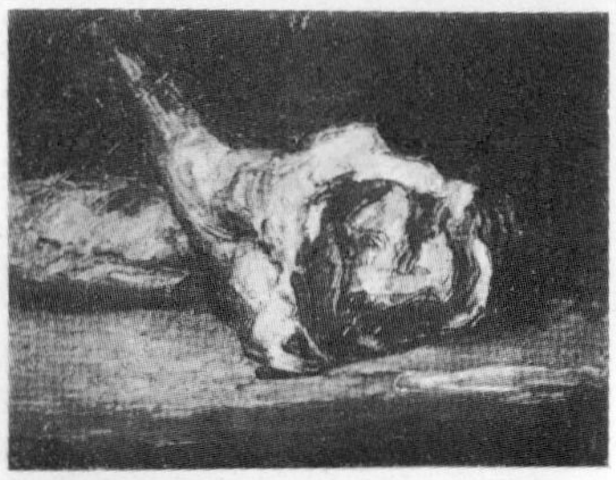
125

126

127

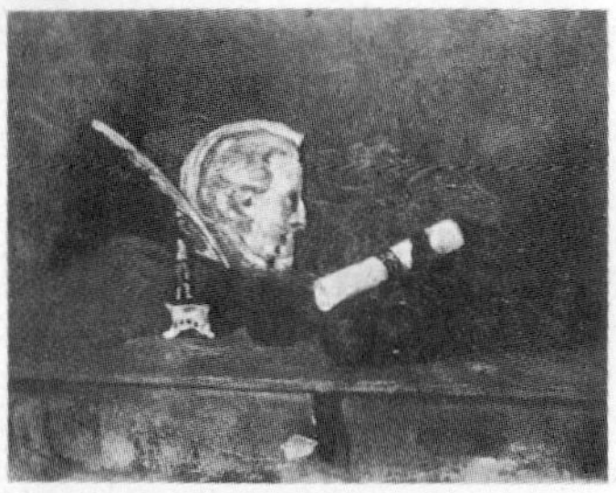
128

129 (plate VI)

130

was to make a bust of Cézanne (1904).

129. Jar, Coffee-Pot and Fruit (Still-Life in Black-and-White)
Paris, Louvre
63 × 80 1870–2 V.70
A tribute to Manet, in composition and treatment of light. The ground and table are in shades of grey. The pot stands out against the white cloth. See plate VI.

130. Vase, Bottle, Cups and Fruit .
Berlin, Nationalgalerie
64 × 80 1871–2 V.71

Impressionist period 1872–7

This important stage in Cézanne's development is marked by his sojourn at Auvers-sur-Oise from 1872 and working contact with Pissarro over at Pontoise. The constructive element is stressed, and this has a counter-part in the art of Pissarro who "unlike others, gave Impressionism a wish to build bigger; this required a structural approach to light itself" (Venturi).

Landscapes

Pissarro's influence is here most active in Cézanne's objective tackling of nature, his study of structure and colours where his personality and technique apply a visual filter. The two men often worked together, sometimes on the same landscape (nos 176 and 181); there is also a Cézanne copy of a Pissarro (no. 134). By slow degrees, the artist thus used light and vibrant colour to "synthesise space and volume . . . which is what gives things a sense of the eternal" (Venturi). The colour impasto is drier and this makes variegated surfaces which reflect light.

131. Water-Mill
41 × 54 1871–2 V.48

132. Mill
38 × 46 1871–2 V.136

133. Garden Wall
22 × 31 1871–2 V.1513

134. Louveciennes
73 × 92 *1872* V.153
Copy of a Pissarro (1871).

135. Farm-Yard
46 × 38 1871–3 V.1511

136. The House of the Hanged Man at Auvers
Paris, Louvre
55 × 66 s 1872–3 V.133
A clear instance of the artist's new style, which has been described as a "process of solidification" (Gowing). "Space becomes compact rather than shapeless, despite the thick paint material; body is given to mass, rather than weight. Fineness of landscape results" (Venturi). Cézanne "takes from Impressionism all he needs to surpass the concept of motionless reality" (Ponente). The painting was shown at the first Impressionist exhibition (April 1874) and regarded as highly controversial. Leroy's contribution to *Charivari*, 25 April 1874, gives a sample of the current reaction. See plates XII-XIII.

137. Woodland Scene
46 × 55 1872–3 V.155

138. Cottages at Auvers
46 × 38 1872–3 V.135

139. Street in Auvers
s 1872–3 V.134

140. Street in the Snow
38 × 46 1872–3 V.137
Probably a wintry scene at Auvers.

141. House and Tree at Auvers
San Francisco (Calif.), Palace of the Legion of Honor (Goetz Bequest)
66 × 55 s 1872–3 V.142

142. House of Père Lacroix at Auvers
Washington, D.C., National Gallery of Art
61 × 51 s d 1873 V.138

143. Dwelling in Trees at Auvers
Parke-Bernet sale 17.4.69
69 × 49 s d 1873 V.139

144. House of Dr Gachet at Auvers
62 × 52 1873 V.144
See *Outline biography*, **1872**.

145. House of Dr Gachet at Auvers
Paris, Louvre
46 × 37·5 1873 V.145

146. House of Dr Gachet at Auvers
56 × 46 1873–4 V.146

147. Dwellings at Auvers
Cambridge (Mass.), Fogg Art Museum
40 × 54 s 1873–4 V.156
View from Val-Harmé.

148. The Four District at Auvers
47 × 51·5 1873–4 V.157

149. Street in Auvers
Ottawa, National Gallery of Canada
55 × 46 1873–4 V.147

150. Winding Road in Trees
Chicago (Ill.), Brewster Collection
55 × 46 1873–5 V.140

151. Track with Trees and Houses
38 × 46 1873–5 V.141

152. House among Trees near Pontoise
60 × 73 1873–5 V.143

153. House among Trees at Auvers
92 × 73 1873–5 V.148

154. View of Auvers, with Paling
New York, Ittleson Collection
44·5 × 34·5 s 1873–5 V.149

155. View of Auvers, from Above
Chicago (Ill.), Art Institute
65 × 81 1873–5 V.150

156. View of Auvers through Trees
48 × 58 1873–5 V.151

157. Valley of the Oise
San Francisco (Calif.), Palace of the Legion of Honor (Goetz Bequest)
72 × 91 1873–5 V.152

158. Houses and Trees on Hillside
1873–7 V.154

159. Boundary Wall
50 × 65 s 1875–6 V.158

160. Pine Tree at L'Estaque
Paris, Musées Nationaux (Walter-Guillaume Bequest)
72 × 58 1875–6 V.163

161. Trees and Village
65 × 46 1875–6 V.165

162. Woodland Scene
54 × 65 1875–6 V.1525

163. Meadow and Trees near Jas de Bouffan
Christie's sale 28 June 1968
39 × 54 1875–6 V.159

164. View at Jas de Bouffan
45 × 59 1875–6 V.1516

165. Trees at Jas de Bouffan
54 × 73 1875–6 V.161

166. Boundary Wall and Trees at Jas de Bouffan
46 × 55 1875–6 V.162

167. Pool at Jas de Bouffan
46 × 55 1875–6 V.160

168. Pool at Jas de Bouffan
52·5 × 56 1875–6 ? V.164

169. Pool at Jas de Bouffan
1875–6 V.167
As in the next item, no. 170, the statue of a dolphin is shown.

170. Pool at Jas de Bouffan
58 × 71 1875–6 V.166

171. View in Paris (Roofs)
58 × 72 1874–7 V.175

172. Sea at L'Estaque
New York, Bernhard Collection
42 × 59 s 1876 V.168
View of the gulf of Marseilles; in the background, Frioul islands. Cézanne wrote in a letter of 2 July 1876 to Pissarro: "It's like a playing card, red roofs on blue sea. The sun so fierce that objects rise up in outline, not just black and white, but blue, red, brown and violet. I may be mistaken, but this seems the model's furthest pole."

173. Trinitarian Monastery at Pontoise (The Retreat)
Moscow, Museum of Modern Western Art
58 × 71 1875–7 V.172

174. Trees and Houses
Zurich, Bührle Collection
58 × 47·5 1875–7 V.169

175. Village in Northern France
60 × 50 s 1875–7 V.171
Perhaps a view of Auvers

176. The Côte des Boeufs at Pontoise
65 × 54 1875–7 V.173

177. The Étang des Soeurs at Osny
London, Home House Trustees
57 × 71 1875–7 V.174

178. Trinitarian Monastery at Pontoise (The Retreat)
44 × 54 1875–7 V.176

179. Winding Road
48 × 59 1875–7 V.177

180. Winding Street in Auvers
60 × 73 1875–7 V.178

181. Bed of Torrent from the Pontoise Retreat
Leningrad, Hermitage
50 × 61 *1877* V.170

182. Houses (Roofs)

131

135

132

138

133

134

136 (plates XII-XIII)

137

139

140

141

142

143

144

145

146

147

148

149

150

151

152

153

154

155

156

157

160

158

159

162

163

161

164

165

166

Berne, Hahnloser Collection
47 x 59 *1877* V.1515

Still-lifes

Unlike the path followed by the Impressionists of the time, Cézanne's investigations of light made him esteem form rather than try to "empty" it. There are a lot of flower paintings at this period (nos 213–25), of near body-like consistency. The knife motif re-echoes Manet (nos 183, 196 and 212).

Fruit and objects

183. Jug, Glass, Knife and Fruit
60 x 73 1873 V.185
Painted in the house of Dr Gachet at Auvers.

184. Bowl with Apples and Pears
25 x 39 1873–4 V.194

185. Faïence Ware and Fruit
Parke-Bernet sale 3 April 1968
40 x 53·5 1873–4 V.189

186. Glass, Cup and Apples
41·5 x 55 1873–7 V.186
See plate VII.

187. Glass, Cup and Apples
33 x 46 1873–7 V.187

188. Glass, Cup and Fruit
38 x 46 1873–7 V.188

189. Apples
19 x 27 1873–7 V.190

190. Apples
Parke-Bernet sale 26 October 1967
12 x 26 1873–7 V.191

191. Apples
Lausanne, Musée Cantonal des Beaux-Arts
16·5 x 23·5 1873–7 V.195

192. Overturned Fruit Basket
Glasgow, Art Gallery and Museum
16 x 32 1873–7 V.211

193. Plate of Grapes and Peach
16·5 x 29 1873–7 V.192

194. Plate of Apricots and Cherries
16 x 22 1873–7 V.193

195. Dish of Apples and Dessert
46 x 55 s 1873–7 V.196

196. Bottle, Glass, Fruit and Dessert (Dessert)
Philadelphia (Pa.), Museum of Art
60 x 73 s 1873–7 V.197

197. Vessels and Lemon
21·5 x 43·5 1873–7 V.221

198. Vessels and Lemon
19 x 30 1873–7 V.219

199. Jug and Cup
Tokyo, Ishibashi Collection
20·5 x 18·5 1873–7 V.220

200. Two Apples and a Half
Merion (Pa.), Barnes Foundation
16·5 x 10 1873–7 V.202
This may be part of a work (Venturi).

201. Three Pears
20·5 x 26 1873–7 V.201

202. Plate of Apples, Orange and Lemon
22 x 33 1873–7 V.204

203. Plate of Four Apples
15 x 31 1873–7 V.205

204. Plate of Fruit
24 x 35 1873–7 V.206

205. Receptacles, Fruit and Biscuits on a Sideboard
Budapest, Szépmüvészeti Múzeum
75 x 81 1873–7 V.208
"Here, reality is on the side of the painter. His own blue, laid on like wadding, his red, his green unshadowed and the reddish black of his bottles of wine" (Rilke to Clara, 1907).

206. Plate of Apples and Sugar Bowl
Philadelphia (Pa.), Annenberg Collection
46 x 55 s 1873–7 V.207

207. Bronze Vase and Sugar-Bowl
27·5 x 51 1875–6 ? V.200
Analogous composition in the centre of no. 625.

208. Biscuits and Fruit-Bowl
53 x 63 *1877* V.209
The hanging in the background, olive yellow with blue flowers, appears in other works (nos 209–12 and 231–2), and may serve for purposes of dating. It is thought to have been part of the household at no. 67 rue de l'Ouest where the artist was living in 1877 (Rivière, followed by Venturi). On the other hand, Cézanne's comings-and-goings are not fully known. It may look like 1877 in style, though other dates have been suggested (Anderson): 1879–80, when the artist was at Melun in a house similarly furnished; or 1881 when he was back at a house in rue de l'Ouest, Paris.

209. Plate of Apples
Chicago (Ill.), Art Institute
46 x 55 s *1877* V.120
See no. 208.

210. Apples and Plate of Biscuits
38 x 55 s *1877* V.212
See no. 208.

211. Jar, Cup and Fruit
New York, Metropolitan Museum of Art
60 x 73 *1877* V.213
See no. 208.

212. Flask, Glass and Fruit
New York, Solomon R. Guggenheim Museum
46 x 55 *1877* V.214
See no. 208.

Flowers

213. Delft Vase with Dahlias
Paris, Louvre
73 x 54 s 1873–5 V.179
Painted at Auvers in the house of Dr Gachet; the vase was there in 1936 (Venturi). Also used as a model by Pissarro.

214. Vase of Geraniums and Coreopsis
52 x 39 s 1873–5 V.180

215. Light-Blue Vase
Moscow, Museum of Modern

167

168

169

170

171

172

173

174

175

177

178

179

176

180

181

182

183

184

185

186 (plate VII)

187

188

189

190

191

192

193

194

195

196

199

197

198

200

201

202

203

204

205

206

207

208

209

210

211

212

Western Art
56 x 46 1873–5 V.182

216. Small Delft Vase
Paris, Louvre
41 x 27 s 1873–5 V.183
The flowers are massed in bright colour tones of red, yellow and black, with a compact look; the volume aspect is accentuated by the clear ground.
See plate X.

217. Vase on a Floral Cloth
61 x 50 s 1873–7 V.181

218. Vase on a Round Table
49 x 36 1873–7 V.216
Painted in the house of Dr Gachet at Auvers.

219. Two Vases
54 x 44 1873–7 V.217

220. Green Vase
Philadelphia (Pa.), Museum of Art
46 x 34 1873–7 V.218

221. Vase of Petunias
Zurich, Bührle Collection
46 x 55 1875–6 V.198
Duranty remarked on this painting: "Obviously Maillobert [i.e. Cézanne] thought a kilo of green would be greener than a gram" (Dorival).

222. Terracotta Vase
31·5 x 36·5 1875–6 V.199

223. Rococo Vase
Washington, D.C., National Gallery of Art
73 x 58 s *1876* V.222
Inspired by a Second Empire print. The vase is elaborately baroque, as if under the impetus of the flowers.

224. Plate and Decorated Vase
37 x 32 1875–7 V.215

225. Glass Vase
41 x 33 1875–7 V.184

Portraits

Observation of the subject is close but detached, after Impressionism. However, the resemblance draws more from the character of the artist than mere technical skill. The violent treatment of earlier days is gone: "Cézanne seemed to be revenging himself on a friend for some secret grudge" (Valabrègue). The approach now is calm; it conveys the sitter's attitude. In particular, nos 242–3 have an introspective air and are among the period's leading achievements.

226. Man with Beard (Self-Portrait?)
48 x 36 s ? V.21
Sometimes considered an early work, because it is rather traditional in style. The artist's son always dated it later. Possibly the piece accepted for the 1882 Salon through Guillemet's good offices (Venturi) and if so, this would account for a style conventionally acceptable.

227. Madame Cézanne
Paris, Louvre
46 x 38 1871–3 V.226

228. Madame Cézanne
55 x 46 1872–7 V.229

229. Madame Cézanne with her Head Inclined
26 x 30 1872–7 V.228
Cézanne made of Hortense a long-suffering model. The group of paintings which feature her comprise some of his best works. A certain "abstract charm" (Venturi) comes from the well-groomed hair, striped bodice and facial oval.

230. Madame Cézanne Leaning on a Table
61 x 50 1873–7 V.278
See plate XI.

231. Madame Cézanne Sewing
58 x 48 *1877* V.291
See no. 208.

232. Madame Cézanne in a Red Armchair
Boston (Mass.), Museum of Fine Arts
72·5 x 56 *1877* V.292
Cézanne's wife was said to be fashion-conscious and a reader of the *Mode Illustrée* (Van Buren). Her dress is in the fashion of 1877, with a straight, uncluttered line. The background hanging, olive yellow and blue-flowered, appears elsewhere (see no. 208).

233. Girl with her Hair Down
1873–7 V.277

234. Country Girl
48 x 40 1873–7 V.285

235. Louis-Auguste Cézanne
55 x 46 1875–6 V.227

236. Self-Portrait in a Beret
Leningrad, Hermitage
55 x 38 1873–5 V.289

237. Self-Portrait on Rose Background
65 x 54 1873–6 V.286
Described in a Rilke letter to Clara (23 October 1907), in these terms: "It is drawn with a pre-eminently confident hand, round and hard, the forehead all of a piece. It is solid even when dissolving planes and forms de-limit a thousand contours within the face itself, spear-headed by the growth of beard which strand by strand responds to an incredible intensity of touch . . ."

238. Self-Portrait in a Straw Hat
34 x 26 1873–6 V.287

239. Self-Portrait Outdoors
64 x 52 1875–6 V.288

240. Self-Portrait
24 x 18 1875–7 V.280

241. Self-Portrait with Head Covered
Munich, Neue Staatsgalerie
55 x 47 1875–7 V.284

242. Self-Portrait
Washington, D.C., Phillips Collection
61 x 46 *1877* V.290

243. Victor Chocquet
46 x 36 s 1876–7 V.283
Shown at the 1877 Impressionist exhibition. It was controversial and called "Billoir en chocolat" (Billoir was a murderer, much in the papers). See also *Outline biography*, **1875**.

Various compositions

These are more in line with the previous period and the detachment from Romanticism is less in evidence. Many signs of Delacroix's influence (nos 250, 251, 262, 263, 267 and 280). Scenes of agricultural labour tie in with Pissarro (nos 274–5). The subject treatment, is new—in a luminous spatial dimension rendered by shorter brush-strokes and clearer colour.

244. Girl in a White Apron, Seated
16 x 13 1871–2 V.1520 B

245. Venus and Cupid
21 x 21 1870–3 V.124
The background view may be the gulf of Marseilles.

246. Courtesans
17 x 17 1871–2 V.122

247. Female Nude with a Looking-Glass
17 x 22 1872 V.111

248. Woman Suckling a Child
23 x 23 *1872* V.233
This may be the artist's wife and son Paul.

249. Man and Seated Woman Outdoors (Conversation Piece)
45 x 54 1872–3 V.231

250. A Modern Olympia
Paris, Louvre
46 x 55 1872–3 V.225
The theme (previously treated with an analogous composition but differing technical solutions, some years before – see no. 36), is taken from Manet (1863). It is a spirited and ironical composition, baroque in design and emotional in content; there are reminders of Delacroix

213

214

215

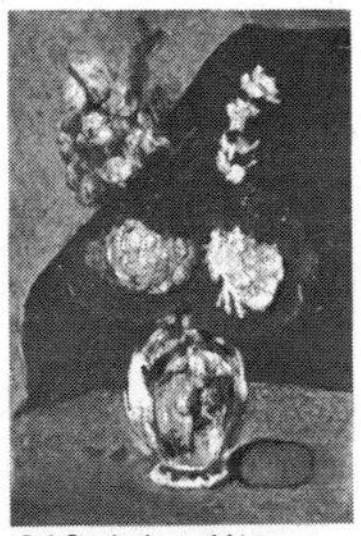
216 (plate X)

217

218

221

219

220

222

223

224

225

226

227

228

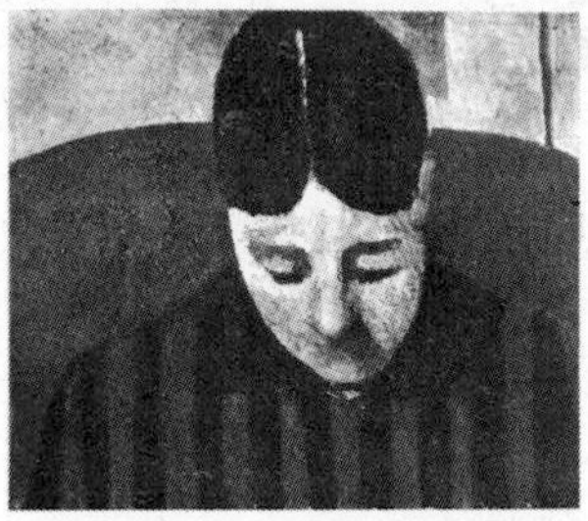
229

230 (plate XI)

231

232

233

234

235

236

237

238

239

240

241

242

243

(Lichtenstein). The pyramidal composition is referable to the same source, also the rich still-life to the left, the sense of colour and the theatrical impetus of the whole. Love, cruelly symbolised by the older painter, turns to idolising on the Baudelaire model. The artist's approach has been described as "romantic still; whereas the technique and visual freedom belong already to the Impressionist school" (Ponente). The beholder in the foreground, against the light, may be Cézanne. See plates IV–V.

251. Afternoon in Naples
30 × 40 1872–5 V.223

A series of oils and water-colours by Cézanne, on the same subject (see also no. 43), may derive from a painting now lost, done in 1863 and turned down for the 1866 Salon (Venturi).

The motif and especially the models and their poses have been identified (Vollard). "The model for this academic piece was a sewage-worker whose wife kept a small dairy. . . . Cézanne asked him to pose which he did, at first under the sheets, in a cotton night-cap – the last touch in the painter's honour. But as there was no point in standing on ceremony with friends, he took off first the night-cap, then the sheets until in the end he posed nude. His wife is in the picture, offering her husband hot wine in a bowl."

Not unlike *A Modern Olympia* (no. 250) in technique; the character of the brushstroke and resplendent palette reflect Impressionism to the full. Mention has been made of Delacroix's influence (Lichtenstein), particularly the *Women of Algiers* at the Louvre, in which similar props were used. But the gestures in Cézanne are not indolent as in Delacroix. They aggressively evoke the erotic concept of the artist, expressed as a personal view.

"How can you like dirty painting!" Thus exclaimed Monet to his friend Guillemet on the subject. But then Guillemet shared the credit with Cézanne for the title (Vollard).

252. Afternoon in Naples
37 × 45 1872–5 V.224

253. Out Fishing
27 × 37 1872–5 V.230

254. A Game of Bowls
17 × 23 1872–5 V.236

255. Drunkards
40 × 50 1872–5 V.235

256. Painter Outdoors
Solothurn, Müller Collection
1872–5 V.237

257. Beside the Seine at Bercy
Hamburg, Kunsthalle
60 × 73 1873–5 V.242

258. "Le déjeuner sur l'herbe"
Paris, Musées Nationaux (Walter-Guillaume Bequest)
21 × 27·5 1873–5 V.238
See nos 31 and 536.

259. Outing (The Pool)
Boston (Mass.), Museum of Fine Arts
47 × 56 1873–5 V.232

260. Outing
17 × 26 1873–5 V.234

244

245

246

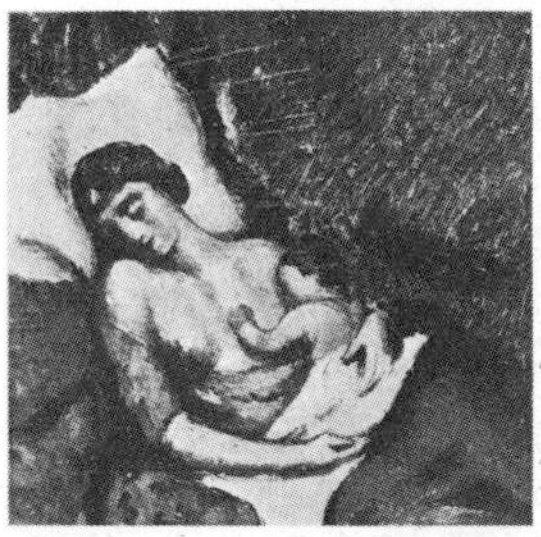
248

247

249

250 (plates IV-V)

251

252

253

254

255

256

257

258

259

260

261

262

263

264

265

266

267

268

269

270

271

272

273

275

276

274

277

278

279

280

261. Figures Outdoors (Sunday Afternoon; July Day; Fishermen)
54 × 81 1873–5 V.243
Shown by Cézanne at the third Impressionist Exhibition (1877), when the theme puzzled Rivière. But the landscape and the attitude of some figures, to the left, may bear comparison with the *Apotheosis of Delacroix* (no. 264).

262. Don Quixote
22·5 × 16·5 1873–5 V.244
As with no. 263, some analogy with *Don Rodrigo*, by Delacroix.

263. Don Quixote
35 × 24 1873–7 V.246

264. The Apotheosis of Delacroix
27 × 35 1873–7 ? V.245
Delacroix is sustained by angels; also, from the right, are represented Pissarro, Monet, Cézanne and his pack, Chocquet and one more figure (unidentified). The dog may stand for envy or critical opinion (Lichtenstein). There is some difference about the dating. The artist wrote to Bernard (12 May 1904): "I don't know if my poor health will ever let me realise the dream of making his Apotheosis" (understood as that of Delacroix). But an 1874 photograph, published in *Amour de l'Art* (October 1935), shows Cézanne by his easel, and resting on it what looks like a similar painting, perhaps the very same.

265. Tiger
29 × 37 s 1873–7 V.250

266. Female Nude in Bed
8·5 × 13 1873–7 V.279

267. Figures Outdoors (Mythological Scene; Sancho Panza in the Water)
46 × 55 1873–7 V.239
Some analogy in terms of composition with *Ovid among the Scythians* by Delacroix.

268. The Temptations of St Anthony
47 × 56 1873–7 V.241
The theme was treated on a previous occasion (see no. 29).

269. The Temptations of St Anthony
Parke-Bernet sale 24 May 1968
25 × 33 1873–7 V.240

270. Love Play
42 × 55 1875–6 V.379

271. Love Play
New York, Harriman Collection
38 × 46 1875–6 V.380

272. Labourer Drilling a Well
20 × 15·5 1873–7 V.1520

273. Rural Life
27 × 35 1875–6 V.251

274. Harvest
46 × 55 1875–6 V.249
Gauguin may have owned the painting; anyhow, he used the motif on a fan (1884) and to decorate ceramics (*c.* 1886–7).

275. Reapers
25 × 39 1875–8 V.1517

276. Man Putting on a Jacket
Merion (Pa.), Barnes Foundation
31 × 24 s 1875–6 V.248

277. Bathsheba (Susanna Bathing)
London, Korda Collection
31·5 × 23·5 1875–7 V.252

278. Bathsheba
29 × 25 1875–7 V.253

279. Bathsheba
20 × 20 1875–7 V.255

280. The Eternal Feminine (The Golden Calf; The Triumph of Woman; "La belle Impéria")
New York, Private collection
43 × 53 1875–7 V.247

Bathers

A "genre" all of its own in Cézanne's painting at this period and even more so later on. The human figures belong to the landscape; the treatment given them, as Venturi observed, like that for water and trees. A crucial stage between representation from reality and pure volume construction, which the artist attained gradually in succeeding periods.

281. Woman Standing
22 × 14 1873–7 V.257

282. Six Women
1873–7 V.265

283. Five Women
50 × 61 1873–7 V.264

284. Woman Sitting
1873–7 V.258

285. Woman Sitting on the Sea-Shore
23·5 × 22 1875–6 V.256
The landscape is of L'Estaque, as again in nos 289 and 290.

286. Four Men
38 × 46 1875–6 V.274
This work and others in the same vein seem to recall the artist's outings in younger days through the Aix countryside (Dorival). Of his companions, Baille and Zola, the latter seems also to have alluded to them in *L'Oeuvre*: "They planned to camp beside the Viosne and live there like savages, in and out of the water all day, needing only a few books for necessities."

287. Four Men
Merion (Pa.), Barnes Foundation
1875–6 V.276

288. Four Men
33 × 41 s 1875–6 V.273

289. Man Standing with Open Arms
23 × 15 1875–6 V.271

290. Man Standing with Open Arms
24 × 16 1875–7 V.259

291. Man Standing with

281

282

283

284

285

286

287

288

289

290

291

292

294

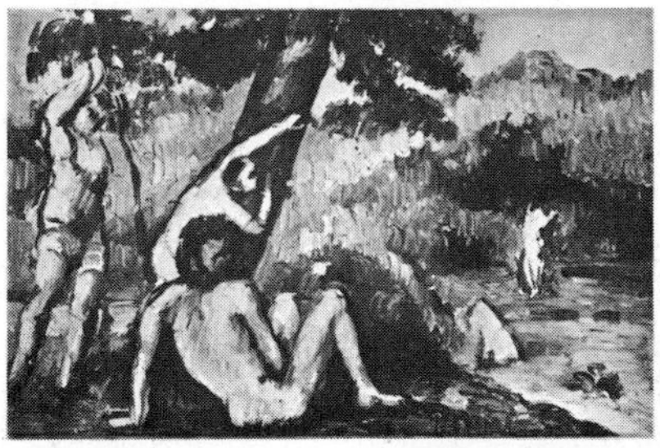
296

297

293

298

299

295

300

301

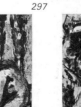

Open Arms
1875–7 V.262

292. Man Sitting
29 × 21 1875–7 V.260

293. Man Standing with Arms Raised
31 × 21 1875–7 V.263

294. Five Men
24 × 25 1875–7 V.268

295. Man Standing with One Arm Raised
1875–7 V.261
A drawing was made of this by Paul Signac.

296. Group of Men
19 × 27 1875–7 V.272

297. Group of Men
14 × 19 1875–7 V.275

298. Three Women
22 × 19 1875–7 V.266

299. Three Women
1875–7 V.267

300. Three Women
1875–7 V.269

301. Three Women
Merion (Pa.), Barnes Foundation
35 × 27 1875–7 V.270

The constructive period

1878–87

The Impressionist exhibition of 1877, in which Cézanne took part, was not a success and marks his departure from the group. He wanted his own work to provide motivation and meaning and to rely on his own resources. A letter to Maus of 25 November 1889 explains: "I made up my mind to work in silence until the day I felt able to explain my working results in terms of theory." In fact, the answers he looked for were forthcoming from the actual work process.

Landscapes

As in the Impressionist period, this was Cézanne's favourite line for taking his investigations further. To "construct", he brought form down to essentials: "by way of simplification, Cézanne reaches to the heart of things" (Venturi). A "primitive" time, when the visual reality was opening up before him and he could leave aside, indeed dispense altogether with preconceived intellectual notions. Mindful of Impressionist teaching, he started painting "sur le motif" – outdoors –, studying and recording the subject by exhausting the possibilities under all kinds of conditions.

His landscape output at this period distinguishes the themes, most significantly involved at subsequent periods in his researches.

302. Pool at Jas de Bouffan
73 × 60 *1878* V.484

303. Viaduct in the Arc Valley
57 × 72 1878–83 V.296

304. Houses and Trees in Provence
Washington, D C., National Gallery of Art
50 × 61 1878–83 V.297

305. Pilon du Roi
Merion (Pa.), Barnes Foundation 1878–83 V.301
Upland near Aix.

306. Tree and Dovecot in Provence
Laren, Boerlage Collection
73 × 92 1878–83 V.300

307. L'Estaque from the Sea
Merion (Pa.), Barnes Foundation
44 × 77 1878–83 V.293

308. Lane in L'Estaque
52 × 64 1878–83 V.294

309. Beach in L'Estaque
53·5 × 54·5 1878–83 V.295

310. Provençal Hills with Tree and Houses
Berne, Hahnloser Collection
58 × 79 1878–83 V.302

311. Houses among the Trees
Zurich, Bührle Collection
46 × 55 1878–83 V.305

312. Hills with Trees and Houses
Zurich, Bührle Collection
54 × 73 1878–83 V.306

313. Hills with Fields and Trees
60 × 73 1878–83 V.303

314. Neighbourhood of Jas de Bouffan
Oslo, Nasjonalgalleriet
60 × 73 1878–83 V.304

315. Médan Castle (The House of Zola)
Glasgow, Art Gallery and Museum
59 × 72 s 1879–81 V.325
Zola bought a house at Médan in 1878 and Cézanne often went to stay with him, certainly in the summer of 1879 and the spring and summer of 1880, so that this painting can be referable to that time. Originally, it belonged to Gauguin.

316. Trees and Hills
Zurich, Bührle Collection
46 × 55 1879–82 V.299
Perhaps a view near Aix.

317. Wooded Country and Hills
65 × 81 1879–82 V.298

318. Houses among the Trees
80 × 64 1879–82 V.308

319. Provencal Village
San Francisco (Calif.) Palace of the Legion of Honor (Goetz Bequest)
60 × 73 1879–82 V.307
Given as northern French countryside (Venturi).

320. Trees and Houses
46 × 55 1879–82 V.309

321. Water-Tank among Trees
Merion (Pa.), Barnes Foundation
1879–82 V.310

322. The Oise Valley
72 × 91 s 1879–82 V.311

323. Hills with Trees and Houses
Stockholm, Nationalmuseum
74 × 93 1879–82 V.317

324. Bridge and Custom House at Pontoise
60 × 73 1879–82 V.316

325. Auvers from Val Harmé
Zurich, Private collection
73 × 92 1879–82 V.318
The landscape is pin-pointed by the artist's technique of accentuating planes. See plate XVIII.

326. Val Harmé Suburb at Auvers
53 × 85·5 1879–82 V.315

327. Square in a Village
Merion (Pa.), Barnes Foundation
51·5 × 64 1879–82 V.321

328. Fortifications (Gennevillers)
54 × 65 1879–82 V.322

329. Hill with Trees and Houses
45 × 53 s 1879–82 V.323
It is uncertain whether this is a view of Auvers or Pontoise.

330. Mill on the Couleuve at Pontoise
Berlin, Nationalgalerie
73 × 92 1879–82 V.324

331. Farm-Yard
Paris, Louvre
63 × 52 1879–82 V.326
Against the bright blue sky, the red roofs and yellow walls of the farm are outlined in light blue. In his search for landscape of a constructive order, Cézanne gave the component elements equal importance; in simplifying, they stand out even

302

303

304

305

307

306

308

309

310

311

312

313

314

315

316

317

318

319

320

321

322

323

324

325 (plate XVIII)

326

327

328

329

330

331 (plate XVII)

332

333

334 (plate XXII)

335

336

337

338

339 (plates XX-XXI)

340

341

343

344

345

346

342

347

348

349

350

351

352

353

354

355

356

357

358 (plate XXVI)

359

360

361

362

stronger. See plate XVII.

332. House among Trees
60 x 73 1879–82 V.331

333. Uphill Road
59 x 71 1879–82 V.333

334. Small Bridge (The Bridge at Maincy)
Paris, Louvre
59 x 72 1882–5 V.396
This is one of Cézanne's best-known landscapes. The brushstroke is very regular, the light and shade modulated in passages from green to blue, to yellow. The stress on geometric form has been observed (Venturi).
See plate XXII.

335. Pool at Jas de Bouffan
Buffalo (N.Y.), Albright-Knox Art Gallery
73 x 60 1882–5 V.417

336. House at Jas de Bouffan
59 x 71 1882–5 V.415

337. Houses at L'Estaque
65 x 81 1882–5 V.397

338. Viaduct at L'Estaque
Basle, Kunstmuseum
44 x 53 1882–5 V.401

339. Rocks at L'Estaque
São Paulo, Museu de Arte
73 x 91 1882–5 V.404
The landscape rock motif takes the artist's attention at this point, with the focus on dynamic form. See plates XX–XXI.

340. Trees and Houses
54 x 65 1882–5 V.403

341. Viaduct at L'Estaque
Helsinki, Ateneumin Taidemuseo
54 x 65 1882–5 V.402

342. Wooded Ravine
Solothurn, Müller Collection
73 x 54 1882–5 V.400

343. Trees and Houses from Above
Basle, Kunstmuseum
60 x 92 1882–5 V.410
A comment from Gasquet. "All self-organised, trees, fields, houses. I see by dabs. The rock-bed, the preparatory drawing, the world above, sinking, bared as if by some catastrophe."

344. Bellevue Houses
Sotheby's sale 4 December 1968
54 x 65 1882–5 V.412
The farm and pigeon-house of Bellevue, near Aix, belonged to Cézanne's brother-in-law Conil. Often a motif of the artist's work.

345. Pilon du Roi from Bellevue
1884–5 V.416

346. Hills with Houses and Trees in Provence
Glasgow, Art Gallery and Museum
49 x 59 1884–5 V.418

347. Countryside with Houses in Winter
1885 V.440

363

364

365

366

367

368

369

370

371 (plate XXXI)

348. Médan Village and Castle
(81 × 65) *1885* V.439
In late July 1885, Cézanne was at Médan again, staying with his friend Zola, one of the last, if not the last occasion that he did so before their friendship ended (see *Outline biography*).

349. Mills at Gardanne
Merion (Pa.), Barnes Foundation
65 × 100 1885–6 V.430

350. Gardanne
New York, Brooklyn Museum
92 × 73 1885–6 V.431

351. Gardanne
81 × 65 1885–6 V.432
A colour-fused painting, with no regular brushstroke. It may have inspired the early Cubist landscapes (1908–9) of Braque, Picasso and also Derain (Richardson).

352. Houses and Trees near Bellevue
Merion (Pa.), Barnes Foundation
81 × 100 1885–7 V.450

353. Fields and Houses near Bellevue
63 × 78 1885–7 V.448

354. Fields and Houses near Bellevue
36 × 50 1885–7 V.449

355. House in Aix Countryside
Merion (Pa.), Barnes Foundation
79 × 85 1885–7 V.451

356. Chestnut-Trees and Farm at Jas de Bouffan
Moscow, Pushkin Museum
73 × 92 1885–7 V.462

357. Chestnut-Trees and Farm at Jas de Bouffan
Providence (R.I.), Rhode Island School of Design
65 × 81 1885–7 V.463

358. House and Farm at Jas de Bouffan
Prague, Národní Galerie
60 × 73 1885–7 V.460
Painting of notable quality, though apparently unfinished. In such instances, the artist's light and colour sensitivity is very patent. The observer gets a keenly accurate impression of the original (Richardson).
See plate XXVI.

359. Farm at Jas de Bouffan
60 × 73 1885–7 V.461

360. Chestnut-Trees and Farm at Jas de Bouffan
31 × 38 s 1885–7 V.465
Vollard says that Cézanne had to "finish" this piece to satisfy an "indiscreet" collector who bought it from the dealer. He did so with reluctance and always regretted it. The treatment of the trees contrasts with the really genuine background (Venturi).

361. Chestnut-Trees and Farm at Jas de Bouffan
51 × 65 s 1885–7 V.464

362. Meadow and Trees at Jas de Bouffan
Ottawa, National Gallery of Canada
65 × 81 1885–7 V.466

363. House with Red Roof
73 × 92 1885–7 V.468
The house has been said to resemble Jas de Bouffan (Venturi), but the lie of the land and the trees look different.

364. At Jas de Bouffan
74 × 55 1885–7 V.470

365. Jas de Bouffan Neighbourhood
65 × 81 1885–7 V.473

366. Village on a Hill
46 × 55 1885–7 V.482

367. Hill with Trees and a House in Provence
65 × 81 1885–7 V.469

368. Hills with Trees and Houses
63 × 94 1885–7 V.486

369. Trees and Houses
1885–7 V.487

370. Hills and Mountains in Provence (Noon at L'Estaque)
54 × 73 1886–90 V.490
This belonged to Gauguin, who used the subject for a fan dedicated to the Danish painter Peter Krohn. It was sold, probably by Mette Gauguin to Brandes (1891) when Gauguin went off to Tahiti. The mountain country may be L'Estaque.

371. Rocks and Hills in Provence
London, Tate Gallery
65 × 81 1886–90 V.491
As has been observed, the artist lays stress on strength of volume in rocky slopes and the interplay of succeeding planes (Venturi). See plate XXXI.

Trees

A growing interest in trees as a rhythmic element is evident in the paintings of this time.

372. Woodland Scene
55 × 46 1879–82 V.314

373. The Forest of Fontainebleau
63 × 79 1879–82 V.332

374. Fontainebleau under Snow
New York, Meyer Collection
73 × 102 1879–82 V.336

375. Poplars
Paris, Louvre
65 × 80 1879–82 V.335
The vertical element is pronounced and this bears a

372

373

374

375 (plate XIX)

376

377

378

379

380

381

383

384

382

385

386

387

388

389

390

391

392

393

394

395

396

397

398

399

400

401

402

403

relation to Cézanne's study of tree structure. See plate XIX.

376. At L'Estaque
73 x 92 1882–5 V.409

377. At Jas de Bouffan
60 x 73 1882–5 V.413

378. Near the Exit from Jas de Bouffan
60 x 73 1882–5 V.414

379. Tree-Trunks and Houses (Gnarled Tree)
Arlesheim, Stoll Collection
46 x 55 1882–5 V.420

380. Gnarled Trees
116 x 81 1882–5 V.419

381. Woodland Scene
Cambridge, Fitzwilliam Museum
62·2 x 51·5 1882–5 V.421

382. Woodland Scene
1882–5 V.422

383. Village through the Trees
Bremen, Kunsthalle
65 x 81 *1885* V.438

384. Orchard on a Farm in Normandy
Paris, Ganay Collection
65 x 81 1885–6 V.447
Gowing thinks this is a landscape painted at Pontoise.

385. Orchard
61 x 50 1885–6 V.442

386. Orchard on a Farm in Normandy
London, Aberconway Collection
50 x 65 1885–6 V.443

387. Orchard on a Farm in Normandy
50 x 65 1885–6 V.445

388. Orchard
65 x 50 1885–6 V.444

389. Wood in Provence
Cardiff, National Museum of Wales
77 x 61 1885–6 V.446

390. Countryside at Arc
New York, Suydam Cutting Collection
81 x 65 1885–7 V.472

391. Great Pine and Red Earth
81 x 100 1885–7 V.459
Painted, like no. 392, in the Arc valley.

392. Great Pine and Red Earth
Moscow, Museum of Modern Western Art
73 x 92 1885–7 V.458

393. Chestnut-Trees at Jas de Bouffan
65 x 81 1885–7 V.467

394. Avenue at Jas de Bouffan
73 x 92 1885–7 V.471

395. Big Trees at Jas de Bouffan
London, Home House Trustees
65 x 81 1885–7 V.475

396. Big Trees at Jas de Bouffan
69 x 58 1885–7 V.474

404

405

406

407

410

408

409

411

412

413

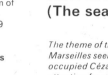

397. Chestnut-Trees at Jas de Bouffan in Winter
Minneapolis (Mi.), Institute of Arts
73 x 92 s 1885–7 V.476
The subject is a farm-house near Jas de Bouffan, and not the great house as previously thought. In the background is the Montagne Sainte-Victoire.

398. Chestnut-Trees at Jas de Bouffan
65 x 81 1885–7 V.478

399. Houses
Paris, Musées Nationaux (Walter-Guillaume Bequest)
54 x 73 1885–7 V.480

400. Houses
68 x 92 1885–7 V.479

401. Houses
Oslo, Nasjonalgalleriet
60 x 81 1885–7 V.481

402. Viaduct
Moscow, Museum of Modern Western Art
92 x 73 1885–7 V.477
Behind the trees is a glimpse of the Montagne Sainte-Victoire.

403. Mill and Tank
Merion (Pa.), Barnes Foundation
81 x 65 1885–7 V.485
View of the wood of Château-Noir; the subject was studied on more than one occasion, especially in the last years of the artist's life.

Bending road

In the years 1879 to 1882, the motif of the bending road occurred frequently. It goes back, however, to some paintings of about 1870 and the artist returned to it several times later.

404. Road at Auvers from Val Harmé
57 x 72 1879–82 V.313

405. Track in a Wood
55 x 46 1879–82 V.320

406. Côte du Galet at Pontoise
60 x 73 1879–82 V.319
According to Badt this painting is of an impression of nature subjected to rigorous order, particularly by means of the vertical stress in the poplars; yet the emphatic bend, known from the Pissarro version of the same subject (1867), is apparently simplified; thus, the S-bend makes a line independent of base directions, embracing the whole field of vision.

407. Wooded Country at Auvers
1879–82 V.312

408. Road with Trees and Pond
81 x 60 1879–82 V.327

409. Village
New York, Wildenstein Collection
54 x 45 1879–82 V.328

410. Hillside Houses
Boston (Mass.), Museum of Fine Arts
59·5 x 72 1879–82 V.329

411. Trees and Houses
60 x 73 1879–82 V.330

412. Trees and Houses
58 x 68 1879–82 V.334

413. At La Roche-Guyon
Northampton (Mass.), Smith College Museum of Art
62 x 75·5 1885 V.441

In the summer of 1885, Cézanne joined Renoir at La Roche-Guyon. It was an unhappy time, for the artist had just been through a brief love affair about which he wrote some letters to Zola.

At L'Estaque (The sea)

The theme of the bay of Marseilles seen from L'Estaque occupied Cézanne's critical attention from 1882 to 1887, the expanses of sea and mountain serving a space-volume function. A different treatment of the theme over the same period is noticeable (nos 307–9

414. Saint-Henri
66·5 x 83 1882–5 V.398

415. Trees and Houses from Above
65 x 81 1882–5 V.399

416. Trees and Houses from Above
60 x 73 1882–5 V.405

417. View through Trees
London, Butler Collection
73 x 60 1882–5 V.406

418. Marseilles Neighbourhood
60 x 73 1882–5 V.407

419. Mount Marseilleveyre and Maire Island
51 x 62 1882–5 V.408

420. The Gulf of Marseilles
Philadelphia (Pa.), Museum of Art
65 x 81 1882–5 V.411

421. The Gulf of Marseilles
Paris, Louvre
58 x 72 1883–5 V.428

422. The Gulf of Marseilles
New York, Metropolitan Museum of Art
73 x 100 1883–5 V.429
In the distance, the outcrops

414

415

416

417

418

419

420

421

422

423

424

425

426

427

428

of Marseilles, Notre-Dame de la Garde, Roucas Blanc and Mount Marseilleveyre.

423. Trees and Houses from Above
-The Hague, Gemeentemuseum
46 × 55 1883–6 V.427

424. Houses and Chimney-Stack from Above
38 × 46 1883–6 V.426

On the horizon are Mount Marseilleveyre and Maire Island.

425. Houses and Chimney-Stack
73 × 92 1883–6 V.425

426. Mountains
Philadelphia (Pa.) Museum of Art
60 × 73 s 1886–90 V.489

Curious clouds and some parts of the promontory are held to have been added later (Venturi). The stroke appears thick and unaccented in contrast with the light and regular work that characterises the painting. The signature too may have been an addition.

427. Rocks and Trees
78 × 97 1886–90 V.492

428. Gulf of Marseilles
Chicago (Ill.), Art Institute
76 × 97 1886–90 V.493

The Montagne Sainte-Victoire

The mountain was a cherished motif with Cézanne from early days. Gasquet remembered him exclaiming, "Look at Sainte-Victoire, what a line what a thirst for the sun !

How sad at evening when the load falls down . . . those blocks were of fire . . . and fire is in them still." It figures, in the period from 1885 to 1887 (given various view-points and the play of relief around), as the expression of his constructive ideal. "The motif is arid and this helps Cézanne simplify and regularise on a mounting scale" (Venturi).

429. Road at the Foot of the Mountain
Merion (Pa.), Barnes Foundation
45 × 53 1882–5 V.424

430. Upland with Houses and Trees
Moscow, Pushkin Museum
60 × 73 1882–5 V.423

431. View from Gardanne
73 × 92 1885–6 V.434

432. Gardanne Neighbourhood
US Government Property (Charles A. Loeser Bequest)
63 × 91·5 1885–6 V.435

433. Gardanne Neighbourhood
67·5 × 91·5 1885–6 V.437

434. Beaurecueil
Indianapolis (Ind.), Herron Museum of Art
65 × 81 1885–6 V.433

435. Gardanne Neighbourhood
60 × 73 1885–6 V.436

436. Viaduct and Big Trees
New York, Metropolitan Museum of Art
65 × 81 1885–7 V.452

437. Viaduct and Big Trees
48 × 59 1885–7 V.453

438. The Great Pine
London, Home House Trustees
67 × 92 s 1885–7 V.454

439. The Great Pine
Washington, D.C., Phillips Collection

429

430

431

432

433

434

435

436

437

438

439

440

442

60 × 73 1885–7 V.455

440. View from the South-West
54 × 65 1885–7 V.456
Probably painted from the Conil property belonging to Cézanne's brother-in-law.

441. View from the South-West
Merion (Pa.), Barnes Foundation
73 × 92 1885–7 V.457

442. View from the South-West
65 × 92 1886–9 V.488

Still-lifes

Cézanne's brush stroke becomes regular and constructive, consonant with his aim to simplify forms. Objects start having volume, at the same time acquiring structure mainly in chromatic terms. It has been observed that intense colours "model by colouring the object" concerned (Bernard).

Fruit and objects

443. Apples and Cloth
25 × 44 1875–80 V.203

444. Vessels, Fruit and Cloth
Moscow, Museum of Modern Western Art
45 × 57 1879–82 V.337

445. Jug, Fruit and Cloth
Moscow, Museum of Modern Western Art
50 × 61 1879–82 V.338

446. Vessels and Orange
New York, Museum of Modern Art
28 × 34 1879–82 V.340

447. Jug, Fruit, Cloth and Glass
Paris, Musées Nationaux (Walter-Guillaume Bequest)
60 × 73 1879–82 V.356

448. Glass, Cloth and Apples
Basle, Kunstmuseum (Staechelin Bequest)
31·5 × 40 1879–82 V.339

449. Fruit-Bowl, Cloth and Apples
Winterthur, Reinhart Collection
55 × 75 1879–82 V.344
There is a knife in the picture, obliquely-angled, after Manet (see also no. 452).

450. Apples and Plate of Biscuits
Paris, Musées Nationaux (Walter-Guillaume Bequest)
46 × 55 1879–82 V.343

451. Cloth and Apples
50 × 61 1879–82 V.346

452. Fruit-Bowl, Cloth, Glass and Apples
46 × 55 s 1879–82 V.341
The painting appears in the *Portrait of Marie Henry* by Gauguin (Chicago (Ill.), Art Institute) and *Hommage à Cézanne* by Denis (Paris, Musée du Luxembourg).

443

444

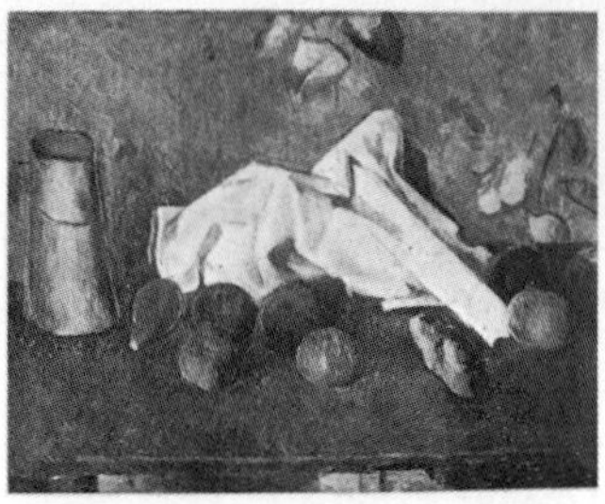
445

446

447

448

449

450

451

452

453

454

455

456

458

457

459

460

461

462

463

464

465

466

467

468

469

470

471

472

473

474

475

476

477

478

479

480

481

482

483

484

485

453. Fruit-Bowl, Cloth and Dish of Apples
Copenhagen, Ny Carlsberg Glyptotek
43·5 × 54 1879–82 V.342

454. Plate of Fruit and Jar
Merion (Pa.), Barnes Foundation
18 × 37 1879–82 V.363

455. Plate of Peaches
New York, Solomon R. Guggenheim Museum
60 × 73 1879–82 V 347

456. Plate of Fruit and Sugar-Bowl
24 × 33·5 1879–82 V.1606

457. Plate of Apples, Pears and Grapes
37 × 44 1879–82 V.345

458. Plate of Fruit
Prague, Národní Galerie
19 × 38 1879–82 V.348

459. Plate of Pears and Glass
18 × 38 1879–82 V.351

460. Plate of Fruit
Merion (Pa.), Barnes Foundation
19·5 × 35·5 1879–82 V.352

461. Plate of Pears
1879–82 V.350

462. Plate with Fig and Peaches
28 × 23 1879–82 V.353

463. Plate with Two Apples and a Pear
27 × 35 1879–82 V.354

464. Two Pears, Jar and Knife
New York, Museum of Modern Art
20 × 30 1879–82 V.349

465. Apples
1879–82 V.364

466. Apples
18 × 23 1879–82 V.355

467. Vessels, Cloth and Pot-Plant in Flower

60 × 73 1882–7 V.357

468. Tureen, Bottle and Basket of Apples
Paris, Louvre
65 × 81·5 1883–5 V.494

469. Salad-Bowl, Plate of Apples, Glass and Mirror
33 × 41 1883–5 V.495

470. Vessels, Fruit and Cloth in front of a Chest
Munich, Neue Staatsgalerie
71 × 90 1883–7 V.496
Probably painted, like no. 471, at Jas de Bouffan.

471. Vessels, Fruit and Cloth in front of a Chest
65 × 81 1883–7 V.497
See no. 470.

472. Plate of Cherries and Peaches, Vase and Cloth
Los Angeles (Calif.), County Museum of Art
50 × 61 1883–7 V.498

473. Pot with Lid and Plate of Fruit
35 × 46 1883–7 V.1518

474. Plate of Peaches and Pears
36 × 45 1883–7 V.504

475. Plate of Pears and Apples
36 × 45 1883–7 V.507

476. Plate of Apples
22 × 26 1883–7 V.509

477. Two Apples
14 × 24 1883–7 V.506

478. Two Pears
1883–7 V.505

479. Apples
1883–7 V.508

480. Hanging, Plate with Jug, Fruit-Bowl and Fruit
43 × 63 1885–7 V.499

481. Jug and Plate with Fruit
43 × 63 1885–7 V.500

482. Two Plates with Big Apples
45 × 59 1885–7 V.502

483. Plate and Two Apples
24 × 33 1885–7 V.503

484. Plate of Apples
38 × 46 1885–7 V.501

485. Plate and Apples on a Cloth
Chicago (Ill.), Art Institute
38 × 46 1886–90 V.510

Flowers

486. Fruit and Vase
Paris, Musées Nationaux (Walter-Guillaume Bequest)
34 × 21 1879–82 V.359

487. Red Vase
40 × 50 1879–82 V.358

488. Vase
46 × 55 1879–82 V.360

489. Light-Blue Vase
41·5 × 22 1879–82 V.361

490. Light-Blue Vase
Paris, Musées Nationaux (Walter-Guillaume Bequest)
29 × 22 1879–82 V.362

491. Green Vase
68 × 57 1883–7 V.511

492. Vase and Two Apples
Zurich, Bührle Collection
55 × 46 1883–7 V.513

493. Vase, Plate, Ink-Well and Fruit (Blue Vase)
Paris, Louvre
61 × 50 1883–7 V.512
The objects are outlined in blue, and blue is indeed the tone of the whole work. The flower-vase, which had hitherto been considered as an entity of its own now forms part of a more complex composition. See Plate XXIII.

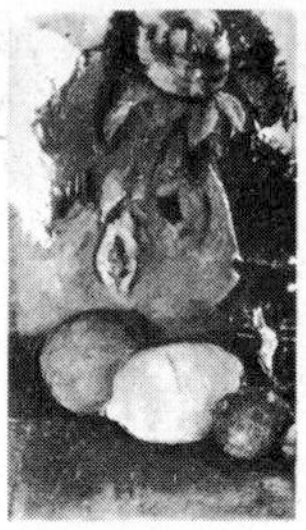
486

487

488

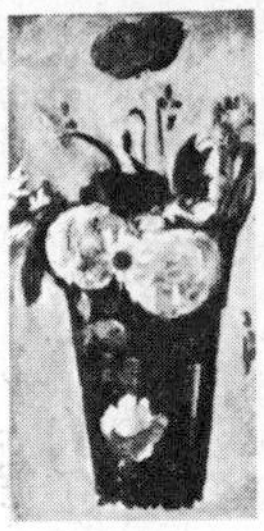
489

490

491

492

493 (plate XXIII)

Portraits

Cézanne, having favoured the direct probe of character – and indeed of soul – in the Impressionist period, now changes his attitude. The pace is altogether slower and steadier. His models now seem to be imbued with "straightforward vegetating life" (Raynal). This applies to his young son Paul, his wife and his friend Chocquet. Thin colour impasto and the fusion of the brushstrokes make for fullness of form, especially in the portraits of Hortense. Composed with a natural grace and spontaneous refinement, the volume dimension has been reduced. (nos 519, 528 and 530).

Self-portraits come with a number of variants. In some of them (for example, nos 509–11), the artist has used a more stylised approach, the figure being neatly detached from the ground; he also seems to be conducting something of an objective analysis of himself.

494. Head of a Boy
22 × 16 1877–80 V.281
This has been said to represent the artist's son Paul, aged 7 (Gowing).

495. Head of a Boy
Parke-Bernet sale 26 October 1967
22 × 13 1877–80 V.282
This may, like the previous number, represent the artist's son.

496. Head of Young Paul
29 × 32 1879–82 V.1522

497. Louis Guillaume
Washington, D.C., National Gallery of Art
56 × 47 1879–82 V.374
The model was the son of a neighbour.

498. Madame Cézanne with a Fan
Zurich, Bührle Collection
92·5 × 73 1879–82 V.369
A garment similar to that worn by Hortense Fiquet has been traced (Van Buren) to the *Journal des Dames* of 15 October 1878. See plate XIV.

499. Madame Cézanne in a Garden
Paris, Musées Nationaux (Walter-Guillaume Bequest)
81 × 65 1879–82 V.370
It appears to be a study; part of the background has not been filled in. See plate XV.

500. Woman in a Fur
53 × 49 1879–82 V.376
This seems to have been inspired by a print in the *Magasin pittoresque* of 1860 which in turn, was after an El Greco, the *Lady in Ermine*. But the features may resemble Cézanne's sister Marie. Cézanne must have modelled his work on the magazine, as he had copied Lancret, for the fame of El Greco in France was less in 1880 than subsequently (Badt).
Sterling states that, as the Louvre had nothing of El Greco until just before or immediately upon Cézanne's death, and as Cézanne had never been to Spain, the resemblance might spring from a visual kinship of perception (Sterling).

501. Victor Chocquet
Columbus (Ohio), Gallery of Fine Arts
46 × 38 1879–82 V.373

502. Victor Chocquet
Upperville (Va.), Mellon Collection
35 × 27 1879–82 V.375

494

495

496

497

498 (plate XIV)

499 (plate XV)

500

501

502

503 (plate IX)

504

505

506

507 (plate XVI)

508

509

510

511

512

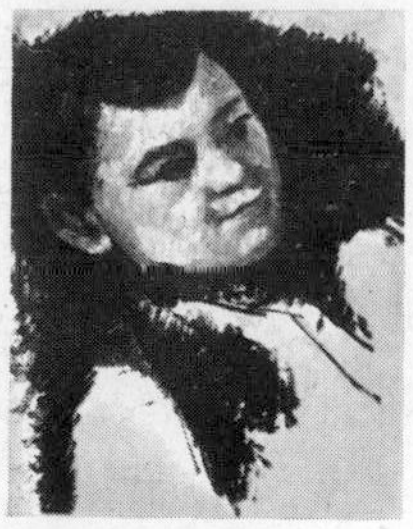
513

515

514

516

517

518

519

520

521

522

523

524 (plate XXIV)

525

526

527

528

529

530

531

532

533

534

503. Self-Portrait in a Hat
Berne, Kunstmuseum
65 × 51 1879–82 V.366
"Cézanne's geometric analysis is explicit here in the play of angles, triangles and parallels; the face stands out on a cylindriform ground without a hint of dryness because the artist was 'drawing with his brush'" (Raynal). See plate IX.

504. Self-Portrait
London, Tate Gallery
34 × 27 1879–82 V.365

505. Self-Portrait
Winterthur, Reinhart Collection
33 × 24 1879–82 V.367

506. Self-Portrait
Moscow, Museum of Modern Western Art
46 × 38 1879–82 V.368

507. Self-Portrait
Paris, Louvre
26 × 15 1880–1 V.371
This belonged to Pissarro. It has a vigorous approach, showing acute self-observation and at the same time, a determination to abstract and simplify. See plate XVI.

508. Self-Portrait
57 × 47 1880–1 V.372
This portrait was painted on wood and taken from the *Portrait of Cézanne* done in pastels by Renoir (1880), and now in Chicago (Ill.) (Ittleson Collection).

509. Self-Portrait
Paris, Goulandris Collection
25 × 25 1883–5 V.517

510. Self-Portrait
34 × 25 1883–5 V.518

511. Self-Portrait in a Bowler-Hat
Paris, Niarchos Collection
41 × 34 1883–5 V.515

512. Self-Portrait in a Bowler-Hat
Copenhagen, Ny Carlsberg Glyptotek
44·5 × 35·5 1883–7 V.514

513. Paul Cézanne
25 × 20 1883–5 V.534

514. Paul Cézanne
Paris, Musées Nationaux (Walter-Guillaume Bequest)
35 × 38 1883–5 V.535

515. Paul Cézanne
19·5 × 11·2 1883–5 V.536

516. Paul Cézanne in a Hat
Washington, D.C., National Gallery of Art
65 × 54 1885 V.519

517. Madame Cézanne
20·3 × 15·8 1883–5 V.533

518. Madame Cézanne
Paris, Berggruen Collection
46 × 38 *1885* V.520

519. Madame Cézanne
Philadelphia (Pa.), Museum of Art
46 × 38 *1885* V.521

520. Madame Cézanne
Philadelphia (Pa.), Museum of Art
46 × 38 1883–7 V.526

521. Madame Cézanne with her Hair Down
Philadelphia (Pa.), McIlhenny Collection
62 × 51 1883–7 V.527

522. Victor Chocquet
46 × 38 1883–7 ? V.532
According to Rivière this was painted in 1902, after the subject's death in 1899 and from a photograph.

523. Head of a Boy
28 × 32 1883–7 V.1521
Painted on paper.

524. Man Seated
Basle, Kunstmuseum (Staechelin Bequest)
55 × 46 1883–7 V.1519
See plate XXIV.

525. Self-Portrait with a Palette
Zurich, Bührle Collection
92 × 73 1885–7 V.516

526. Jules Peyron
25 × 31 1885–6 V.1607

527. Jules Peyron
46 × 38 1885–7 V.531

528. Madame Cézanne in Half Bust
73 × 60 1885–7 V.529

529. Madame Cézanne
47 × 39 1885–7 V.530

530. Madame Cézanne in a Shawl
Merion (Pa.), Barnes Foundation
89 × 71 1885–7 V.522

531. Madame Cézanne
Ardmore (Pa.), White Collection
46 × 38 1885–7 V.524

532. Madame Cézanne
New York, Solomon R. Guggenheim Museum
50 × 46 1885–7 V.525

533. Madame Cézanne with Clasped Hands
99 × 77 1885–7 V.528

534. Madame Cézanne in a Pleated Bodice
Paris, Musées Nationaux (Walter-Guillaume Bequest)
81 × 65 1885–90 V.523

Various compositions

Some of the subjects here seem to relate to literature or mythology, some to themes already treated earlier (no. 536 for example). But the real purpose was to work out the figure-space interrelation (see nos 539–40), or problems of structure and rounded forms in the female nude.

535. Female Nude with a Mirror
Merion (Pa.), Barnes Foundation
32 × 25 * 1878 * V.254
This was inspired by a painting of Delacroix, with additional component elements.

536. "Le déjeuner sur l'herbe"
34 × 39 1877 × 82 V.377
The subject was previously treated by the artist (nos 31 and 258). The debt to Manet is now in the title only.

537. Outing by Boat
1879–82 V.378

538. Reclining Boy
Worcester (Mass.), Art Museum
54 × 65 1882–7 V.391

539. Water-Maidens
35 × 44 1883–5 V.538

540. The Judgment of Paris
52 × 62 1883–5 V.537

541. Leda and the Swan
Merion (Pa.), Barnes Foundation
60 × 73 1886–90 ? V.550
According to Vollard the inspiration was drawn from *Lady with a Parrot* by Courbet.

535

536

537

538

539

540

541

542

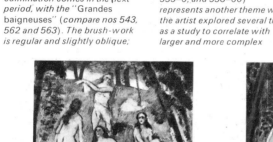

542. Reclining Female Nude
40 × 55 1886–90 ? V.551
On the left, a still-life painted with the canvas the other way round. It is said to be an illustration of Zola's *Nana*. (Vollard). But Venturi's thesis is that the novel was finished in 1880 at Médan, whereas the style of painting looks later than that date.

Bathers

The image construction relying especially on colour becomes rhythmical, and this creates a counter-point between figures and landscape. The culmination comes in the next period, with the "Grandes baigneuses" *(compare nos 543, 562 and 563). The brush-work is regular and slightly oblique; plastic mass is read from the foreground to the back and this adds to dynamic stress to the composition, more meaningful in the outcome than the poses of the various figures.*
The Bather Standing *(nos 555–6, and 558–60) represents another theme which the artist explored several times: as a study to correlate with larger and more complex paintings, or else as an essay in realism. Here, the strength of composition relies on geometric structure in terms of horizontal, perpendicular and oblique lines.*

543. Three Women
Paris, Petit Palais
58 × 54·5 1879–82 V.381
Given to the museum by Matisse, who bought it in his youth.

544. Four Women
46 × 38 1879–82 V.384

545. Four Women
27 × 35 1879–82 V.386

546. Five Women
Merion (Pa.), Barnes Foundation
40 × 42 1879–82 V.383

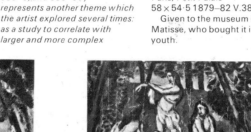

547. Five Women

543

544

545

546

547

548

549

550

551

552

553

554

555

556

557

558

559

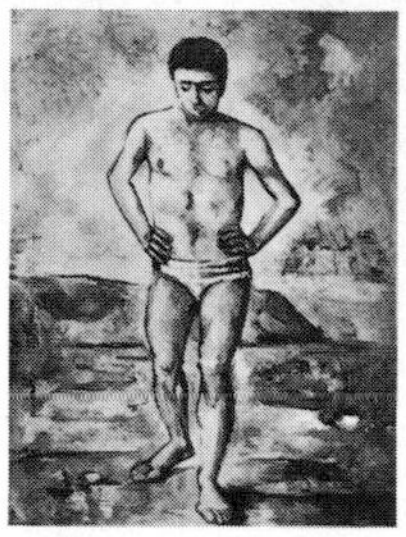
560

43 × 53 1879–82 V.385

548. Five Women
38 × 41 1879–82 V.382

549. Seven Men
38 × 46 1879–82 V.387

550. Five Men
19 × 26 1879–82 V.388

551. Five Men
35 × 39 1879–82 V.389

562

563

564

561

565

566 *(plate XXV)*

552. Five Men
60 × 73 1879–82 V.390

553. Two Men
Zurich, Bührle Collection
42·5 × 33 1879–82 V.392

554. Three Men
35 × 22 1879–82 V.395

555. Man Standing, Rear View
33 × 22 1879–82 V.393

556. Man Standing, Rear View
27 × 17 1879–82 V.394

557. Six Men
39 × 53 1883–7 V.541

558. Man Standing, Arms Extended
33 × 24 1883 V.544
In the background is a landscape of L'Estaque as in no. 559.

559. Man Standing, Arms Extended
73 × 60 1885–7 V.549

560. Man Standing, Hands on Hips
New York, Museum of Modern Art
126 × 95 1885–7 V.548

561. Women in Front of a Tent
Stuttgart, Staatsgalerie
63 × 81 1883–5 V.543

562. Eight Women
28 × 44 1883–7 V.540
The stretcher is inscribed, in the hand of Cézanne, with the following words: "Hommage respectueux de l'auteur à la Reine des Félibriges, P. Cézanne 5 Mai 1896."

563. Eight Women
28·5 × 51 1883–7 V.539

564. Five Women
20 × 21 1883–7 V.545

565. Four Women
39 × 35 1883–7 V.547

566. Five Women
Basle, Kunstmuseum
65·5 × 65·5 1885–7 V.542
The composition focuses on the female figures; now much simplified, they impress one as solemn and monumental.
See plate XXV.

Period of synthesis

1888–1906

Cézanne began seeing less of people. The reasons were various, one being his persistent quest of style control. Living withdrawn, his preference turned more and more in the direction of Aix and the countryside around it, where he made long stays before finally settling down.

Young artists, such as Bernard and Camoin, paid him visits. The critical attention which his work eventually attracted made them want to hear his views and see him at work. But he guarded his solitude, preferring to paint on alone and travel daily to a chosen spot "sur le motif", somewhere outdoors.

The subjects are sometimes new: the *Card-Players* (nos 630–40), or the masked figures (nos 621–4). In the main, his interests continue unchanged, as throughout his working life. The aim was still to perfect and synthesise, and confront the problems inherent in the demands he made of himself.

Portraits

In Cézanne's painting of this period, the function of the model is stressed. Features are carefully delineated, the underlying logic firmly constructive, to the exclusion of pleasing individual facts. As a result, he arrives at a kind of characterisation of a particular type of human being (see nos 567, 574, 599, 601, 610 and most especially no. 612). The form is concise, the geometrics sound; the effect is of a solemn and monumental order (nos 569, 572 and especially no. 578). The attitude is quite natural (nos 579 and 580), achieving a synthesis relative to the figure and the ground. The colour, especially in the later work, of a thinner flowing paste, consonant with the artist's long experience in watercolour technique. Where the action of light governs the material (nos 616 and 620), the figure loses nothing of its solidity.

567. Gardener with a Hoe
Merion (Pa.), Barnes Foundation
64 × 53 1886–90 V.546

568. Victor Chocquet
81 × 65 1889 V.562

569. Madame Cézanne in the Conservatory
New York, Metropolitan Museum of Art
92 × 73 *1890* V.569
One of the best-known portraits of Hortense. A good deal of canvas is left uncovered, but the effect is at once elegant and graceful. "The continuous line of the brow, the facial oval beneath the concave area of hair, the nose, mouth and chin of formal regularity, reveal the artist's geometric ideal" (Venturi).

570. Madame Cézanne in a Yellow Chair
Chicago (Ill.), Art Institute
81 × 65 1890 V.572
The red dress contrasts with the yellow chair; in the ground are various tones of light-blue. The portrayal of the artist's wife has been described as follows. "The lady's character is clear, calm, satisfied, simple and attractive; turned forty and very nineteenth-century, she is eminently middle-class" (Venturi).
See plate XLVI.

571. Madame Cézanne in a Yellow Chair
81 × 65 1890–4 V.571

572. Madame Cézanne in Red
São Paulo, Museu de Arte
89 × 70 1890–4 V.573
The simple pose, the crystal clarity of light mould the figure superbly; the oval rhythm works slowly but overall, gentle yet massive like a new Giotto" (Valsecchi).
In the red-dress portraits of about 1890, the "perspective cube of traditional representation has quite disappeared" (Ponente). The painter in fact "achieves a new synthesis between figure and setting, making the image come across with greater monumentality".
See plate XLI.

573. Madame Cézanne in a Yellow Chair
116 × 89 1890–4 V.570

574. Madame Cézanne in a White Dressing-Jacket
55 × 46 1890–4 V.577

575. Self-Portrait in a Soft Hat
1890–4 V.579

576. Self-Portrait
46 × 40 1890–4 V.578

577. Labourer Seated
55 × 46 1890–4 V.565

578. Woman with a Coffee-Pot
Paris, Louvre
130 × 97 1890–4 ? V.574
According to the artist's son this was painted in 1887. Venturi thinks it is later, and it is dated 1892 by Gowing, and 1890–2 by Cooper. The sitter was a servant at Jas de Bouffan.

567

568

569

570 *(plate XLVI)*

571

572 *(plate XLI)*

573

574

575

576

577

578 *(plate XXXII)*

See plate XXXII.

579. Boy in a Red Waistcoat, Side View
81 × 65 1890–5 V.680
Traditionally said to represent an Italian boy called Michelangelo Di Rosa.

580. Boy in a Red Waistcoat Leaning on his Elbow
Zurich, Bührle Collection
79·5 × 64 1890–5 V.681
The boy's arm, very long in proportion to the body, expresses a sense of utter relaxation on the part of the model.
See plates XLIX–L.

581. Boy in a Red Waistcoat, Standing
92 × 73 1890–5 V.682

582. Boy in a Red Waistcoat, Front View
Merion (Pa.), Barnes Foundation
65 × 54 1890–5 V.683

583. Girl with a Doll
92 × 73 1892–6 V.675

584. Woman Seated with a Book
Merion (Pa.), Barnes Foundation
92 × 73 1892–6 V.575

585. Bust of Seated Woman
65 × 54 1892–6 V.576

586. Madame Cézanne in a Hat
Merion (Pa.), Barnes Foundation
100 × 81 1894–5 V.704

587. Girl in Half-Bust
55 × 46 1894–5 V.676

588. Bust of a Young Man
73 × 60 1894–5 V.677

589. Gustave Geoffroy
116 × 89 1895 V.692
Painted in the Belleville house, between April and July 1895. See also *Outline biography*, **1894**.

590. Boy with a Skull
Merion (Pa.), Barnes Foundation
130 × 97 1894–6 V.679
There is a Giulio Campagnola engraving, similarly composed. As in Delacroix, death was often present in the work of Cézanne (Lichtenstein). The tragic view of life was part of the Romantic concept of Love.
"It was a canvas that he loved . . . one of the few he sometimes mentioned after the work had been given away" (Gasquet).

591. Boy with a Book
1894–6 V.678
The same young man of no. 590 was the model.

592. Italian Girl Leaning on a Table
New York, Bakwin Collection
92 × 73 *1896* V.701
Probably painted in Montmartre, rue Gabrielle; the model was a relative of Michelangelo Di Rosa, the *Boy in a Red Waistcoat* (nos 579–82).

593. Girl in a Straw Hat
69 × 58 1896 V.700

594. Girl in a Straw Hat
81 × 65 1896 V.698

595. Joachim Gasquet
Prague, Národní Galerie
65 × 54 1896–7 V 694
Gasquet was a poet from Aix, later among the artist's biographers; Cézanne met him in 1896. Here, again the element of form is stressed and in consequence the definition of planes and volume content, the whole being achieved by contrasting chromatic values.
See plate LIV

596. Henri Gasquet
55 × 46 1896–7 V.695
The sitter was the father of Joachim Gasquet.

597. Woman Sitting at a Table
64 × 53 1895–1900 V 1611

598. Man with Folded Arms (The Clockmaker)
New York, Solomon R. Guggenheim Museum
92 × 73 1895–1900 V.689

599. Man with Folded Arms
Annapolis (Ma.), Mitchell Collection
92 × 73 1895–1900 V.685

600. Man with a Pipe, Leaning on a Table
Mannheim, Städtische Kunsthalle
92 × 73 1895–1900 V.684

601. Man with a Pipe, Leaning on a Table
Leningrad, Hermitage
92 × 73 1895–1900 V.686

602. Man with a Pipe Leaning on a Table
Moscow, Museum of Modern Western Art
92 × 73 1895–1900 V.688

603. Drinker
46 × 37 1895–1900 V.690

604. Bust of a Seated Peasant
81 × 65 1895–1900 V.687
On the right is a sketch of female figure.

605. Peasant Seated
1895–1900 V.691

606. Ambroise Vollard
Paris, Petit Palais
100 × 81 1899 V.696
The sitter was a collector, art-dealer and writer. Shortly before 1894, he came and settled in the rue Lafitte, Paris where the galleries were. Rewald writes that "Vollard's taste in matters artistic was not over-confident and at first he was relatively undiscerning. But, knowing his shortcomings, he welcomed advice from other people. By good fortune, it happened to come from Pissarro and sometimes Degas. On this, he was quick to act. At Pissarro's insistence, he got in contact with Cézanne who sent in no less than 150 paintings. This was more than Vollard could exhibit at any one time. The Vollard exhibition opened in the autumn of 1895. Cézanne had not shown in

579

580 (*plates XLIX-L*)

581

582

583

584

585

586

587

588

589

590

591

592

593

594

595 (*plate LIV*)

596

597

598

599

600

601

602

603

604

605

606

607

608

609

610

611

612 (plates LVII-LVIII)

613

614

615

616 (plate LXIII)

617

618

619

620

Paris for nearly twenty years, so the result was little short of startling. The public as usual took offence, the critics continued to give him bad notices but the artists of the avant-garde and his old colleagues hailed him as a master."

Vollard wrote the first Cézanne biography, richly anecdotal and with a chapter on this very portrait.

607. Man Seated with a Paper
Oslo, Nasjonalgalleriet
100 × 73 1898–1900 V.697

608. Self-Portrait with Beret and Beard
65 × 54 1898–1900 V.693

609. Girl with a Doll
73 × 60 1900–2 V.699

610. Lady in Blue
Moscow, Museum of Modern Western Art
88 × 71 1900–4 V.705

The model is the same as in no. 611.

611. Lady with a Book
65 × 50 1900–4 V.703

612. Old Woman with a Rosary
London, National Gallery
85 × 65 1900–4 V.702

Cézanne spent eighteen months at work on this old lay-sister to whom he habitually gave alms. Gasquet recalled Cézanne having seen "a touch of Flaubert" in the picture, "a mood, something indefinable, a flow of colour red and bluish, which I think belongs to Madame Bovary". See plates LVII and LVIII.

613. Peasant Seated, with a Stick
72 × 58·5 1900–4 V.713

614. Peasant Seated, with a Soft Hat
Ottawa, National Gallery of Canada
92 × 73 1900–4 V.712

615. Peasant Seated Outdoors
65 × 54 1900–6 V.714

616. Vallier Full-Length (The Gardener)
London, Tate Gallery
63 × 52 1900–6 V.715

Vallier the gardener was the model for Cézanne's last portraits. The brushstroke is free and fluid, in token of the ever-increasing mastery of watercolour technique. See plate LXIII.

617. Vallier Full-Length
65 × 54 1904–6 V.1524

618. Beggar (Vallier)
Washington, D.C., National Gallery of Art
107·4 × 74·5 1904–5 V.716

This portrait has been said to result from the following combination: an old beggar, who served as model; and after he left, Cézanne himself – who put on old clothes in order that the work might continue (Gasquet). The resemblance to Vallier, however, is too plain to disregard (Venturi).

619. Beggar (Vallier)
100 × 81 1904–5 V.717

620. Vallier in a Straw Hat
65 × 54 1906 V.718

The paint here is thick and creamy, the brush-work very free. It is deemed Cézanne's final portrait (Venturi).

Various compositions

In this field too, Cézanne's growing preoccupation with the human figure is apparent. A brief series of costumed figures (nos 621–4) belong to a world apart rather than to the realm of humour; their vigour is impressive. Delacroix was still admired by Cézanne; see the copy (no. 629) of one of his works. The Card-Players *motif deserves separate mention; it is not wide-ranging in itself, but significant within the limited number of master-themes.*

621. Mardi-Gras
Moscow, Museum of Modern Western Art
100 × 81 1888 V.552

The date was supplied by Chocquet, the painting's original owner. According to the artist's son, however, it was done in the Paris studio, rue du Val-de-Grâce. A piece of Cézanne's thought it painted at Jas de Bouffan. The models were: for Harlequin, the painter's son Paul, and for Pierrot, Louis Guillaume. The two figures have also been held to represent Cézanne and Zola (Badt).

The influence of the French popular theatre has also been suggested (Sterling), because of the set, innocent expressions; a link with the spirit of Le Nain's day and the ingenious gravity of Épinal's colour prints.

622. Harlequin
92 × 65 1888–90 V.553

623. Harlequin
92 × 65 1889–90 V.554

624. Harlequin
1888–90 V.555

625. Preparing a Banquet
45 × 53 *1890* V.586

626. Boat and Bathers
30 × 124 1890–4 V.583

The canvas is now in three pieces, the sides in the Walter-Guillaume Bequest collection, Musées Nationaux, Paris and the centre portion, whereabouts unknown.

It was intended for Chocquet's apartment, like no. 627; probably as an over-door painting. Commissioned in 1888 it was however unfinished by Chocquet's death (1891); it was included in the Chocquet sale of 1899.

627. Fountain (Trough with a Peacock)
30 × 124 1890–4 V.584

On the art market, New York. See no. 626.

628. Female Nude
Geneva, Waechter Collection
93 × 71 *1895* V.710

The model is said to have been one Marie-Louise (G. Rivière); or perhaps the artist's wife (Venturi).

629. Hagar in the Wilderness
50 × 65·5 1899 V.708

Copy of a Delacroix which had belonged to Chocquet; in 1899, Vollard bought it and gave it to Cézanne (Venturi).

Card-players

Painted about 1890–2 at Aix, the subjects were local peasants. Portrait studies (nos 630, 631, 633, 636, 637 and 640) precede the composite work, when each individual assumes universal significance. It is done by conclusive handling of form, synthesised gesture and intense colour areas creating a serried whole. "Zonal rhythm" (Venturi) stands instead of the modelling of form. As Cézanne explained to Larguier, "Painting does not mean making a slavish copy of the object in view; it is capturing the harmony between

621

622

623

624

629

625

626

627

628

variously related things."

630

631

632

634

633

636 (plate XXXIV)

637

640

635 (plate XXXV)

638

639 (plates XXXVI-XXXVII and XXXVIII-XL)

630. Peasant Standing with Folded Arms
Merion (Pa.), Barnes Foundation
1888–9 V.561

631. Man with a Pipe and Folded Arms
39 × 30 1890–2 V.563

632. Five Card-Players
Merion (Pa.), Barnes Foundation
134 × 181 1890–2 V.560

633. Card-Player
Worcester (Mass.), Art Museum
32 × 35 1890–2 V.568

634. Four Card-Players
65 × 81 1890–2 V.559

635. Two Card-Players
London, Home House Trustees
58 × 69 1890–2 V.557
The man on the left is the gardener "père Alexandre". Strikingly put together, the elementary colour contrasts are supported by endless gradations. The yellow-brown of the player on the right, the violet blue of the one on the left; behind, the slate-blue of the landscape background. See plate XXXV.

636. Man with a Pipe
London, Home House Trustees
73 × 60 1890–2 V.564
A study of "père Alexandre" the gardener, see also nos 635, 638–9. The figure is built by means of elementary planes and the arrangement of colours is complex. "A Cézanne peasant is individual in the portrayal and universal in the idea; monumental without and unshakably convinced within" (Venturi). See plate XXXIV.

637. Man with a Pipe
26 × 20·5 1890–2 V.566

638. Two Card-Players
97 × 130 1890–2 V.556

639. Two Card-Players
Paris, Louvre
45 × 57 1890–2 V.558
The two players of nos 635 and 638 reappear. The treatment of volume and plane is simpler and at the same time stronger; the effect, more life-like still. The landscape background is barely hinted at in tonal values of violet, grey-blue and white. See plates XXXVI–XXXVII, XXXVIII, XXXIX and XL.

640. Peasant
55 × 46 1890–2 V.567

Bathers

Over the previous years, this theme had been given varied treatment. The aim now is to balance landscape with figure content until the latter becomes integral (see no. 657). There are some rather statuesque nudes as earlier. But by degrees, an extraordinary expressive synthesis is achieved (no. 652) and dynamic strength (nos. 653 and 655). The fusion of figures and landscape architecture results. The colour material is luminous and fluid, light-bluish areas of shade; the line is moist and soft (no. 658). Patiently aligning the means of expression, a consensus is reached embracing all components (of especial significance in this regard is no. 657).

641. Five Men
54 × 65 1888–90 V.582

642. Four Men
Paris, Louvre
22 × 33 1890–4 V.585
See plate XLII.

643. Group of Men and Women
22 × 35 1890–4 V.589

644. Group of Men and Women
Philadelphia (Pa.), Museum of Art
21 × 30·8 1892–4 V.591

645. Five Men
Moscow, Museum of Modern Western Art
27 × 41 1892–4 V.588

646. Four Men
Merion (Pa.), Barnes Foundation
30·5 × 40·5 1892–4 V.590

647. Six Men
52 × 63 1892–4 V.581

648. Group of Men
Paris, Louvre
60 × 81 1892–4 V.580
The attitudes are human, not idealised; though Cézanne's rounded form makes the nudes lyrical, it remains subordinate to the monumental effect (Raynal). See plate XLIII.

649. Group of Men
22 × 33 1892–4 V.587

650. Six Men
27 × 46 *1895* V.724

651. Group of Men
30 × 44 *1895* V.727
A lithograph of this was made by Roussel, and published in the *Album Cézanne* issued by Bernheim-Jeune, 1914.

652. Group of Men and Women
24 × 27 1900–4 V.728
Published by Venturi when it belonged to Ambroise Vollard, and seen as powerfully expressive.

653. Group of Men
20 × 33 1900–6 V.729

654. Four Women
Copenhagen, Ny Carlsberg Glyptotek

641

642 (plate XLII)

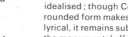

643

644

645

646

647

648 (plate XLIII)

649

650

651

652

653

654

656

655

657 (plate LV)

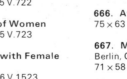

660

662

658 (plates LX-LXI)

659

661

73×92 *1900* V.726

655. Group of Women
73×92 1898–1905 V.725
Probably the preparatory study for no. 657.

656. Four Women
New York, Juviler Collection
33·5×20·5 1895–8
Not listed by Venturi; published by Richardson in 1956. It seems directly associable with no. 657, interposing the reclining figure in the group on the right.

657. Group of Women ("Les grandes baigneuses" – I)
Philadelphia (Pa.), Museum of Art
208×249 1898–1905 V.719
This "masterpiece of architectonic fantasy" (Venturi) is traditionally said to have taken seven years to paint. A niece of Cézanne's has recently recalled him working it out at the Lauves studio, specially built for him. Certainly it is the most perfectly concluded of the *Bathers* series. All is fused; in the colour atmosphere, relative mass is harmonious everywhere, everything has a place and purpose; its architecture is sublime" (Ponente).
The breathing space between the two groups leads the eye through to a vast landscape background. This is not distinct from the figures; it includes them, projects them continually back against the distance; the images evoke the landscape and bring it into being (Waldfogel). The arc movement joins the two groups along the line it describes; it also links the various planes and view in the background. Thus, the interval itself which acceeds to the background performs a unifying function. See plate LV.

658. Group of Women ("Les grandes baigneuses" – II)
London, National Gallery
130×195 1900–5 V.721
Referred to 1904–5 by Gowing, since colour and stroke are directly comparable with his 1905 style. The line is moist and soft, the whole immersed in light-bluish shade; even the usual violet half-tones are muted.
The problem of relating figures and background so that they become integral has been solved even more brilliantly through the medium of a sole reclining figure (Waldfogel): a focus between foreground and background, the first plane of vision and the second, the right-hand and the left-hand group. See plates LX–LXI.

659. Group of Women ("Les grandes baigneuses" – III)
Merion (Pa.), Barnes Foundation
133×207 1900–5 V.720

660. Group of Women
Chicago (Ill.), Art Institute
50×61 1900–5 V.722

661. Group of Women
29×36 1900–5 V.723

662. Sketch with Female Figures
65×81 1900–6 V.1523

Landscapes

Nature view, in Cézanne's late period, gain in unity of composition by use of fluid and transparently fused colour. The landscape is at one, whether there is water in it or otherwise. The leafy trees of Chantilly are painted with close criss-crossing brush-work (nos 666–7). The areas of colour are vibrantly luminous throughout. This does not diminish the structural entity; it makes the composition, more synthesised and dynamic (see nos 690, 692, 704 and 730), especially in the case of motifs from the loved Aix countryside of Lauves, Bibémus and Château-Noir.

663. House and Mountain
Zurich, Bührle Collection
73×91 1885–95 V.483

664. Avenue at Chantilly
23×17 1888 V.626

665. Avenue at Chantilly
Toledo (Ohio), Museum of Art
81×65 1888 V.627

666. Avenue at Chantilly
75×63 1888 V.628

667. Meadow and Trees
Berlin, Cassirer Collection
71×58 *1888* V.633

668. Château de Marines
73×92 1888–90 V.636

669. Chestnut Avenue at Jas de Bouffan
81×65 1888–90 V.649

670. Pool and Trough at Jas de Bouffan
65×81 1888–90 V.648

671. Bellevue House and Dove-Cot
Essen, Museum Folkwang
65×81 1888–92 V.651

672. Bellevue House and Dove-Cot
54×73 1888–92 V.652

673. Bellevue Dove-Cot
1888–92 V.653

674. Bellevue Dove-Cot
Cleveland (Ohio), Museum of Art
65×81 1888–92 V.650

675. Bellevue Dove-Cot
58×78 1888–92 V.654

676. "La Colline des Pauvres"
New York, Metropolitan Museum of Art
63×81 1888–94 V.660

677. Lines of Apple Trees
Merion (Pa.), Barnes Foundation
1890–4 V.642

678. Provençal House
Merion (Pa.), Barnes Foundation
65×81 1890–4 V.643

679. House and Trees
Merion (Pa.), Barnes Foundation
65×81 1890–4 V.646

680. Woodland Scene
1890–4 V.645

681. Woodland Scene
1890–4 V.647

682. Bellevue Houses
60×73 1890–4 V.655
The planes are clearly defined and the brushstroke moves freely especially in the foliage. See plate XXXIII.

683. Pilon du Roi
Winterthur, Reinhart Collection
80×98 1890–4 V.658

684. Hunting Lodge in Provence
Merion (Pa.), Barnes Foundation
54×81 1890–4 V.671

685. Trees and Road
73×60 1890–4 V.672

686. Ruined House
New York, Haupt Collection
65×54 1892–4 V.657

687. Deserted House
49×58·5 1892–4 V.659

688. The Great Pine
São Paulo, Museu de Arte
84×92 1892–6 V.669
Painted at Montbriant on the property of Cézanne's brother-in-law. See plate XLVII.

689. Clearing
100×81 1892–6 V.670

690. Château-Noir
Winterthur, Reinhart Collection
73×92 1894–6 V.667
The artist had a studio by Château-Noir, a fine house near Aix. He was often at work there in the late period.

691. Rocks in a Wood
New York, Metropolitan Museum of Art
73×93 1894–8 V.673
Perhaps a view of the forest of Fontainebleau (Venturi).

692. Rocks in a Wood
Zurich, Kunsthaus
48·5×59·5 1894–8 V.674
Perhaps a view of the forest of Fontainebleau. However, "the actual setting goes for little, given the picture's autonomy. The rebounding perspectives, continually re-aligning, produce a newly-probed depth of emotive content" (Ponente).
Cézanne's words are relevant in this context, as recalled by

663

664

665

666

668

667

669

670

671

672

673

674

675

676

677

678

679

680

681

682 (plate XXXIII)

683

684

685

686

687

688 (plate XLVII)

689

690

691

692 (plate XLVIII)

693

694

695

699

700

701

696

697

698

702

703

704 (plate LVI)

705

706 (plate LIX)

707

709

708

710

711

712

713

714

715

716

717

718

719

720

721

722

723

724

725

726

727

728

Gasquet : "Nature is always the same though nothing remains of what we see now. Art must have impact on nature in recording the elements and appearance that go with each change. Thus, art lets us sample eternal nature." See plate XLVIII.

693. Maison Maria on the Château-Noir Road
65 x 81 1895–8 V.761

694. Big Trees
London, Klessler Collection
81 x 65 1895–8 V.760

695. Woodland Scene
81 x 65 1895–1900 V.1527

696. Woodland Scene
73 x 57 1895–1900 V.1526

697. Montgeroult at Sunset
81 x 65 1899 V.668
Montgeroult was a little village near Pontoise, where Cézanne lived for a while in 1899.

698. Farm at Montgeroult
64 x 52 1899 V.656

699. Rock Cave at Bibémus
Essen, Museum Folkwang
65 x 81 1898–1900 V.767

700. Rock Cave at Bibémus
79 x 63·5 1898–1900 V 772

701. Rock Cave at Bibémus
Merion (Pa.), Barnes Foundation
90 x 71 1898–1900 V.773

702. Mill in Château-Noir Grounds
Philadelphia (Pa.), Museum of Art
73 x 92 1898–1900 V.768
The mill was still on site in 1936.

703. Sea at L'Estaque
97 x 78 1898–1900 V.770

704. Trees and Rocks
New York, Museum of Modern Art
81 x 65 *1900* V.774
The location is the Aix neighbourhood, between Bibémus and Château-Noir (Venturi). The wood in a storm is a landscape motif dear to the artist. Tones of light-blue, violet and orange predominate. See plate LVI.

705. Trees and Rocks
79 x 64 *1900* V.775

706. Trees and Rocks (The Red Rock)
Paris, Musées Nationaux (Walter-Guillaume Bequest)
91 x 66 1900 V.776
To the right is the square orange-red rock, positioned, like the blue-green foliage, against a pale blue sky. The violet shadows and orange-red reflected light from the sun give the picture warmth. See plate LIX.

707. Rock Cave at Bibémus
Zurich, Bührle Collection
65 x 54 *1900* V.777

708. Rock Cave at Bibémus
65 x 54 *1900* V.778

709. Bibémus
New York, Solomon R. Guggenheim Museum
71·5 x 90 *1900* V.781

710. Water-Tank in Château-Noir Park
73 x 60 *1900* V.780

711. Château-Noir Park
Paris, Musées Nationaux (Walter-Guillaume Bequest)
92 x 73 *1900* V.779

712. Château-Noir Park
60 x 81 *1900* V.784

713. Château-Noir Park
93 x 74 *1900* V.787

714. Bibémus
44 x 53 1900–2 V.782

715. Rocks and Trees at Bibémus
50 x 61 1900–4 V.785

716. Rocks and Trees at Bibémus
65 x 54 1900–4 V.786

717. Rocks and Trees in Château-Noir Park
92 x 73 1900–4 V.788

718. Village Church
92 x 71 1900–4 V.1531

719. Houses on a Hill
65 x 81 1900–6 V.1528

720. Bending Road
73 x 92 1900–6 V.1532

721. Provence Woodland
1900–6 V.791

722. Trees and Rocks
61 x 50 1900–6 V.792

723. Bending Road in a Wood
81 x 65 1900–6 V.789

724. Bending Road
Munich, Neue Pinakothek
81 x 65 1900–6 V.790

725. Trees and Houses (Landscape in Blue)
Moscow, Museum of Modern Western Art
102 x 83 1900–6 V.793

726. Forest
Ottawa, National Gallery of Canada
80 x 65 1902–4 V.1530

727. Les Lauves
64 x 80 1902–6 V.1610
The district is in the neighbourhood of Aix.

728. Château-Noir
Washington, D.C., National Gallery of Art
73·7 x 96·6 1904 V.796

729. Château-Noir
London, Clark Collection
70 x 82 1904–6 V.797

730. Château-Noir
73 x 92 1904–6 V.795

731. Château-Noir
73 x 92 1904–6 V.794

732. House and Trees ("Le Cabanon de Jourdan")
Milan, Private collection
65 x 81 1906 V.805
The painting is unfinished; it is Cézanne's last painting in oils. "The representation of the dwelling shows the painter's obsessive geometry at work again, when technically freedom of mastery was being attained. Yet in the surrounding trees, the treatment of form is supremely lyrical: it explodes under the thrust of colour feeling. To his dying day, Cézanne knew a tyranny of conflict between mind and feeling." (Raynal) See plate LXIV.

River and lake-side themes

Interest in such themes became marked about 1880–90. Cézanne's main concern was rendering the reflections "transparent enough and so ordered as to have a volume value too" (Venturi). Subsequently, similar themes came in for fresh treatment; the difference is gradual, tending always to abstract and simplify (nos 745, 747 and 749).

733. Banks of the Marne
50 x 61 *1888* V.629

734. Banks of the Marne
Leningrad, Hermitage
65 x 81 *1888* V.630

735. Houses on the Banks of the Marne (Fishermen)
63 x 79 *1888* V.632

736. Bridge over the Marne at Créteil
Moscow, Pushkin Museum
71 x 90 *1888* V.631
An extraordinary feat according to Venturi. The colours reflected in the water have all been ordered in pictorial terms of pure mass. "The free brushstrokes, transparent as watercolour, do not follow the form of objects . . . instead they run parallel. The different passages of the painting are fused as a result; the whole is consonant and evokes a sense of the universal infinite" (Malizkaia). See plate XXVII.

737. House on a River Bank
81 x 65 1888–90 V.635

738. Trees and Houses on a River Bank
73 x 92 1888–90 V.634

739. Trees on a River Bank (Waters and Boughs)
75 x 63 1888–90 V.638

740. Trees and Houses on a River Bank
73 x 92 1888–90 V.637

741. Trees and Houses on a River Bank
65 x 92 1888–90 V.639

742. Aqueduct and Lock
73 x 92 1888–90 V.640

743. Bridge over a Pool
Moscow, Museum of Modern Western Art
64 x 79 1888–90 V.641

744. Trees on a River Bank
50 x 61 1888–94 V.644
The colours are unfamiliar in Cézanne; therefore deemed (Venturi) a copy of a Romantic School work.

745. Lake Annecy
London, Home House Trustees
64 x 81·3 1896 V.762
A view of Château de Duingt on Lake Annecy, seen from Talloires where Cézanne spent the summer of 1896. The tree-trunk in the foreground sets the rest of the landscape further back; the transparent air-space is thus fused with the composition's massively solid quality and the unity of vision is complete (Venturi). See plates XLIV–XLV.

746. Torrent in a Wood
Cleveland (Ohio), Museum of Art
60 x 81 1898–1900 V.783

747. Trees and Houses on a River Bank
65 x 81 *1900* V.771

748. Houses on a River Bank
73 x 60 1900–6 V.769

729

730

731

732 (plate LXIV)

733

734

735

736 (plate XXVII)

737

738

739

740

741

742

743

Held to be a landscape in the Paris region (Venturi).

749. Trees on a River Bank
64 × 81 1900–6 V.1533

744

745 (plates XLIV-XLV)

746

747

748

749

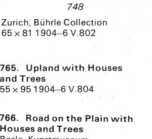

The Montagne Sainte-Victoire

The mountain motif was a favourite with the artist in his later years. Intense chromatic quality is aligned with the breakdown of space in perspective terms (nos 752 and 753). Tonal values, where most warm, make the view draw nearer; the cold hues of the foreground make it step back (nos 764 and 767). Space is thus taken apart in a way that is entirely original. In the artist's own words, "Everything – in art especially – is theory worked out and applied by contact with nature."

750. View From the South-West, with Trees
54 × 65 1890–4 V.661

751. View From the South-West, with Wooded Hill
65 × 81 1890–4 V.662

752. View From the South-West, with Trees and a House
Moscow, Museum of Modern Western Art
81 × 100 1890–1900 V.663

753. Clearing at the Mountain Foot
72 × 91 1897 V.763
The date has been assigned on the strength of family recollection. The artist left the painting in a Tholonet restaurant, whence his sister Marie later retrieved it.

754. From the South-West
55 × 46 1897 V.764

755. Road in the Valley
78 × 96 1894–1900 V.664

756. From the South-West, with Trees
Cleveland (Ohio), Museum of Art
68 × 90 1894–1900 V.666

757. From the South-West
65 × 81 1894–1900 V.665

758. Château-Noir
Tokyo, Ishibashi Collection
1898–1900 V.765

759. View From Bibémus
Baltimore (Ma.), Museum of Art
65 × 81 1898–1900 V.766

760. View From Les Lauves
Philadelphia (Pa.), Museum of Art
73 × 91 1904–6 V.798

761. Road on the Plain with Houses and Trees
65 × 81 1904–6 V.799

762. Meadow and Trees
Kansas City (Mo.), Rockhill Nelson-Atkins Museum
65 × 81 1904–6 V.800

763. Plain with Houses and Trees
Zurich, Kunsthaus
65 × 81 1904–6 V.801
The artist's affection for this landscape motif can be felt in the skill of the composition where the luminous effects are achieved by leaving the canvas bare in places. See plate LXII.

764. Plain with Houses and Trees
Zurich, Bührle Collection
65 × 81 1904–6 V.802

765. Upland with Houses and Trees
55 × 95 1904–6 V.804

766. Road on the Plain with Houses and Trees
Basle, Kunstmuseum
60 × 72 1904–6 V.1529

767. Plain with Houses and Trees
Moscow, Museum of Modern Western Art
60 × 73 1905 V.803
This view of the Montagne Sainte-Victoire was included by Maurice Denis in his portrait of Cézanne, painted in 1905, in which the artist was depicted along with his son Paul and Roussel.

Still-lifes

Cézanne stresses the volume of objects; keenly perceptive of form, he achieves definition by the synthesised and simplificatory handling of outlines (see no. 772). The still-life gains a monumental aspect, partly due to a restive arrangement of elements comprised, reminiscent of the Baroque type (nos 770, 771, 774, 779, 794 and 807). A dynamic whirl of composition results. As Cézanne wrote to Bernard, there is a focal point – be it in an apple or a sphere or a head – where particular light-and-shade effects make the edges of things seem to recede and merge at vanishing-point over the horizon. Each component has been transformed by brilliant colour; the brushstrokes merge (nos 796 and 807). The space-volume interrelation is governed by a central urge (nos. 834–5).

Fruit and objects

768. Wine-Jug and Plate with Fruit
49 × 59 1888–90 V.609

769. Wine-Jug and Plate with Fruit
38 × 46 1888–90 V.622

770. Vessels, Basket and Fruit (The Kitchen Table)
Paris, Louvre
65 × 80 s 1888–90 V.594
The monumental, synthesised character is brought out by the complex receding planes of vision. See plates XXVIII–XXIX and XXX.

771. Sugar-Bowl, Jug and

750

751

752

753

755

756

754

757

758

759

760

761

762

763 *(plate LXII)*

764

765

766

767

Plate of Fruit
Moscow, Museum of Modern Western Art
61 × 90 1888–90 V.619

772. Jug and Plate with Fruit
Oslo, Nasjonalgalleriet
73 × 60 1888–90 V.593

773. Fruit, Plate and Bottle (The Liqueur Bottle)
New York, Museum of Modern Art
60 × 73 1888–90 V.606

774. Curtain, Fruit-Bowl, Carafe and Fruit
Merion (Pa.), Barnes Foundation
73 × 92 1890–1 V.592

775. Curtain, Wine-Jug, Fruit-Bowl and Fruit
Merion (Pa.), Barnes Foundation
58 × 71 1890–4 V.601

776. Plate of Fruit and Wine-Jug on a Cover
Boston (Mass.), Museum of Fine Arts
32·5 × 41 1890–4 V.612

777. Plate of Peaches and Cover
Winterthur, Reinhart Collection
31 × 40 1890–4 V.607

778. Plate of Fruit and Bottles
50·5 × 52·5 1890–4 V.604

779. Basket with Apples, Bottle, Biscuits and Fruit
Chicago (Ill.), Art Institute
65 × 81 s 1890–4 V.600

780. Bottle and Fruit
Merion (Pa.), Barnes Foundation
50 × 73 1890–4 V.605

781. Vessels, Fruit and Cover (The Peppermint Bottle)
Washington, D.C., National Gallery of Art
65 × 81 1890–4 V.625

768

769

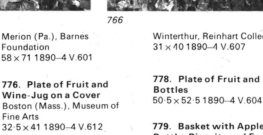

770 *(plates XXVIII-XXIX and XXX)*

771

772

773

774

775

776

777

778

779

780

781

782

783

784

785

786

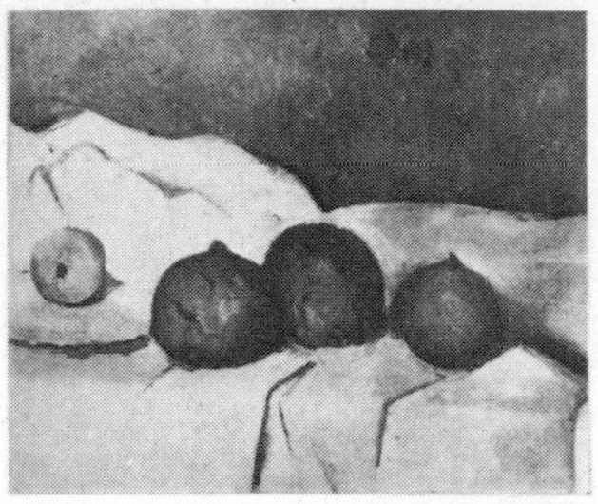
787

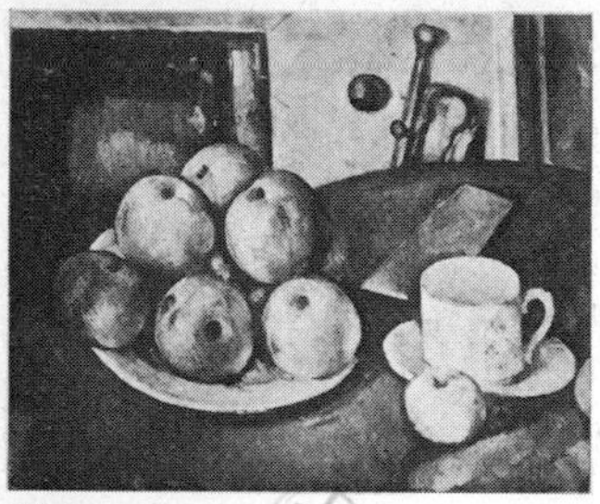
788

789

790

791

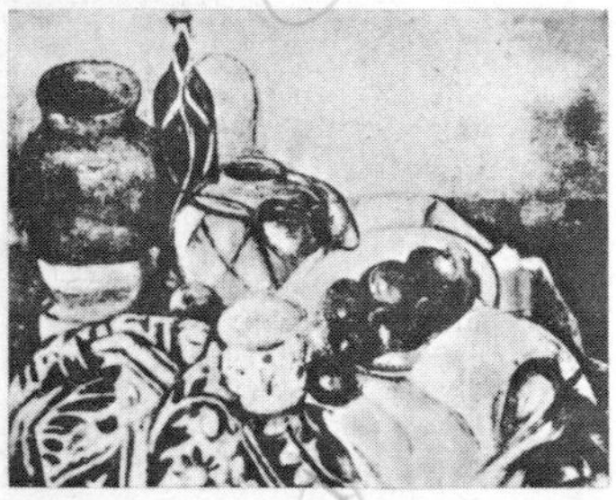
792

793

794

795 (plates LII-LIII)

796

797

798

799

800

801

802

803

804

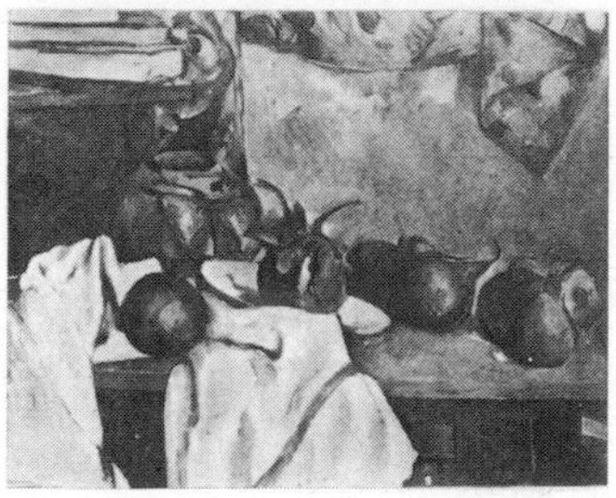
805

806

807 (plate LI)

808

809

810

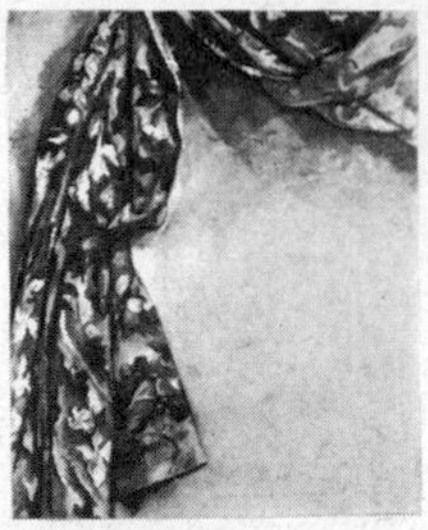

811

812

813

814

815

816

817

818

782. Apples and Cover
Merion (Pa.), Barnes Foundation
45 x 54 1890–4 V.611

783. Cover, Sugar-Bowl and Plate with Fruit
Philadelphia (Pa.), McIlhenny Collection
51 x 62 1890–4 V.624

784. Straw-Cased Jar and Plate with Fruit
33 x 46 1890–4 V.595

785. Straw-Cased Jar and Plate with Melons
44 x 61 1890–4 V.596

786. Jug and Fruit
The Hague, Gemeentemuseum
50 x 61 1890–4 V.615

787. Fruit on a Cloth
Tokyo, Ishibashi Collection
1890–4 V.603

788. Plate with Apples and Cup (Big Apples)
46 x 55 s 1890–4 V.621

789. Plate with Fruit
1890–4 V.608

790. Plate of Peaches
Merion (Pa.), Barnes Foundation
23 x 35 1890–4 V.614

791. Straw-Cased Jar, Sugar-Bowl and Plate with Apples
Paris, Musées Nationaux (Walter-Guillaume Bequest)
35 x 45 1890–4 V.616

792. Vessels and Plate with Fruit on a Cover
1890–4 V.598

793. Cover, Vessels, Plate with Fruit and Aubergines
73 x 92 1890–4 V.597

794. Curtain, Carafe and Plates with Fruit
Leningrad, Hermitage
54 x 73 1895 V.731

795. Curtain, Fruit-Bowl, Carafe and Plate with Fruit
Paris, Louvre
73 x 92 1895–1900 V.732
"The naturalistic motif is here completely transcended; the artist's vision is affirmed, autonomous, with all the means at his disposal. There are several perspective view-points, differentiated so as to emphasise object structure in terms of volume" (Ponente). See plates LII–LIII.

796. Curtain, Vessels and Fruit
New York, Museum of Modern Art
68 x 92 1895–1900 V.736

797. Curtain, Carafe and Plate with Fruit
Merion (Pa.), Barnes Foundation
65 x 81 1895–1900 V.745

798. Straw-Cased Jar and Fruit
Merion (Pa.), Barnes Foundation
71 x 42 *1895* V.737

799. Plate of Fruit, Sugar-Bowl and Straw-Cased Jar on a Cover
New York, Museum of Modern Art
60 x 73 1895–1900 V.738

800. Plate with Pears
The Hague, Gemeentemuseum
38 x 46 1895–1900 V.744

801. Plate with Peaches
The Hague, Gemeentemuseum
36 x 46 1895–1900 V.743

802. Plate with Fruit (Big Pear)
Merion (Pa.), Barnes Foundation
46 x 55 1895–1900 V.740

803. Wine-Jug and Plate with Fruit
London, Tate Gallery (Stoop Bequest)
53 x 71 1895–1900 V.749

804. Tilted Plate with Fruit
Merion (Pa.), Barnes Foundation
46 x 55 1895–1900 V.746

805. Books, Straw-Cased Jar and Fruit
46 x 55 1895–1900 V.733

806. Skull and Fruit
Merion (Pa.), Barnes Foundation
54 x 65 1895–1900 V.758

807. Onions, Bottle, Glass and Plate
Paris, Louvre
66 x 81 1895–1900 V.730
A clear presage of the Cubist approach (Raynal), even though the artist sets the objects on a uniform ground. See plate LI.

808. Jug and Plate with Fruit
1895–1900 V.750

809. Jug, Glass and Plate with Fruit
55 x 46 1895–1900 V.735

810. Woman and Table with Fruit, Glass and Water-Jar
60 x 73 *1900* V.739

811. Curtain
1900 V.747

812. Skull
1900 V.751

813. Three Skulls
34 x 60 *1900* V.1567

814. Pyramid of Skulls
1900 V.753

815. Three Skulls on Oriental Covering
54 x 65 1904 V.759
Seen in Aix by Émile Bernard, on one of his visits to Cézanne in February 1904.

816. Cover, Plate with Fruit and Tea-Pot
58 x 70 1900–5 V.734

817. Curtain and Tilted Plate with Fruit
73 x 92 1900–6 V.741

818. Curtain, Tilted Plate with Fruit, Carafe and Glass
Winterthur, Reinhart Collection
73 x 100 1900–6 V.742

Flowers

819. Fruit and Vase
Berlin, Nationalgalerie
65 x 81 1888–90 V.610

820. Earthenware Pots
Merion (Pa.), Barnes Foundation
1888–90 V.602

821. Plate with Fruit and Earthenware Pot
London, Home House Trustees
46 x 55 1890–4 V.623

822. Fruit and Pot of Geraniums
73 x 92 1890–4 V.599

823. Fruit and Foliage
29 x 29 1890–4 V.613
This work belonged to Matisse and he made a lithograph of it.

824. Vase of Tulips and Fruit
Chicago (Ill.), Art Institute
60 x 42 1890–4 V.617

825. Vase of Tulips and Fruit
72·5 x 42 1890–4 V.618
Painted on wood.

826. Mass of Flowers
81 x 100 1890–4 V.620

827. Vase in a Garden
65 x 54 1895–1900 V.756

828. Flowers and Greenery
Moscow, Museum of Modern Western Art

819

820

821

822

823

824

825

826

827

828

829

830

831

832

77 × 64 *1900* V.754
Copy of a Delacroix watercolour.

829. Decorated Vase
Merion (Pa.), Barnes Foundation
67 × 55 1900 V.755

830. White Vase
40·5 × 29·5 1900–6 V.752

831. Light-Blue Vase
V.748

832. Two-Handled Vase
Washington, D.C., National Gallery of Art
101·2 × 82·2 1902–3 V.757
Mentioned by Cézanne in two letters, dated 2 April 1902 and 9 January 1903, both to Vollard who published them.

Plaster Casts

833. "Anatomy" by Michelangelo
35 × 16·5 *1895* V.709
A lost sculpture, attributed to Michelangelo and much in vogue during last century. Cézanne owned a plaster-cast of it, which served as a model not only in the present instance but as a detail in composition no. 834. Cézanne's treatment of the cast is stylised in the El Greco manner (Venturi).

834. Plaster Cupid and the "Anatomy"
London, Home House Trustees
71 × 57 *1895* V.706
On the right is the lower part of the *Anatomy* (see no. 833). The plaster statuette is a copy from Puget. It was remembered in Cézanne's studio by Vollard and Denis. Puget was greatly admired by Cézanne and Delacroix. Delacroix wrote an article, also a letter about his work, praising its strength and vigour. These were the very qualities to recommend it to the painter of Aix.

835. Plaster Cupid
Stockholm, Nationalmuseum
63 × 81 1895 V.707

836. Plaster Cupid
57 × 27 1895 V.711

837. Plaster Cupid
47 × 31 1895–1900 V.1608

838. Plaster Cupid
45 × 30 1895–1900 V.1609

833

834

835

836

837

838

Appendix

839. Clearing
New York, anonymous charitable foundation
64.8 × 54 *1867* V.1514

840. The Ferry at Bonnières
Aix-les-Bains, Musée France
38.5 × 60.1 1867-70

841. The Crossroads of the Rue Rémy at Auvers
Paris, Louvre (Gachet)
38 × 45.5 *1873*

842. Still Life: Pear and Green Apples
Paris, Musées Nationaux (Walter-Guillaume Bequest)
21 × 32 1873-5

843. Flowers with Yellow Dahlia
Paris, Louvre (Gachet)
54 × 64 *1873*
Painted at Auvers at the house of Dr Gachet.

844. The Brook
Tokyo, private collection
16.5 × 22.5 1873-5

845. Still Life: Fruit and Casserole
Montreal, Museum of Fine Arts
50.8 × 61 1874-8

846. Fruit Picking
15.5 × 22.5 1876-7
Sold at Sotheby's London 6.5.1959.

847. Still Life: Apples
Providence, Rhode Island School of Design
23 × 39.5 1879-82

848. Portrait of Paul Cézanne, Son of the Artist
New York, Henry Pearlman Collection
17.2 × 15.2 1880

849. House and Trees at Jas de Bouffan
Los Angeles, the Norton Simon Foundation
92 × 73 *1885*

850. House on a River Bank
Chicago, Art Institute (Winterbotham)
51.2 × 61 1885-90

851. Study for a Card Player
Beverly Hills, S. R. Barlow Collection
50.2 × 45.7 1890-1

852. Study for Woman with a Coffee-Pot
Great Britain, private collection
36 × 32 1890-4
Sketch for no. 578.

853. Still Life with Apples and Peaches
Washington, National Gallery (Meyer)
81.2 × 100.6 *1895*

854. Montagne Sainte-Victoire
New York, Henry Pearlman Collection
83.8 × 65.1 1903-4

855. Trees at Tholonet
Houston, Menil Collection
81.3 × 65 1904-6

856. Tholonet
New York, Henry Pearlman Collection
101.6 × 81.3 1906

857. Road, Landscape with Guillaumin
Dallas, Museum for Contemporary Arts
23 × 30 *1863*

858. House on the Banks of the Marne
Washington, White House
65 × 81 1880-9

859. Still Life: Fruit and Flowers
39 × 47 1870-1
Previous owners include Dr Gachet and E. G. Bührle.

860. Still Life: Skull and Candlestick
Stuttgart, Staatsgalerie
61 × 50 1895-1900
Returns to the subject of no. 123.

861. Avenue
Göteborg Kunstmuseum
73.5 × 60.5 *1885*
Previously owned by Gauguin.

862. Landscape
Frankfurt on Main, Städelsches Kunstinstitut
53.7 × 65

863. Romantic Landscape (Landscape with Fishermen)
Aix-en-Provence (Jas de Bouffan), Dr Corsy Collection
c. 400 × 300 1860-2
Unknown to Venturi because it was covered with wallpaper at that time. See no. 6.

864. Provençal Houses
New York, Henry Pearlman Collection
33 × 48.2 *1885*

Table of concordance

The corresponding numbers are given here in tabular form, as between the Cézanne paintings (oils only) in the present volume (CWA) and the standard authority (V.): Lionello Venturi, Cézanne, son art, son oeuvre *(Paris, 1936).*

CWA	V.	CWA	V.	CWA	V.	CWA	V.	CWA	V.	CWA	V.	CWA	V.	CWA	V.	CWA	V.	CWA	V.
1	1–3	85	28	169	167	253	230	337	397	421	428	505	367	589	692	673	653	757	665
2	8	86	29	170	166	254	236	338	401	422	429	506	368	590	679	674	650	758	765
3	10	87	31	171	175	255	235	339	404	423	427	507	371	591	678	675	654	759	766
4	11	88	32	172	168	256	237	340	403	424	426	508	372	592	701	676	660	760	798
5	9	89	27	173	172	257	242	341	402	425	425	509	517	593	700	677	642	761	799
6	4	90	30	174	169	258	238	342	400	426	489	510	518	594	698	678	643	762	800
7	5	91	1510	175	171	259	232	343	410	427	492	511	515	595	694	679	646	763	801
8	6	92	33	176	173	260	234	344	412	428	493	512	514	596	695	680	645	764	802
9	7	93	34	177	174	261	243	345	416	429	424	513	534	597	1611	681	647	765	804
10	16	94	35	178	176	262	244	346	418	430	423	514	535	598	689	682	655	766	1529
11	13	95	37	179	177	263	246	347	440	431	434	515	536	599	685	683	658	767	803
12	14	96	36	180	178	264	245	348	439	432	435	516	519	600	684	684	671	768	609
13	15	97	38	181	170	265	250	349	430	433	437	517	533	601	686	685	672	769	622
14	24	98	46	182	1515	266	279	350	431	434	433	518	520	602	688	686	657	770	594
15	83	99	1512	183	185	267	239	351	432	435	436	519	521	603	690	687	659	771	619
16	87	100	41	184	194	268	241	352	450	436	452	520	526	604	687	688	669	772	593
17	84	101	49	185	189	269	240	353	448	437	453	521	527	605	691	689	670	773	606
18	86	102	43	186	186	270	379	354	449	438	454	522	532	606	696	690	667	774	592
19	100	103	45	187	187	271	380	355	451	439	455	523	1521	607	697	691	673	775	601
20	92	104	44	188	188	272	1520	356	462	440	456	524	1519	608	693	692	674	776	612
21	93	105	53	189	190	273	251	357	463	441	457	525	516	609	699	693	761	777	607
22	94	106	42	190	191	274	249	358	460	442	488	526	1607	610	705	694	760	778	604
23	64	107	54	191	195	275	1517	369	461	443	203	527	531	611	703	695	1527	779	600
24	96	108	39	192	211	276	248	360	465	444	337	528	529	612	702	696	1526	780	605
25	101	109	40	193	192	277	252	361	464	445	338	529	530	613	713	697	668	781	625
26	105	110	47	194	193	278	253	362	466	446	340	530	522	614	712	698	656	782	611
27	115	111	51	195	196	279	255	363	468	447	356	531	524	615	714	699	767	783	624
28	121	112	55	196	197	280	247	364	470	448	339	532	525	616	715	700	772	784	595
29	103	113	57	197	221	281	257	365	473	449	344	533	528	617	1524	701	773	785	596
30	116	114	58	198	219	282	265	366	482	450	343	534	523	618	716	702	768	686	615
31	107	115	50	199	220	283	264	367	469	451	346	535	254	619	717	703	770	787	603
32	117	116	52	200	202	284	258	368	486	452	341	536	377	620	718	704	774	788	621
33	118	117	56	201	201	285	256	369	487	453	342	537	378	621	552	705	775	789	608
34	108	118	12	202	204	286	274	370	490	454	363	538	391	622	533	706	776	790	614
35	104	119	59	203	205	287	276	371	491	455	347	539	538	623	554	707	777	791	616
36	106	120	60	204	206	288	273	372	314	456	1606	540	537	624	555	708	778	792	598
37	119	121	63	205	208	289	271	373	332	457	345	541	550	625	586	709	781	793	597
38	113	122	68	206	207	290	259	374	336	458	348	542	551	626	583	710	780	794	731
39	114	123	61	207	200	291	262	375	335	459	351	543	381	627	584	711	779	795	732
40	90	124	62	208	209	292	260	376	409	460	352	544	384	628	710	712	784	796	736
41	120	125	65	209	210	293	263	377	413	461	350	545	386	629	708	713	787	797	745
42	1520	126	69	210	212	294	268	378	414	462	353	546	383	630	561	714	782	798	737
43	112	127	66	212	213	295	261	379	420	463	354	547	385	631	563	715	785	799	738
44	123	128	67	212	214	296	272	380	419	464	349	548	382	632	560	716	786	800	744
45	125	129	70	213	179	297	275	381	421	465	364	549	387	633	568	717	788	801	743
46	—	130	71	214	180	298	266	382	422	466	355	550	388	634	559	718	1531	802	740
47	18	131	48	215	182	299	267	383	438	467	357	551	389	635	557	719	1528	803	749
48	25	132	136	216	183	300	269	384	447	468	494	552	390	636	564	720	1532	804	746
49	20	133	1513	217	181	301	270	385	442	469	495	553	392	637	566	721	791	805	733
50	19	134	153	218	216	302	484	386	443	470	496	554	395	638	556	722	792	806	758
51	17	135	1511	219	217	303	296	387	445	471	497	555	396	639	558	723	789	807	730
52	1509	136	133	220	218	304	297	388	444	472	498	556	394	640	567	724	790	808	750
53	22	137	155	221	198	305	301	389	446	473	1518	557	541	641	582	725	793	809	735
54	95	138	135	222	199	306	300	390	472	474	504	558	544	642	585	726	1530	810	739
55	75	139	134	223	222	307	293	391	459	475	507	559	549	643	589	727	1610	811	747
56	73	140	137	224	215	308	294	392	458	476	509	560	548	644	588	728	796	812	751
57	80	141	142	225	184	309	295	393	467	477	506	561	543	645	591	729	797	813	1567
58	82	142	138	226	21	310	302	394	471	478	505	562	540	646	590	730	795	814	753
59	74	143	139	227	226	311	305	395	475	479	508	563	539	647	587	731	794	815	759
60	79	144	144	228	229	312	306	396	474	480	499	564	545	648	581	732	805	816	734
61	76	145	145	229	228	313	303	397	476	481	500	565	547	649	580	733	629	817	741
62	77	146	146	230	278	314	304	398	478	482	502	566	542	650	724	734	630	818	742
63	72	147	156	231	291	315	325	399	480	483	503	567	546	651	727	735	632	819	610
64	81	148	157	232	292	316	299	400	479	484	501	568	562	652	728	736	631	820	602
65	126	149	147	233	277	317	298	401	481	485	510	569	569	653	729	737	635	821	623
66	102	150	140	234	285	318	308	402	477	486	359	570	572	654	726	738	634	822	599
67	91	151	141	235	227	319	307	403	485	487	358	571	571	655	725	739	638	823	613
68	99	152	143	236	289	320	309	404	313	488	360	572	573	656	—	740	637	824	617
69	98	153	148	237	286	321	310	405	320	489	361	573	570	657	719	741	639	825	618
70	23	154	149	238	287	322	311	406	319	490	362	574	577	658	721	742	640	826	620
71	85	155	150	239	288	323	317	407	312	491	511	575	579	659	720	743	641	827	756
72	88	156	151	240	280	324	316	408	327	492	513	576	578	660	722	744	644	829	755
73	78	157	152	241	284	325	318	409	328	493	512	577	565	661	723	745	762	829	755
74	89	158	154	242	290	326	315	410	329	494	281	578	574	662	1523	746	783	830	752
75	110	159	158	243	283	327	321	411	330	495	282	579	680	663	483	747	771	831	748
76	109	160	163	244	1520	328	322	412	334	496	1522	580	681	664	626	748	769	832	757
77	97	161	165	245	124	329	323	413	441	497	374	581	682	665	627	749	1533	833	709
78	127	162	1525	246	122	330	324	414	398	498	369	582	683	666	628	750	661	834	706
79	128	163	169	247	111	331	326	415	399	499	370	583	675	667	633	751	662	835	707
80	131	164	1516	248	233	332	331	416	405	500	376	584	575	668	636	752	663	836	711
81	130	165	161	249	231	333	333	417	406	501	373	585	576	669	649	753	763	837	1608
82	132	166	162	250	225	334	396	418	407	502	375	586	704	587	648	754	764	838	1609
83	129	167	160	251	223	335	417	419	408	503	366	587	676	671	651	755	664		
84	26	168	164	252	224	336	415	420	411	504	365	588	677	672	652	756	666		

Index of subjects and titles

Topographical index

Works not cited in the present index may be regarded as whereabouts unknown.